POSTCARD HISTORY SERIES

New Smyrna Beach

ON THE FRONT COVER: CANAL STREET. The East Coast Bargain House is shown in this card that was postmarked in September 1908. The store specialized in dry goods, shoes, and clothing. In the distance is the Indian River. On the left side of the card, note the small wooden bridge that would have crossed the Turnbull-era canal, for which the street was named. (Courtesy Dorothy Moore.)

ON THE BACK COVER: RIVERVIEW HOTEL. This view shows the proximity of the Riverview to the north bridge. Traveling west, the cars facing the viewer are headed toward the mainland. The Riverview is now an upscale hotel with a high-quality restaurant, the Grill at Riverview, and a spa, the Spa at Riverview, on premises. (Author's collection.)

POSTCARD HISTORY SERIES

New Smyrna Beach

Robert Redd

ARCADIA PUBLISHING

ISBN 978-1-4671-1746-3

Published by Arcadia Publishing
Charleston, South Carolina

Printed in the United States of America

Library of Congress Control Number: 2016937015

For all general information contact Arcadia Publishing at:
Telephone 843-853-2070
Fax 843-853-0044
E-mail sales@arcadiapublishing.com
For customer service and orders:
Toll-Free 1-888-313-2665

Visit us on the Internet at www.arcadiapublishing.com

This book is dedicated to my wife, Christina. Without her love and support, this work would not have been possible.

Contents

ACKNOWLEDGMENTS

The city now known as New Smyrna Beach can trace its roots to 1768, when Dr. Andrew Turnbull settled the area with a group of over 1,200 indentured servants. While the settlement lasted only nine years, the legacy of Turnbull and these settlers lives on today. Descendants still live in town, and it is quite common to have visitors who can trace their lineage to the Turnbull era.

In the 250-odd years since settlement, much has happened. History has been recorded by the likes of Zelia W. Sweett and her son Larry, Carita Doggett Corse, Daniel Pleasant Gold, and of course, Gary Luther. My goal is to live up to the standards of these individuals.

I am lucky to be employed by the Southeast Volusia Historical Society. Every day, I get to work at a wonderful museum, and on many days, I get to talk history with our visitors and volunteers. While I value all of them, I feel I must single out a few for special recognition. Irene Beckham is a wealth of knowledge and one of the most humble people you will ever meet. She is my go-to resource. Dave Miner has helped organize our library, making things much easier to find. I am truly lucky to work with such wonderful people.

I want to thank all those at Arcadia for their continued support, particularly my editor, Henry Clougherty, for all his help and encouragement.

To my parents, Ted and Bonnie Redd, thank you for the support you have provided. I promise I will continue to try and "do good work."

My wife, Christina, has been a constant support. Between my writing and her trying to keep up with three needy dogs, her home life is full. She is well loved by all of us.

Unless otherwise noted, all images are courtesy of the author's collection.

Introduction

The gem along Florida's east coast called New Smyrna Beach has not always been the thriving community it is today. In fact, the year-round population did not reach 10,000 until 1970. Today, the population is rapidly approaching 25,000 as transplants, many of them Northern visitors who have decided to make the city their permanent home, transform the landscape. With this increase in population comes the corresponding growth in businesses, such as restaurants, grocery stores, gas stations, and other service industries. While many of the jobs associated with these industries are low wage, a surge in the health care industry provides solid, well-paying jobs, which look to be here for the long term.

In 1768, Dr. Andrew Turnbull, along with more than 1,200 indentured servants from Minorca, Greece, Spain, and Italy, sailed through Mosquito Inlet on their way to start an agricultural plantation community. Turnbull and his partners, Sir William Duncan and Sir Richard Temple (acting for his brother Lord George Grenville), received grants totaling 40,000 acres, with Turnbull slated to act as plantation manager. The primary crops were to be indigo, hemp, and cotton.

Problems arose from the beginning, however. The settlement was only built to accommodate 500 people. An immediate lack of housing, clothing, and other provisions met the colonists, many of whom were already in poor health after the journey across the Atlantic. What did await them were heat, work, and unhappiness.

By 1777, a small group had fled to St. Augustine to air their grievances to Patrick Tonyn, the governor of East Florida. Tonyn and Turnbull were not what would be called friendly, and ultimately, Tonyn granted the indentured servants their freedom. By June 1777, the Smyrna settlement had almost been abandoned. Turnbull was heavily in debt to his partners and was ultimately jailed by Tonyn. After being released from prison in 1781, and before being required to appear in court again, Turnbull and his family left Florida, taking residence in Charleston. He would live out the rest of his life there, passing away in 1792 at the age of 73.

There are plenty of other stories that contribute to the fascinating history of New Smyrna, later New Smyrna Beach. In 1830, the partnership of Henry Cruger and William Depeyster erected the building that would lead to decades-long controversy. Cruger and Depeyster were the owners of what is now known as a sugar mill. The mill was sacked and burned in 1835 during the Second Seminole War. Years later, property owner Washington E. Connor gifted the land to his second wife, Jeanette Thurber Connor. Jeanette became the leading proponent that the ruins were those of a Spanish mission and possible dated to 1696. This theory took root, and it took the work of Charles Coe and later archaeologists to disprove. To this day, however, the ruins are located just off Mission Road, leading some to continue to believe the incorrect story.

During the Civil War, Florida threw in its lot with the Confederacy. During the 1860s, New Smyrna was a small populated area, but one with strategic value. In 1862, the Union navy sent troops through Mosquito Inlet in search of a blockade-runner by the name of *Kate*. On their return north through the New Smyrna area, the Union men were attacked by Confederate troops, leaving two officers and six soldiers dead. An African American guide was captured and later killed as well. The bodies of the officers were returned under a flag of truce the following day. The Union navy returned to New Smyrna in 1863 and bombed the city in an unprovoked attack, destroying the Sheldon Hotel, which sat on the ruins in Old Fort Park. The Sheldon family later returned to the property and rebuilt on a smaller scale. While it is often repeated that the 1863 attack was waged in retaliation for the Union deaths in 1862, there is no documentary evidence to support this claim.

Perhaps the most common mistake made in relating the history of New Smyrna Beach is how the word "Beach" came to be added to its name. Until 1937, there were two distinct cities by the names of New Smyrna and Coronado Beach. That year, the residents of New Smyrna voted to add the "Beach" designation to the city name, and on August 1, 1937, the city officially became known as New Smyrna Beach. It is important to realize that the city of Coronado Beach was still in existence. The two cities lived side by side, with only the Indian River separating them, until 1945, when the state government allowed the two cities to hold elections as to whether they would merge. On May 15, 1945, both New Smyrna Beach and Coronado Beach citizens went to the polls to determine their future. The referendum passed in both cities, with Coronado Beach approving the merger by a mere 29 votes. Florida governor Millard Caldwell signed the law allowing the two cities to become one, and on April 1, 1946, Coronado Beach was merged into New Smyrna Beach. The stage was now set for future growth in industry and tourism.

In the following years, New Smyrna Beach has seen its share of ups and downs. The rail industry was a major employer in the town for decades until the Florida East Coast (FEC) Railway strike of the 1960s eliminated passenger service through the town and also dramatically impacted the moving of freight on the lines. Along with this strike came the growth of the Kennedy Space Center and the resulting exodus of many locals who left for higher-paying jobs to the south.

Today, New Smyrna Beach is on the upswing economically. Plans are afoot for development on the beachside, on the North Causeway, and along the busy SR 44 corridor. While this expansion does not please everybody, including many who have lived in the city for many years, the rise in out-of-town visitors, many who decide to make their homes here, is spurring this along.

What is certain, however, is that those who call Florida's "Smartest Little City" home love it and cannot imagine living elsewhere. Let's take a step back in time, through postcards, and see where New Smyrna Beach has been and how it has changed.

One

World's Safest Bathing Beach

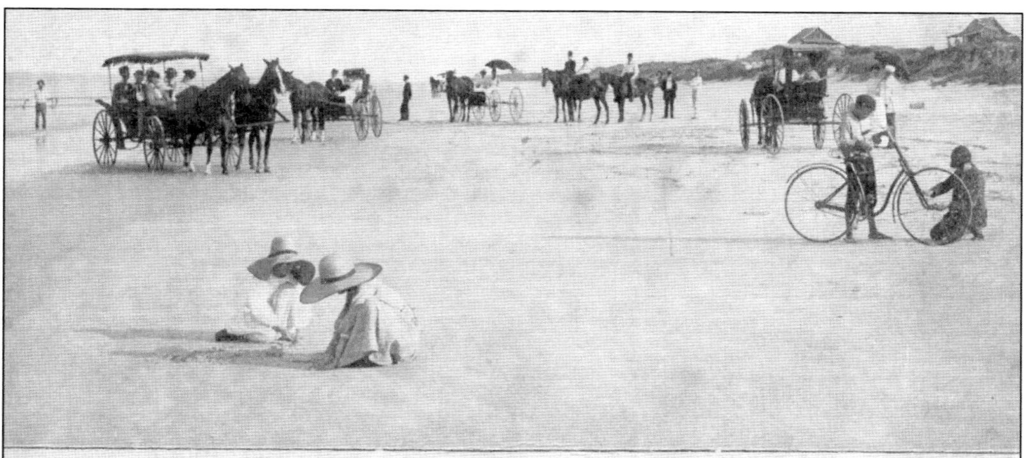

Coronado Beach Opposite New Smyrna. Published by M.A. Galbreath & Co., this card shows that going to the beach in the days before motorized vehicles was little different from today. Bicycling was popular, and note the young children in front, playing in the sand. They might have been looking for shells or perhaps building a sand castle. The big difference today is that horses are not allowed on the beach.

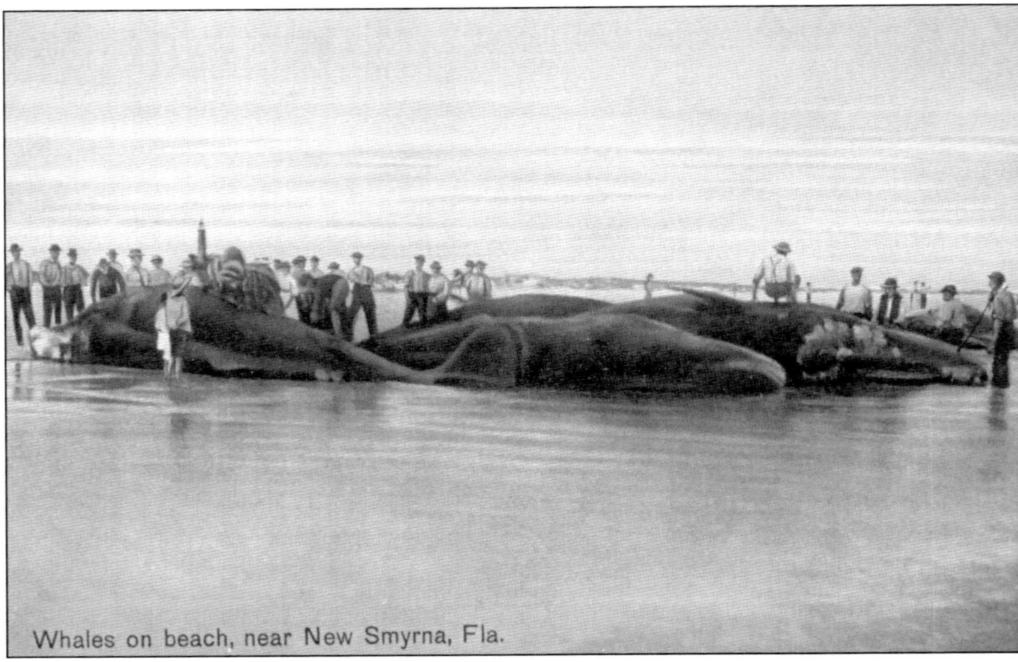

Whales on the Beach. These cards, both published by the Hugh C. Leighton Co., picture a highly unusual occurrence. Nine whales, which ranged from 35 to 43 feet long, beached themselves or washed ashore in June 1908. A party of men, including noted locals Frank Sams and Simmons Bennett, decided to extract oil from the carcasses. Their efforts had little success, and the resulting stench hung over the city for some time. The remains were taken back to the sea for disposal. In the wider view, note the Ponce Inlet lighthouse in the distance.

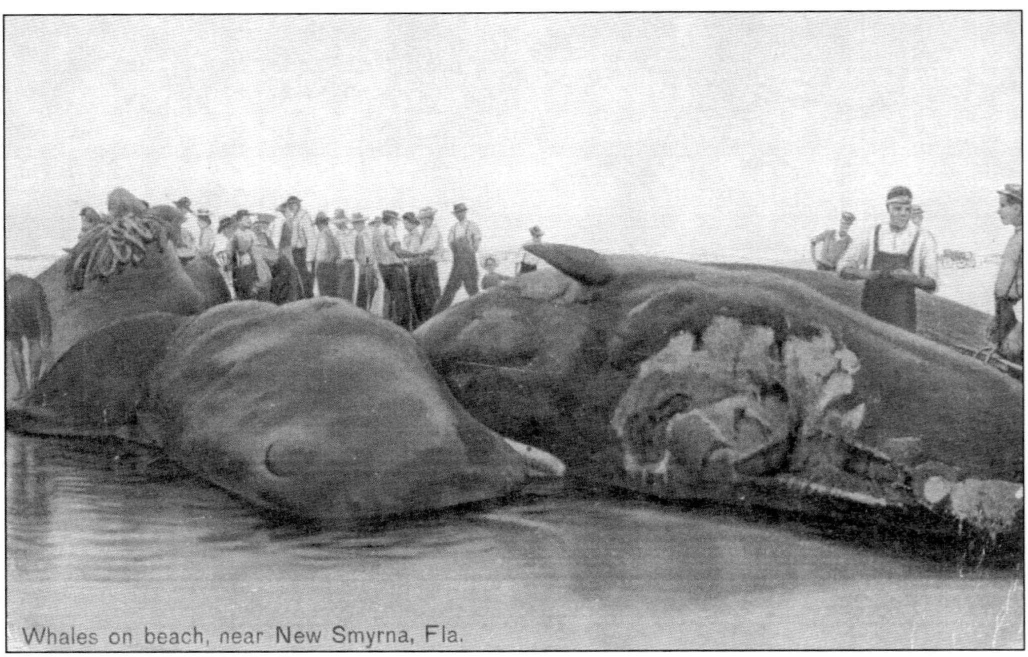

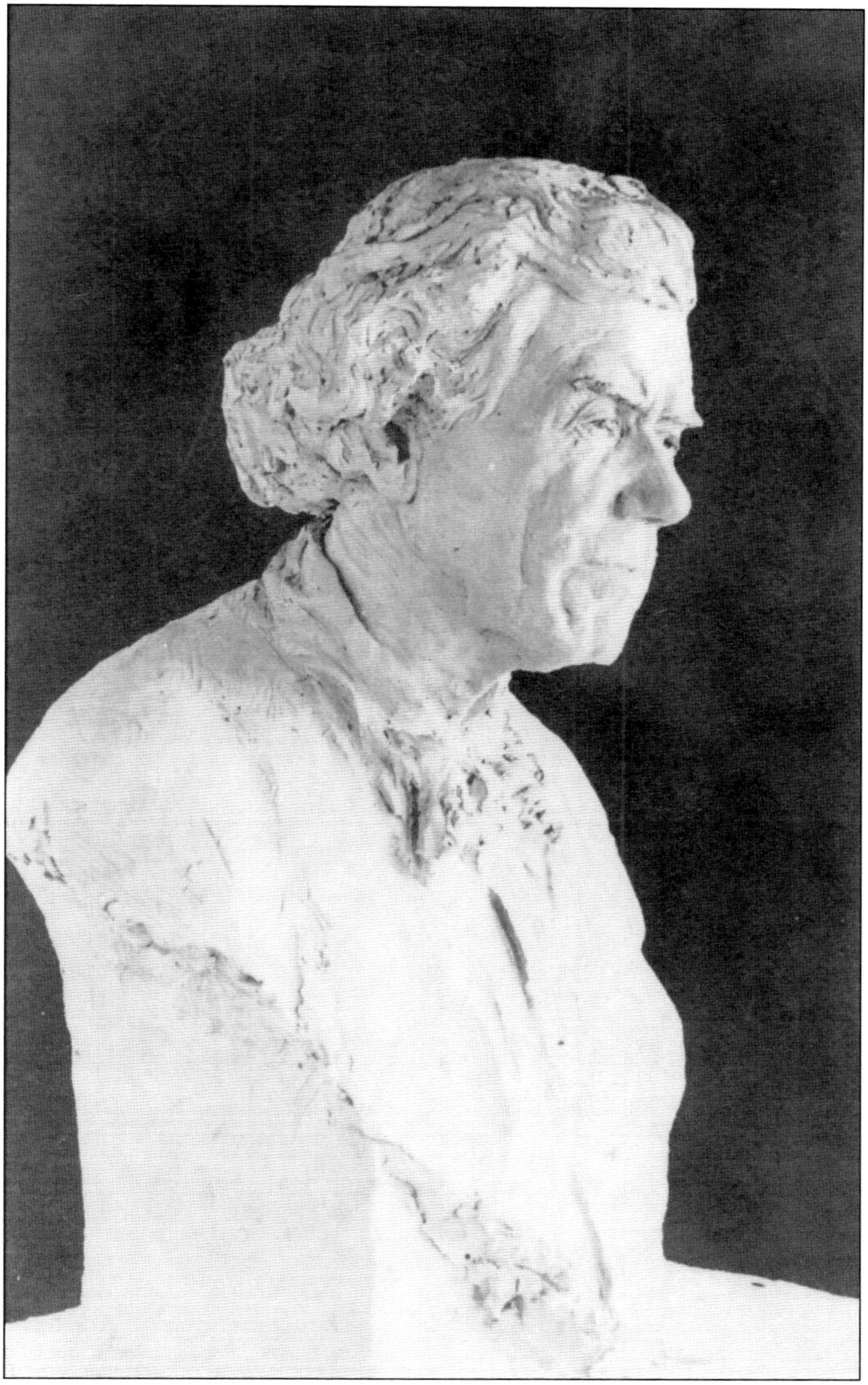

JOHN Y. DETWILER. As one of the earliest settlers of the Coronado Beach area, Detwiler was purchasing beachside property long before it became fashionable to do so. He is most often remembered for three parts of his life: first, he and his wife donated the land that became the Detwiler Park Cemetery; second, he was a staunch believer that New Smyrna Beach was older than St. Augustine; lastly, he was the father of Hannah Bonnet, the first female mayor of New Smyrna Beach.

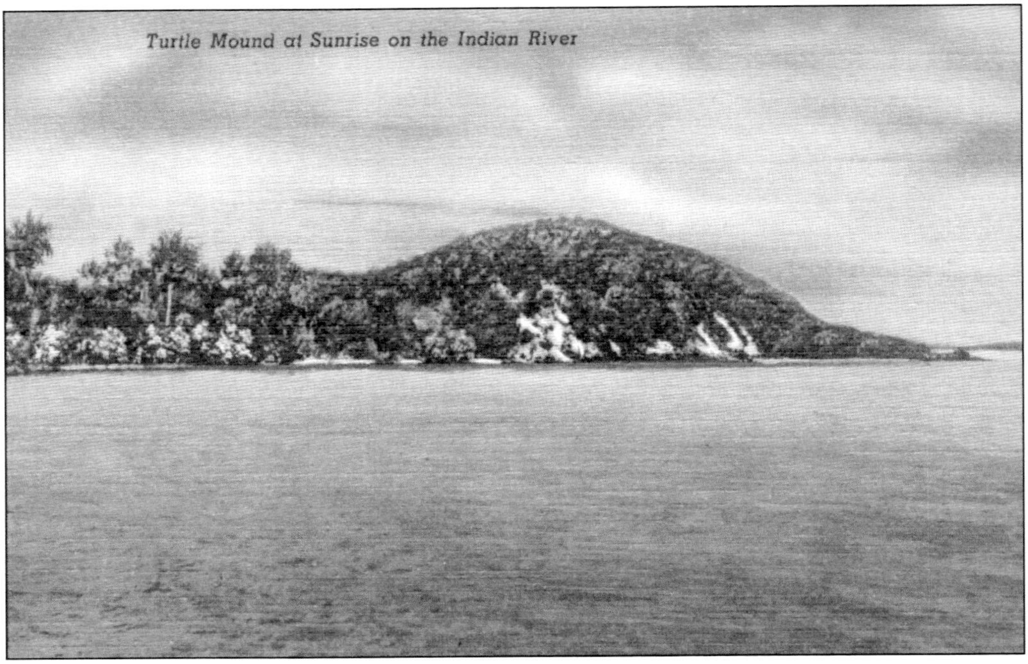

Turtle Mound. Located at the far southern end of the beachside, Turtle Mound is now part of Canaveral National Seashore. The caption on the back of the card states, "Built by the Surocs as a shipyard and lookout post." Turtle Mound is commemorated locally as part of a monument dedicated to the Watch and Warn program from World War II. (Courtesy Dorothy Moore.)

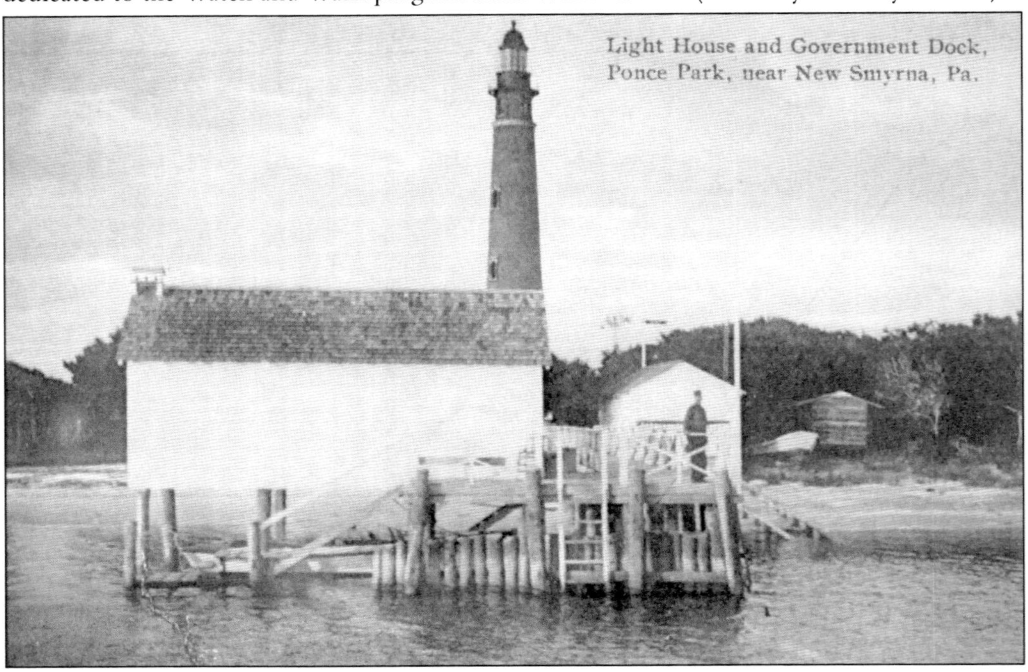

Lighthouse and Government Dock. Located on the north side of Ponce Inlet, formerly known as Mosquito Inlet due to the large number of the pesky insect, the lighthouse was officially lit in 1887. The lighthouse is now owned by the City of Ponce Inlet. Visitors are invited to climb the 203 steps to the top.

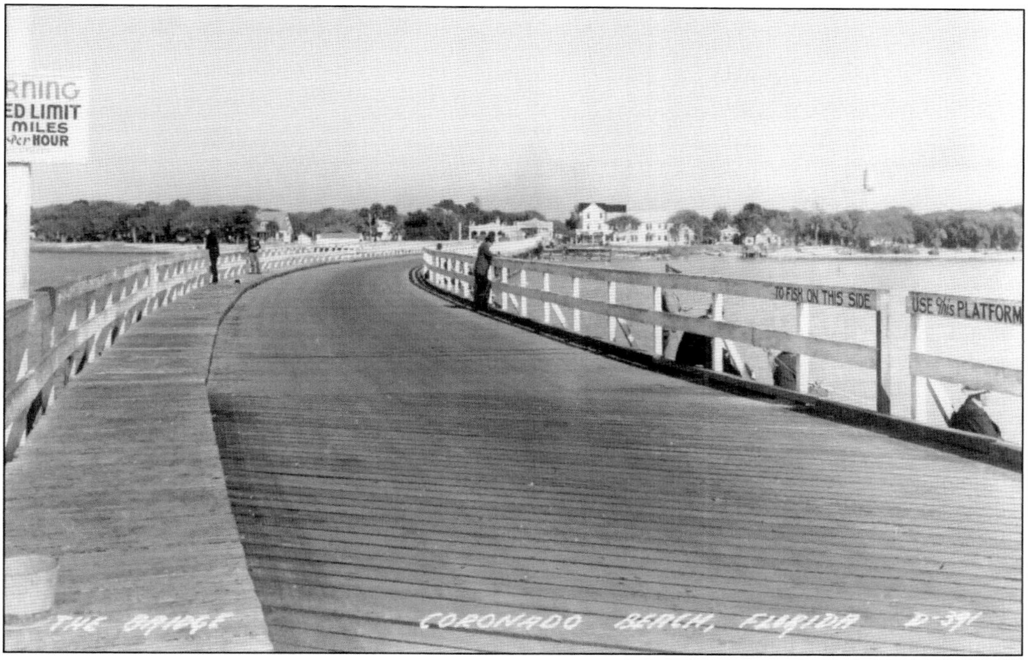

THE BRIDGE. This old wooden bridge used to be the way to get to Coronado Beach. This swivel bridge has since been replaced, and there is now a much larger drawbridge for travelers to cross. In the distance, note the Riverview Hotel, the three-story white building, as well as the water tower in the upper right corner.

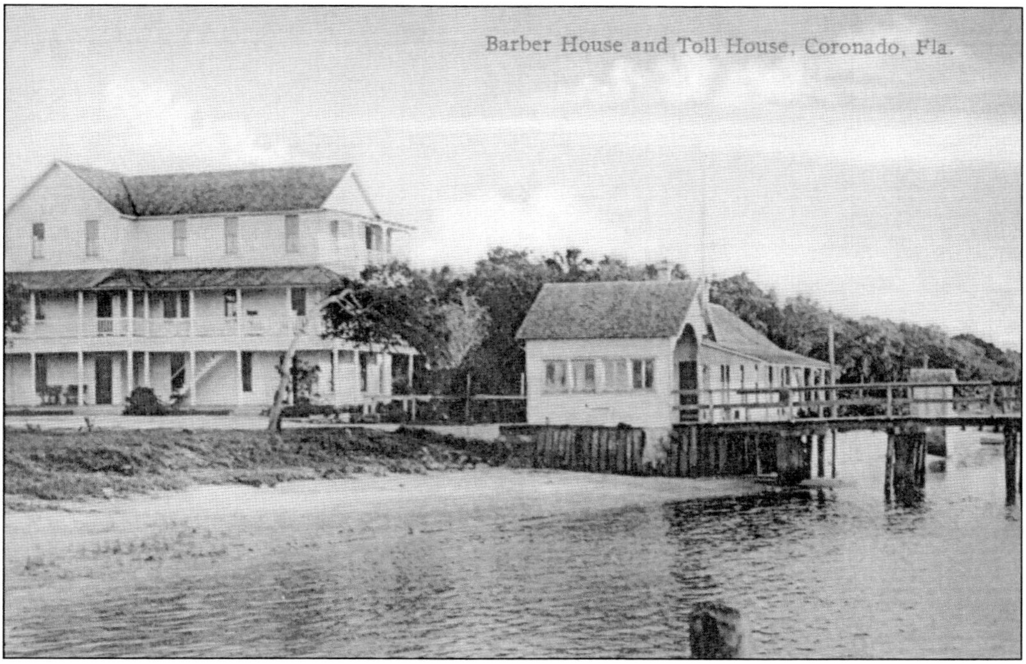

BARBER HOUSE AND TOLL HOUSE. When first constructed, the second "north" bridge was a toll bridge owned by Washington E. Connor. The toll to cross was 1¢ each way, whether on foot, by bike, or by automobile. The Barber House was originally owned by bridge keeper S.T. Barber. The name was later changed to the Riverview, which is still in use today.

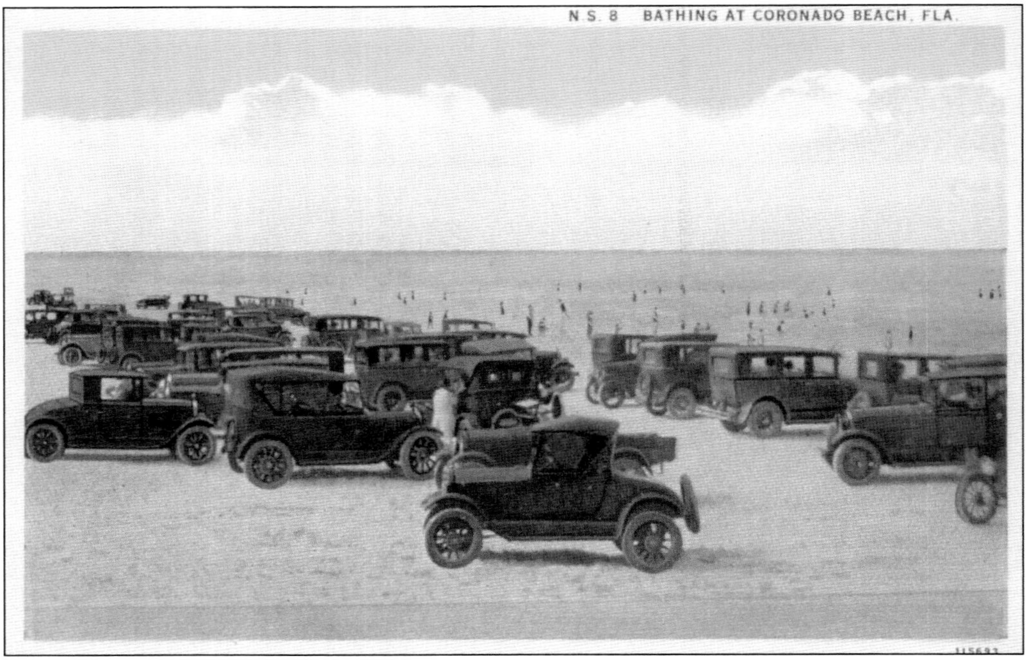

BATHING AT CORONADO BEACH. This early card shows that, despite the claims of many current locals, New Smyrna (Beach) has always been a popular destination. What has changed are the vehicles, the bathing suits, and the parking, which is more organized.

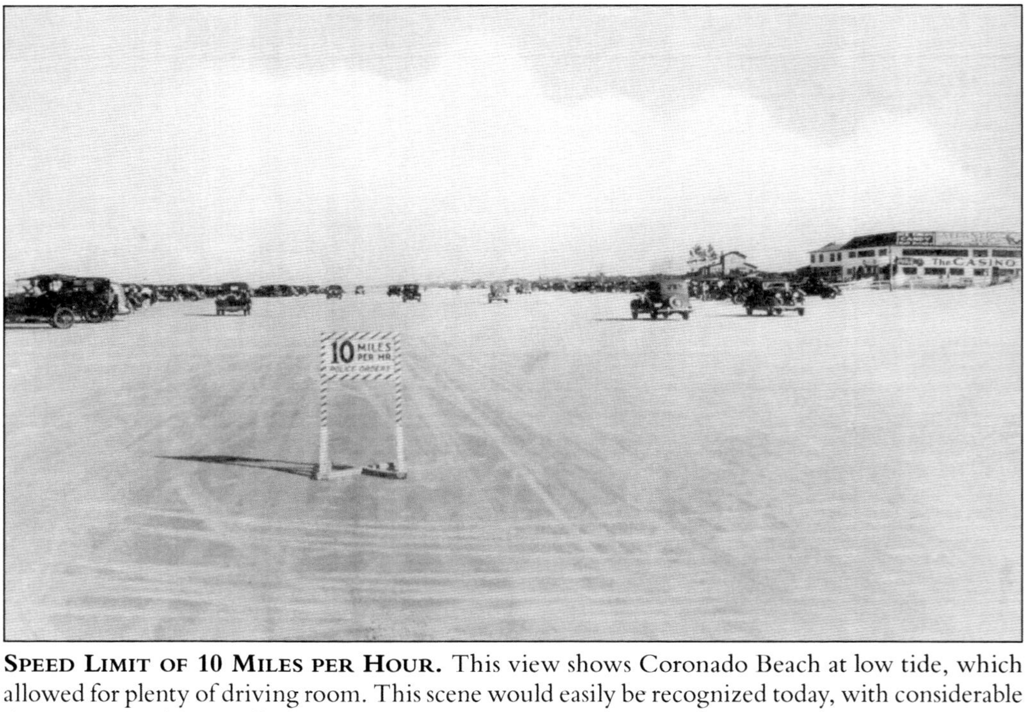

SPEED LIMIT OF 10 MILES PER HOUR. This view shows Coronado Beach at low tide, which allowed for plenty of driving room. This scene would easily be recognized today, with considerable driving and parking traffic, as well as the speed limit sign of 10 miles per hour. The only difference is seen in the density of buildings. Notice how few are shown. The site of what was the casino is now a parking lot.

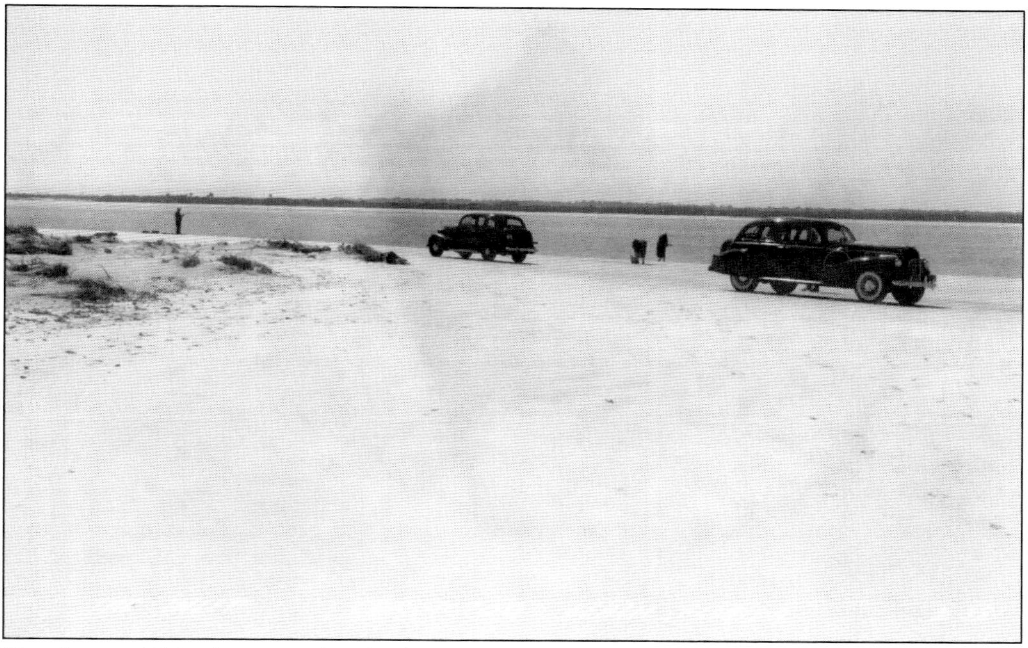

The Inlet. This view was taken looking north across what is now called Ponce Inlet, formerly Mosquito Inlet. Today, the area is known as Smyrna Dunes Park and serves as a beach where dog owners can take their four-legged friends to play in the water. Driving is no longer permitted in the area. Fishing is still a popular pastime in the area, however.

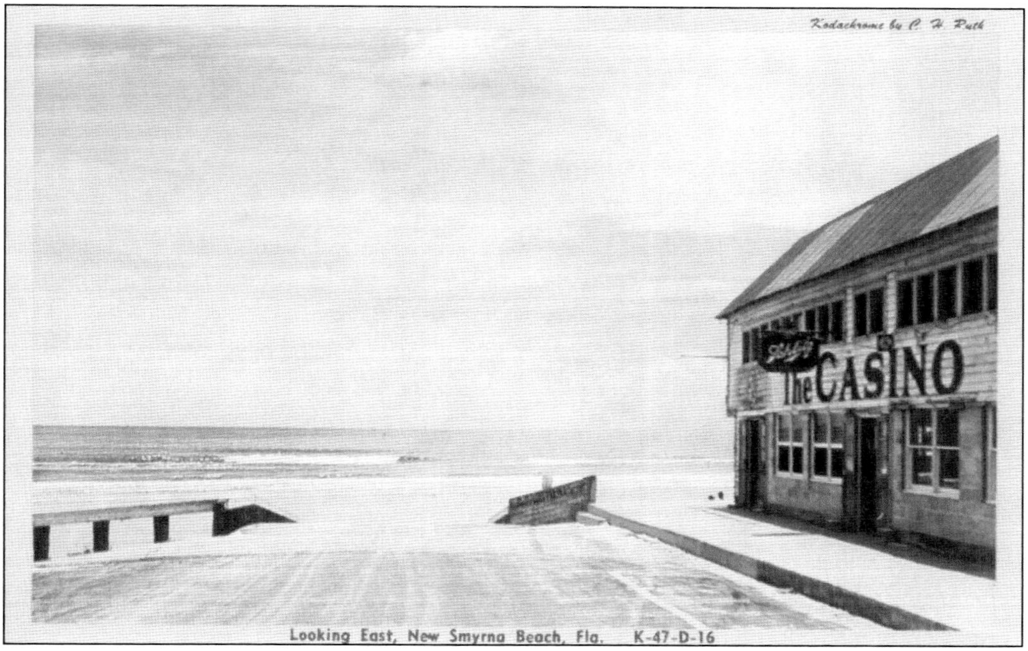

The Casino. New Smyrna Beach has never had a casino in the way the term is used today. Instead, this building served as a popular hangout for beachgoers. The first floor contained a snack bar and dance floor, while the upstairs was used as apartments. An October 1947 storm undermined the seawall, leading to massive erosion and the ultimate destruction of the building. This location now serves as a parking lot.

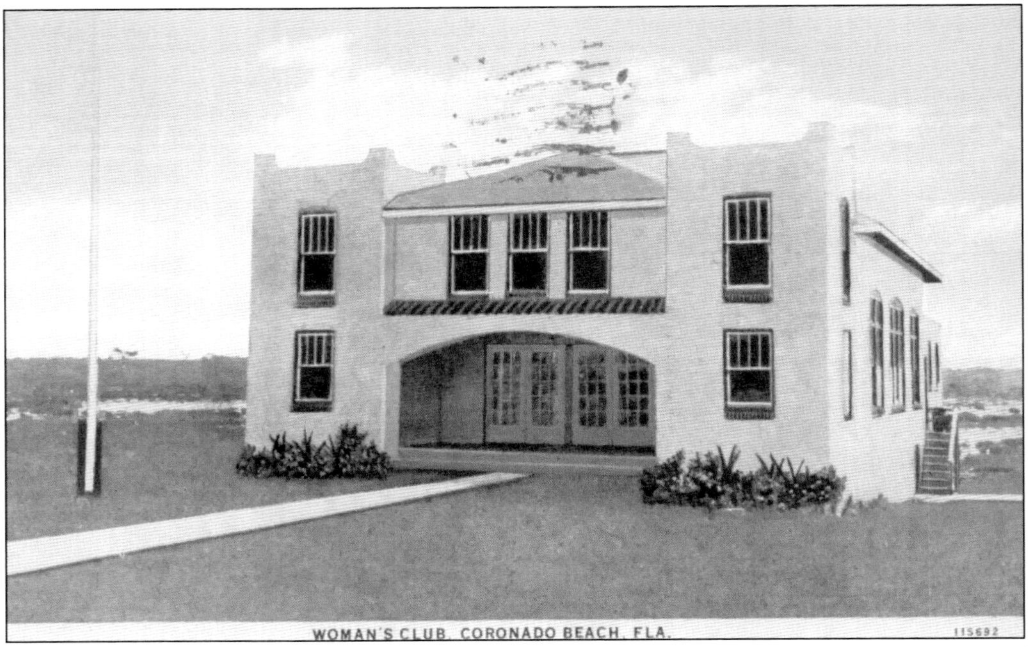

WOMAN'S CLUB. Postmarked in 1937, this card features the now defunct Woman's Club of Coronado Beach. According to longtime residents, this building was located south of what is now Third Avenue. There is currently a Woman's Club building located on the mainland that is listed in the National Register of Historic Places.

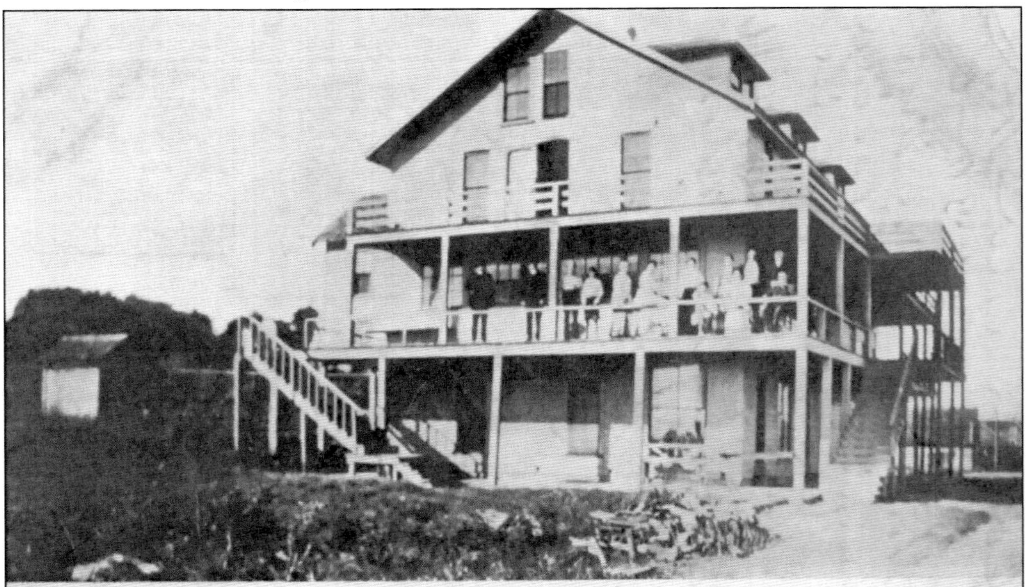

ATLANTIC HOUSE. The Atlantic House was located near the southeast end of Flagler Avenue, near today's city parking lot. William H. Newell was the original owner of the house but sold it to T.B. Demaree several years before it burned to the ground in 1916. Newell later served as mayor for New Smyrna from 1911 to 1916. This card, posted to Columbia City, New York, in December 1910, discusses the fine weather the sender was enjoying. (Courtesy Rick Newell.)

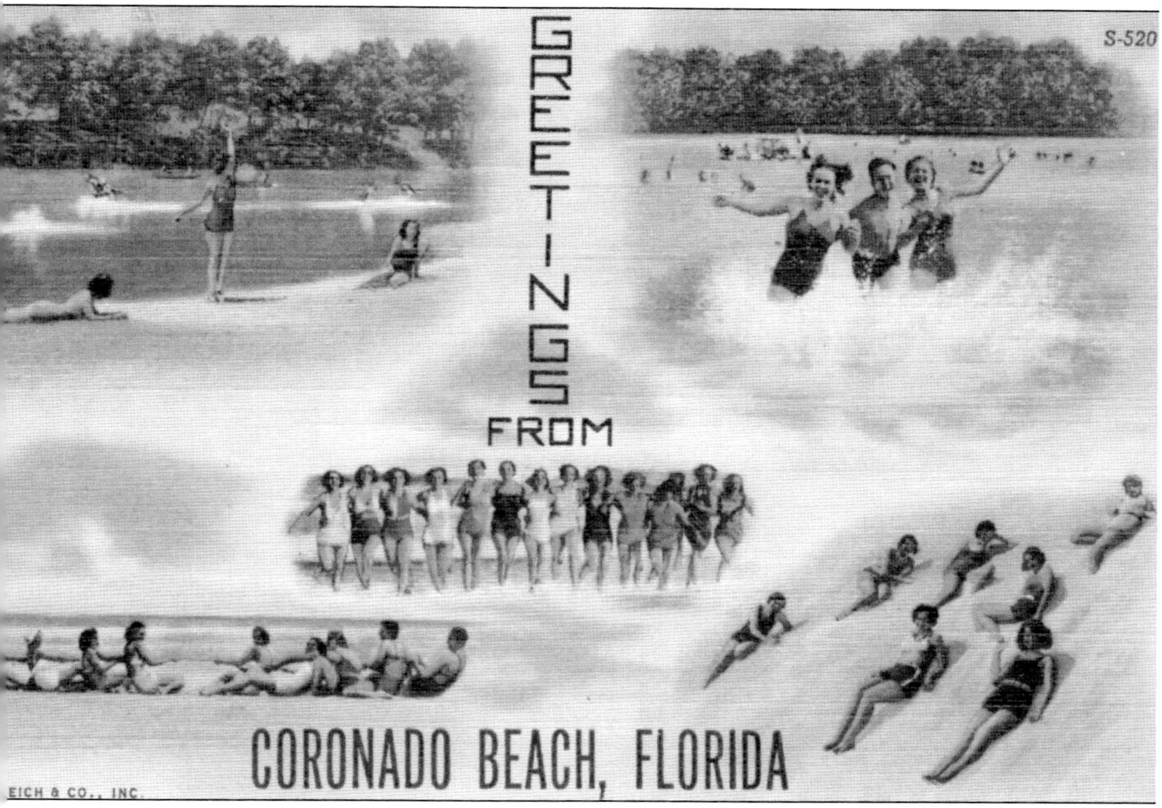

GREETINGS FROM CORONADO BEACH. Despite a 1944 postmark, this card shows that fun could be had at the beach even during wartime. It should be noted that very few men are seen on this card, possibly as a result of the number of young men serving in the military at the time. (Courtesy Dorothy Moore.)

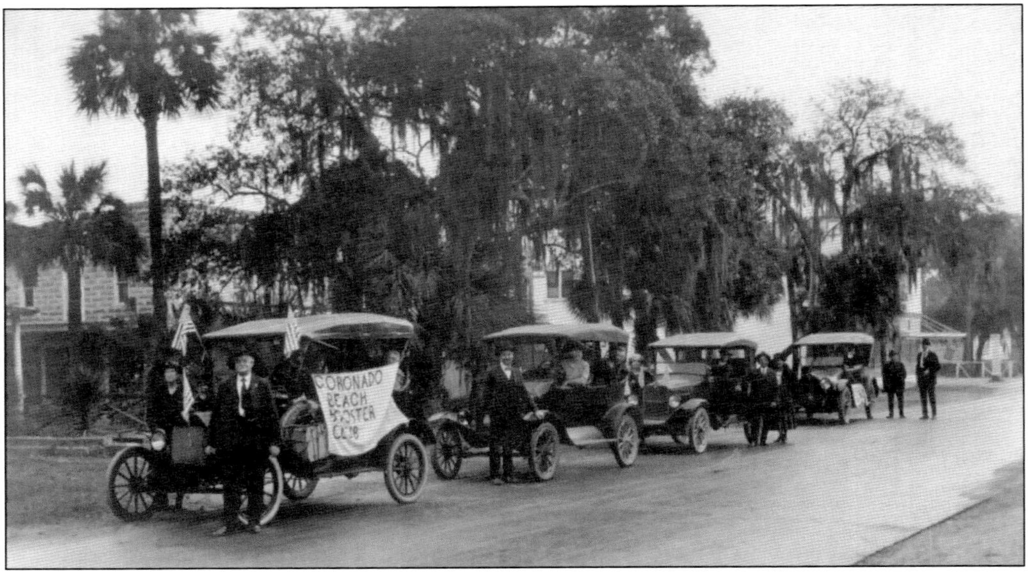

Coronado Beach Booster Club. This real-photo postcard, which was addressed to Grand Rapids, Michigan, is captioned as follows: "E.E. Brown leading a party to Tampa Fair. February 6, 1923." Ephraim E. Brown and his wife, Matilda, who are known to have lived in Coronado Beach during the 1930s, are shown with the lead car at the left in this image. Brown was a veteran of the Civil War, having served in the 64th New York Infantry and would have been approximately 79 years old at the time this image was taken.

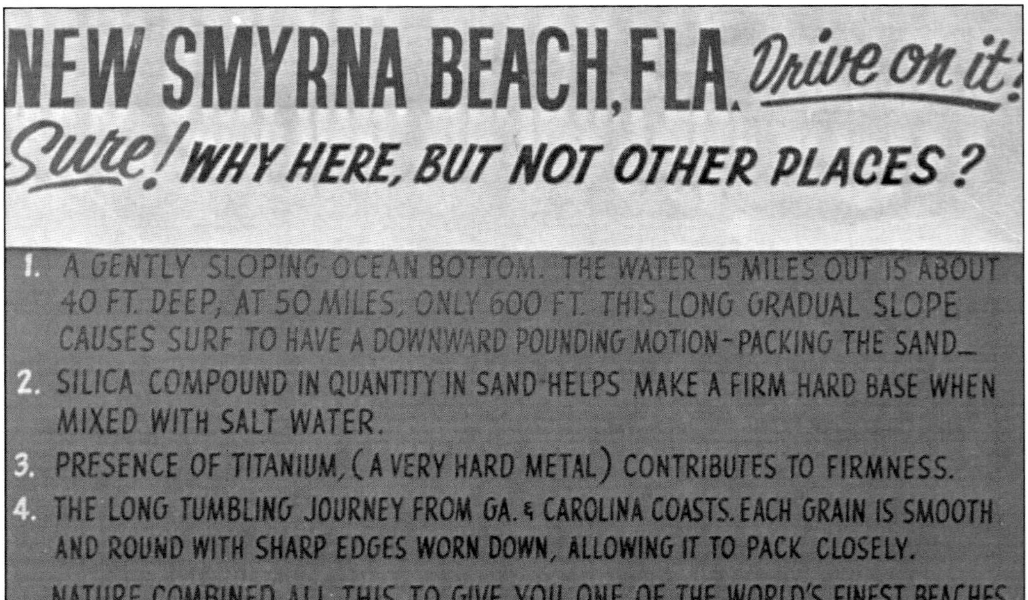

Drive on It? As this postcard attests, the beaches of Volusia County are unique in that they can be driven upon. This card outlines the natural forces at play that allow cars to safely pass at lower tides. In more recent years, the debate of beach driving has intensified. Many feel it is their right to drive on the beach, while others wish to preserve the natural beauty. Still others want uncluttered views for the tenants of nearby hotels and condominiums. In addition, the nesting areas of endangered sea turtles must be considered in the debate.

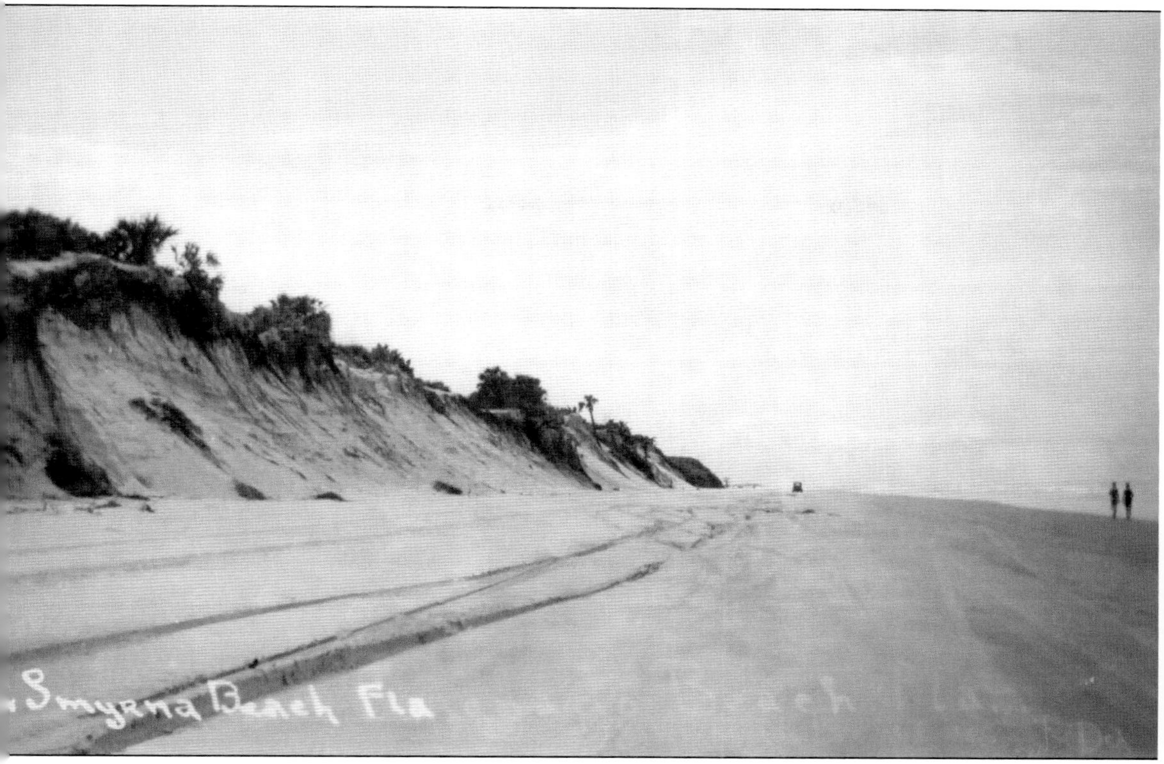

A Nearly Empty Beach. This real-photo postcard shows the tradition of driving on the beach. The hard-packed sands are disturbed only by the tire tracks left by the car shown in the distance and the footprints left by the walkers shown at the waterline.

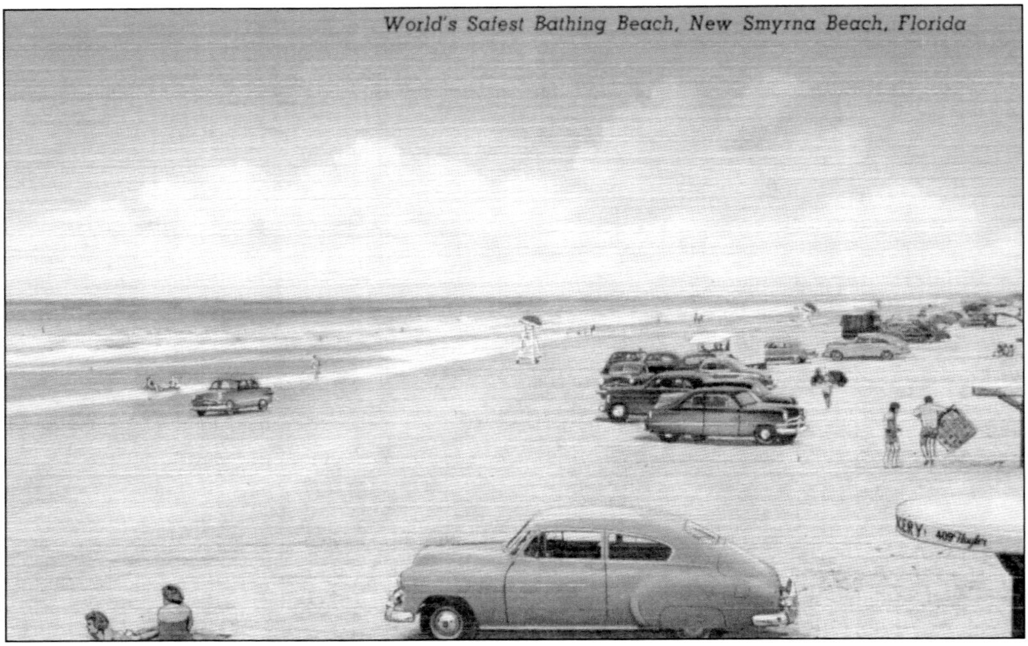

WORLD'S SAFEST BATHING BEACH. This slogan from long ago has been replaced by the somewhat sarcastic "Shark Bite Capital of the World" due to the seemingly high number of shark encounters, mostly near the inlet. According to a *Daytona News-Journal* article, nearly 15 percent of worldwide shark bites occur in the waters off New Smyrna Beach, which amounts to only 10 bites, however. WSBB are also the call letters for a popular local AM radio station.

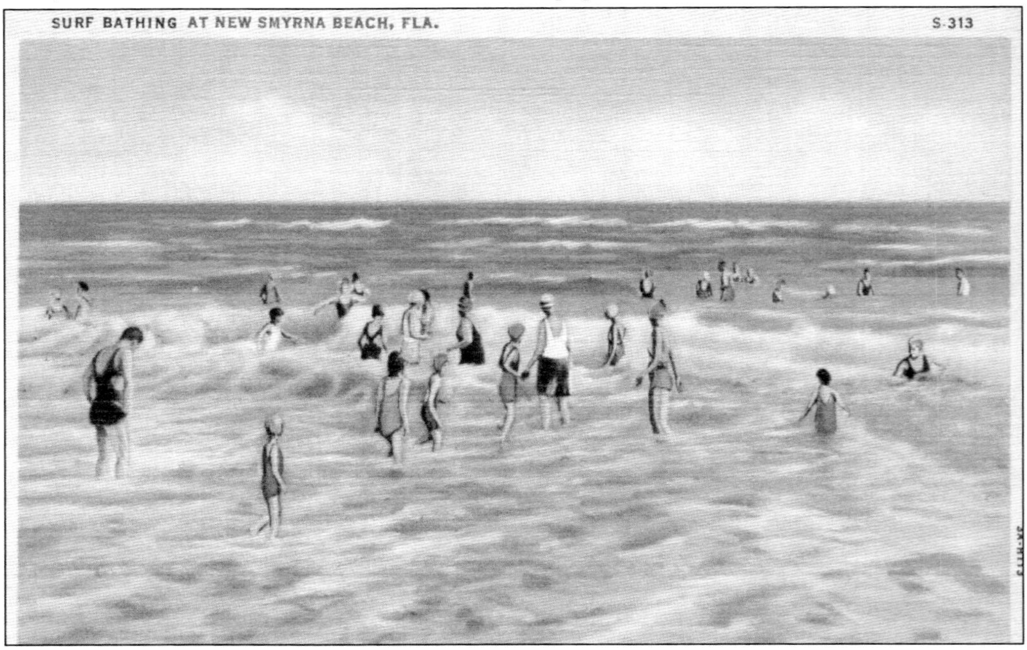

SURF BATHING. This card, postmarked in 1944, shows that the beach was a popular destination for locals and vacationers even during the war years. The sender bragged to his friends in Connecticut that he was able to swim in 8- to 10-foot surf and go horseback riding after dark on a beach 400 feet wide and miles long.

Two

A Stroll through Town

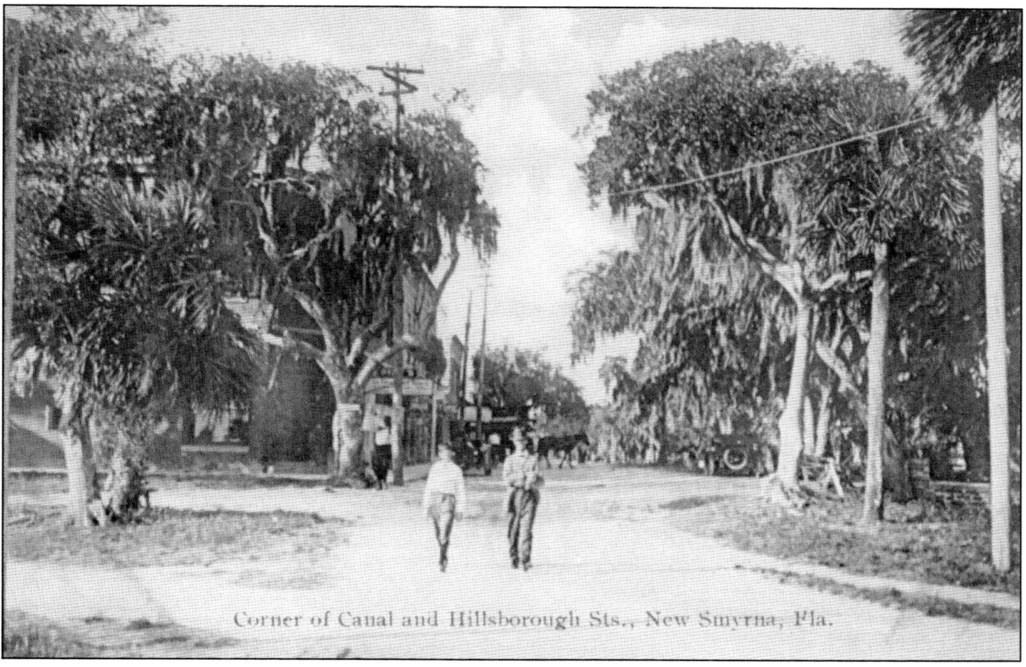

Corner of Canal and Hillsborough Streets. The corner of Canal and Hillsborough Streets is still a major area in town. Behind the viewer is the Indian River. The area to the right of the men in the card is now home to county offices. Where the car is parked is now the approximate location of the Southeast Volusia Chamber of Commerce. Where the horse and carriage are crossing the road is the approximate location of either Sams Avenue or Magnolia Street.

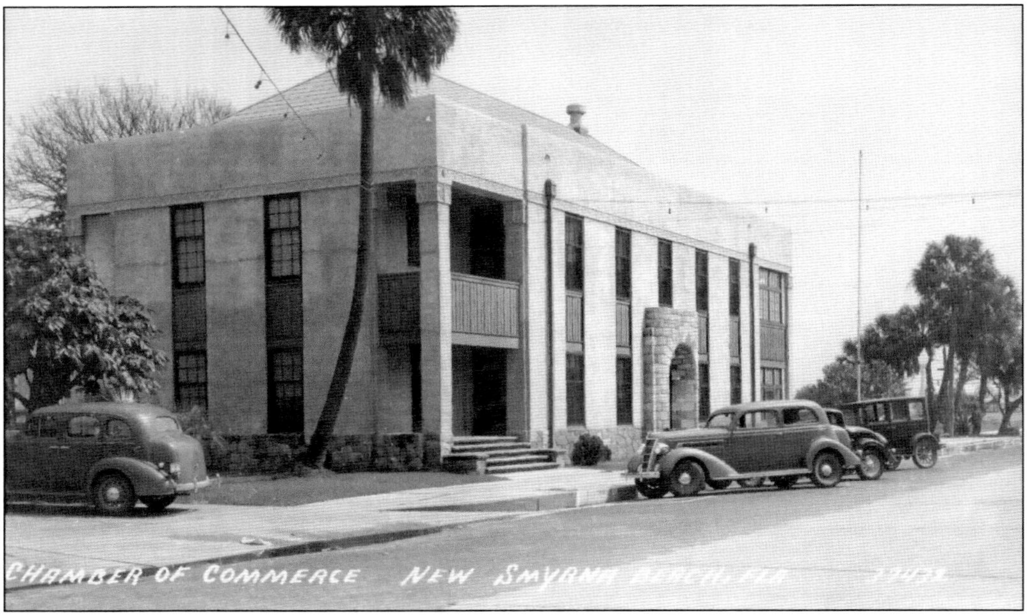

CHAMBER OF COMMERCE. The Southeast Volusia Chamber of Commerce building is located near the northeast end of Canal Street. The chamber began in 1915 as a local board of trade, and its formal charter was approved in 1932 with a goal of the "promotion of civic, economic, and social welfare of the people of New Smyrna and the vicinity." In 2012, the building was restored to its original condition, and the facilities were upgraded. The angled parking shown here is a thing of the past. In addition to chamber offices, the building is also home to the Artist's Workshop, a co-op gallery and studio.

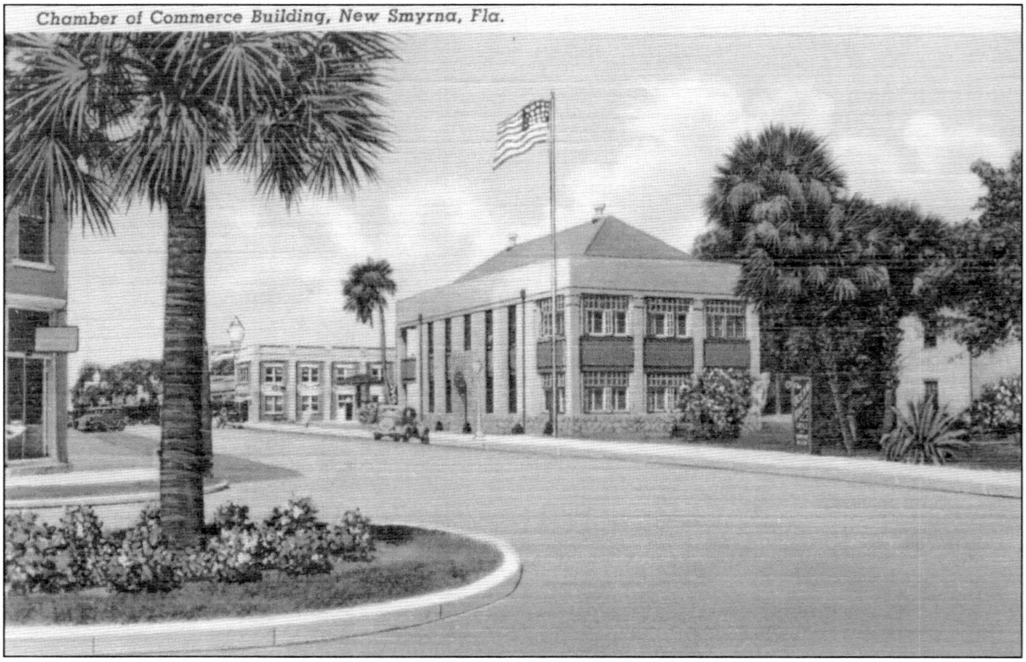

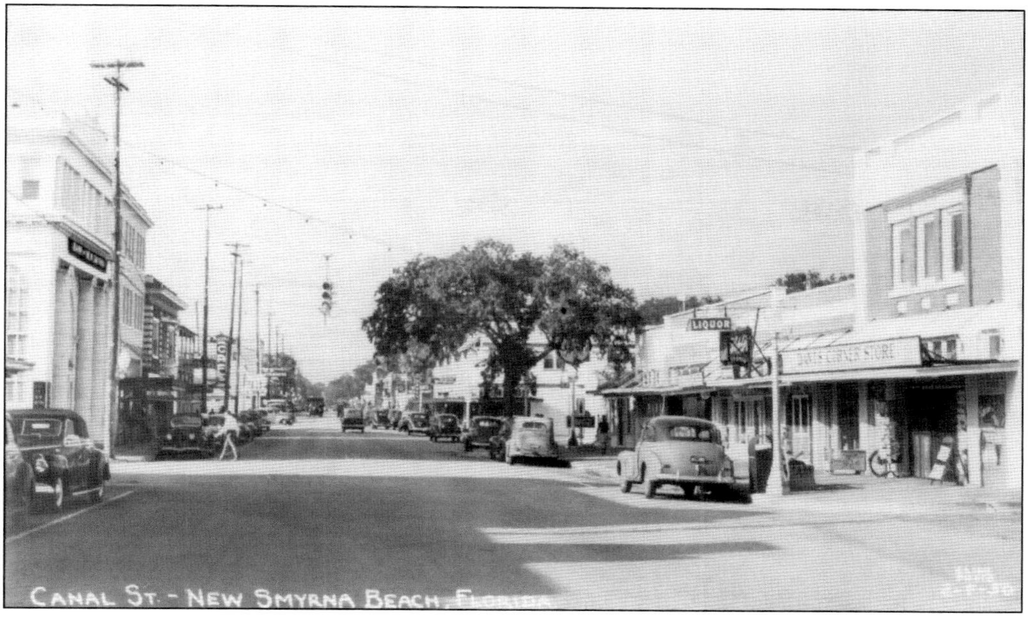

CANAL STREET. These two views were taken from opposite ends of Canal Street and show some of the main shops in town during the 1950s. The Bank of New Smyrna was the major bank of the area. The Davis Corner Store, McCrory's, and Morris Drugs were popular places to shop. The photograph above shows the Royal Café, a popular eatery. The Bank of New Smyrna building, with the columns, is now home to the Utilities Commission, while the Davis Corner Store is now home to the popular Jason's Corner restaurant. Street scenes of today are very similar, with two lanes of traffic and parking on both sides of the road.

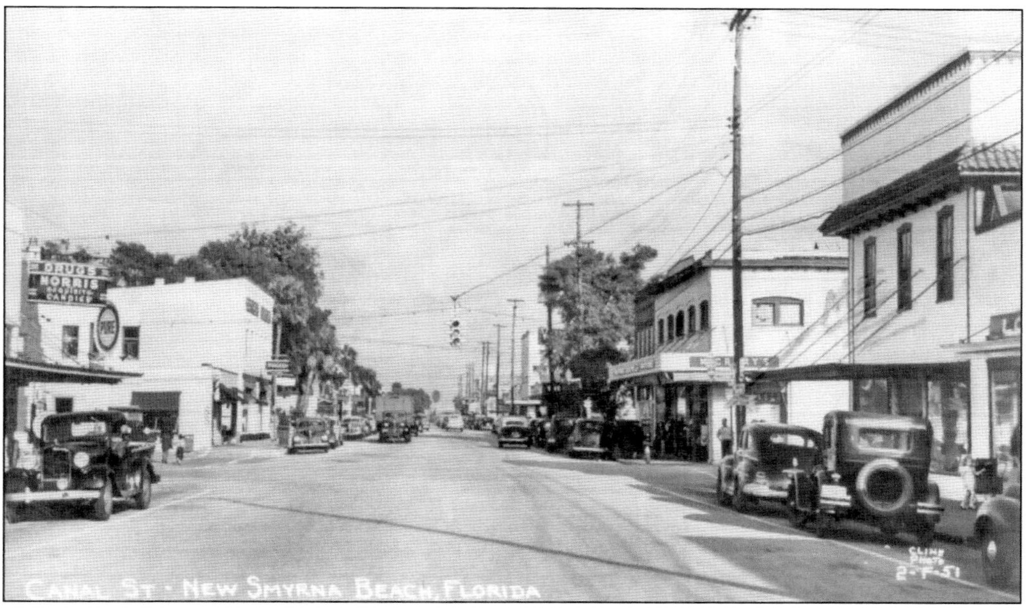

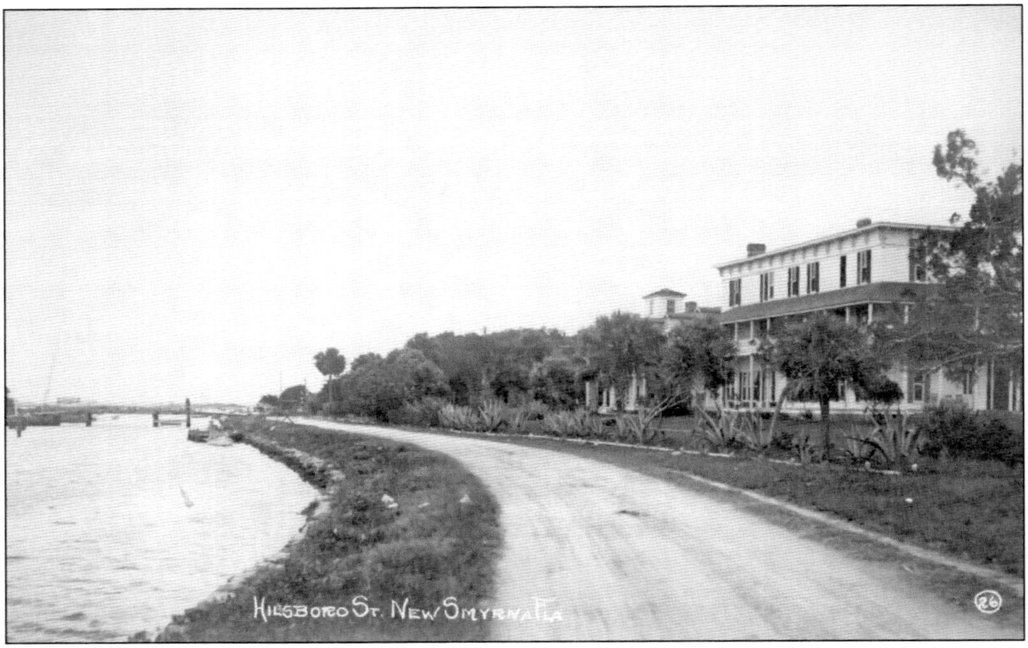

HILLSBORO STREET. Hillsborough Street (note that this is the correct spelling of the street name) is now known as Riverside Drive. Many large and beautiful homes face the Indian River and the tranquil views it provides. The grand structure shown above is the Ocean House, an early hotel originally built by the Lowd family in 1868, then later owned by Frank W. Sams. The Ocean House is no longer standing, and in its place are county offices, including a courthouse annex. Several of the large homes that faced the river can be seen below.

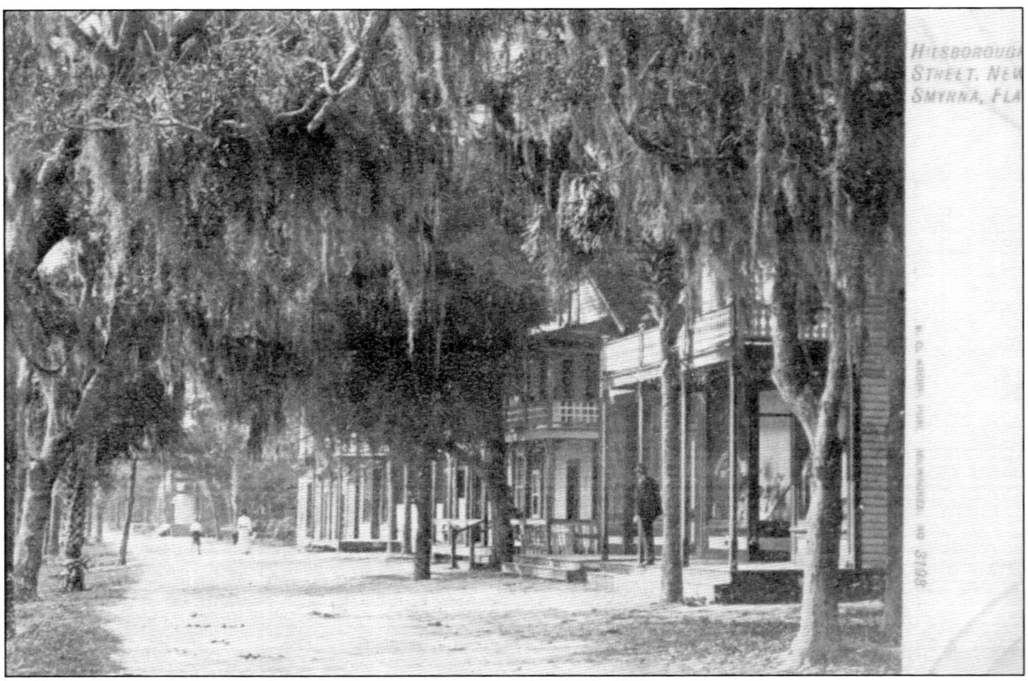

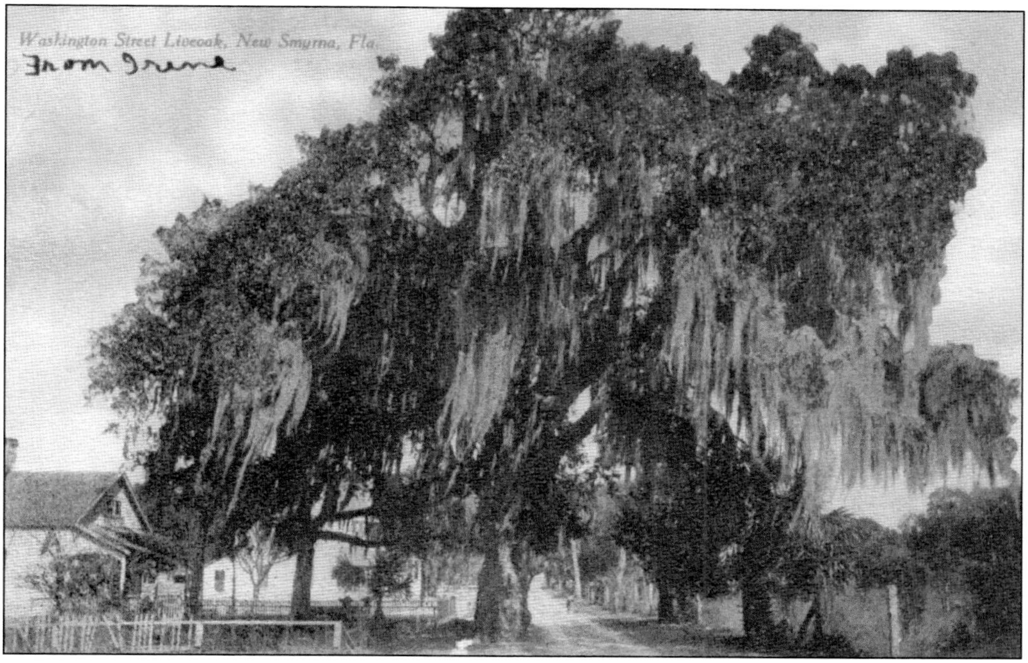

TREES WITH SPANISH MOSS. The plant known as Spanish moss is not actually moss but rather a flowering plant from the bromeliad family. It grows in warm climates with high humidity. It is most often found in live oak and bald cypress trees. The live oak tree has played an important role in the economic history of the area. The US government paid handsomely for live oak timbers to be used in shipbuilding. Teams of cutters swarmed southern states during the cool months in the late 1700s and later to cut and sell the valuable timber, which was often used for creating the structure of ships due to the curved nature of the tree. (Above, courtesy Dorothy Moore.)

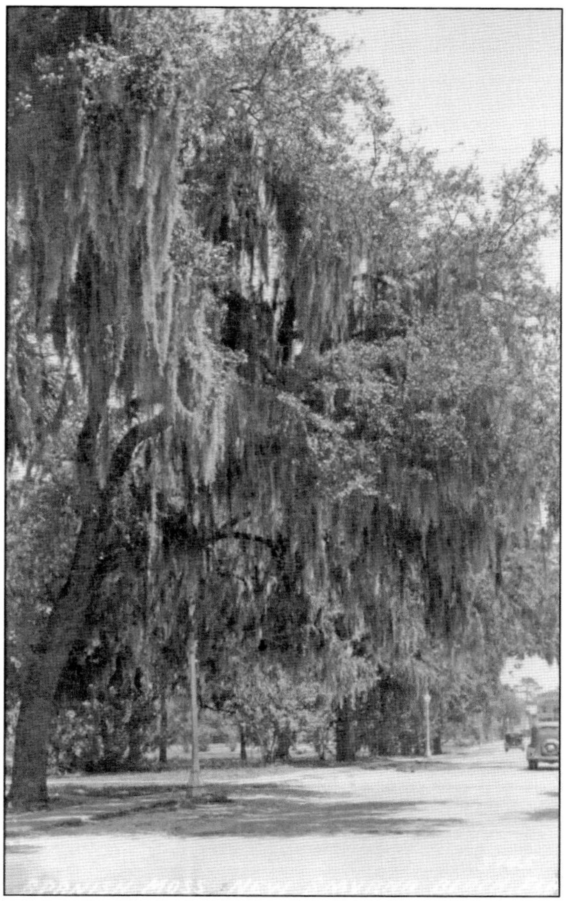

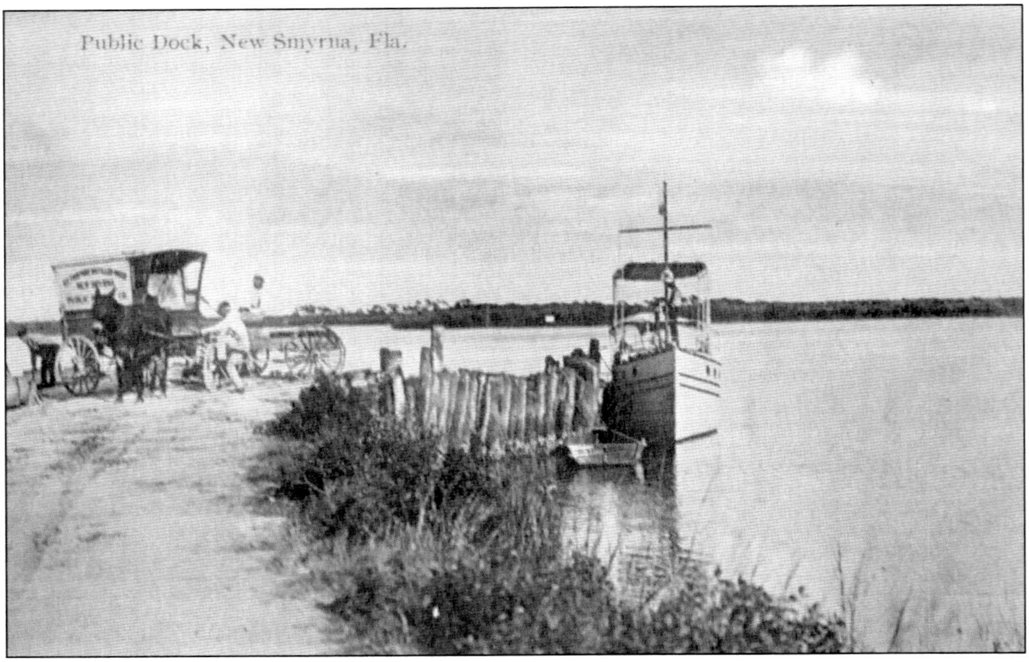

Dock Scenes. When Andrew Turnbull created the Smyrna settlement, he was sure to have a wharf, the remains of which can be seen off Riverside Drive at low tide. The public dock shown above looks to have been an area where local fishermen could unload their day's catch. The markings on the horse and buggy are unidentifiable. The Blue Spring, Orange City & Atlantic (BSOC&A) Railroad had built a line stretching from the St. Johns River to the Indian River at Lytle Avenue, as seen below. Lytle now turns into the Harris M. Saxon Bridge, or the south bridge. Much of the old BSOC&A railbed has been used for the Rails-to-Trails program.

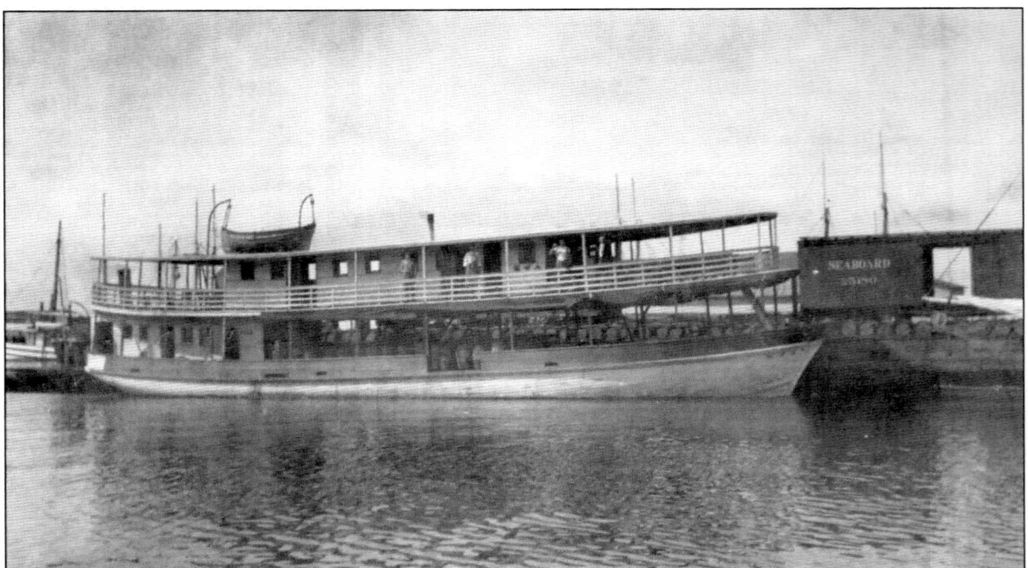

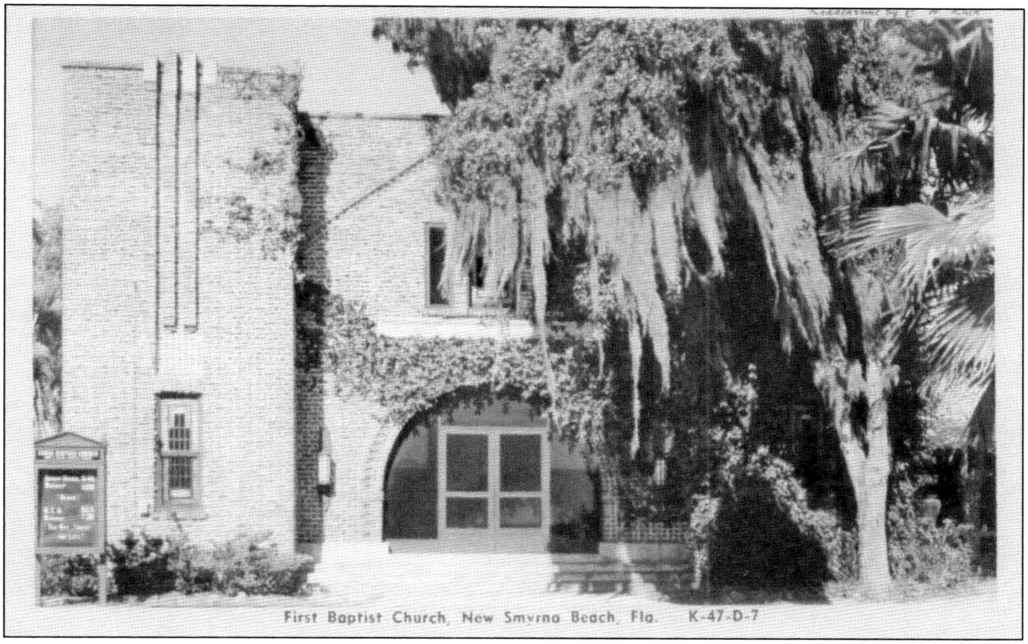

FIRST BAPTIST CHURCH. From its humble beginnings in 1906 to the construction of a beautiful brick building in 1929 to today, the First Baptist Church has been a mainstay in the community. Unfortunately, maintenance costs have skyrocketed, and the building is no longer used for services. The City of New Smyrna Beach will be purchasing the historic structure and converting it into office and meeting space.

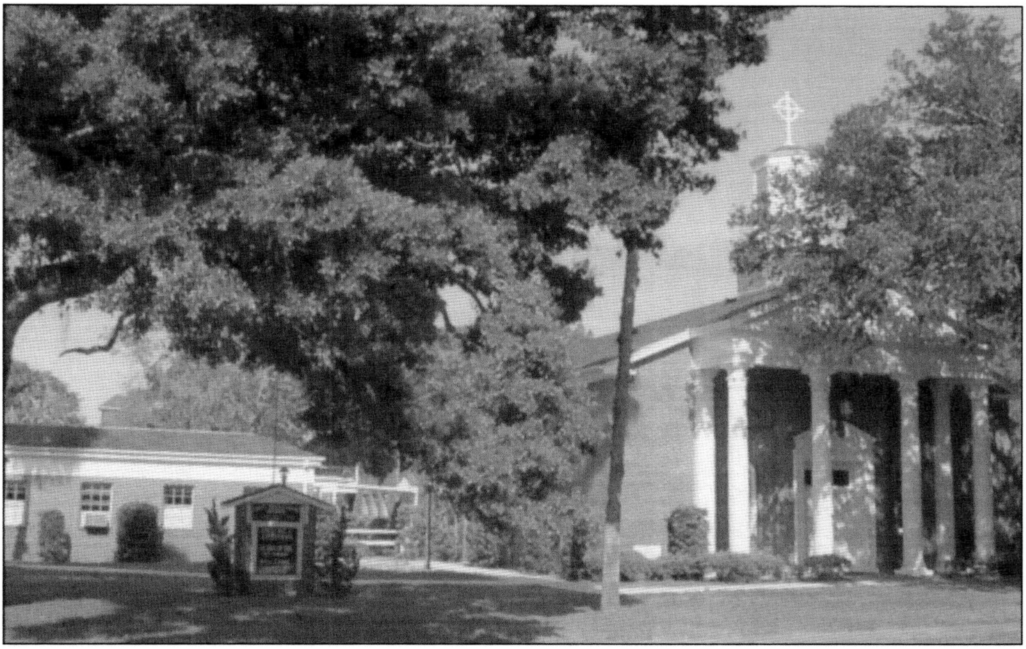

FIRST PRESBYTERIAN CHURCH. The First Presbyterian Church of New Smyrna Beach can trace its roots to 1875, when it was organized in Coronado Beach. The original building was dedicated in 1876. The church moved to the mainland in 1934, with Rev. G.V. Albertson serving as pastor. The present sanctuary on Magnolia Street was constructed between 1960 and 1961.

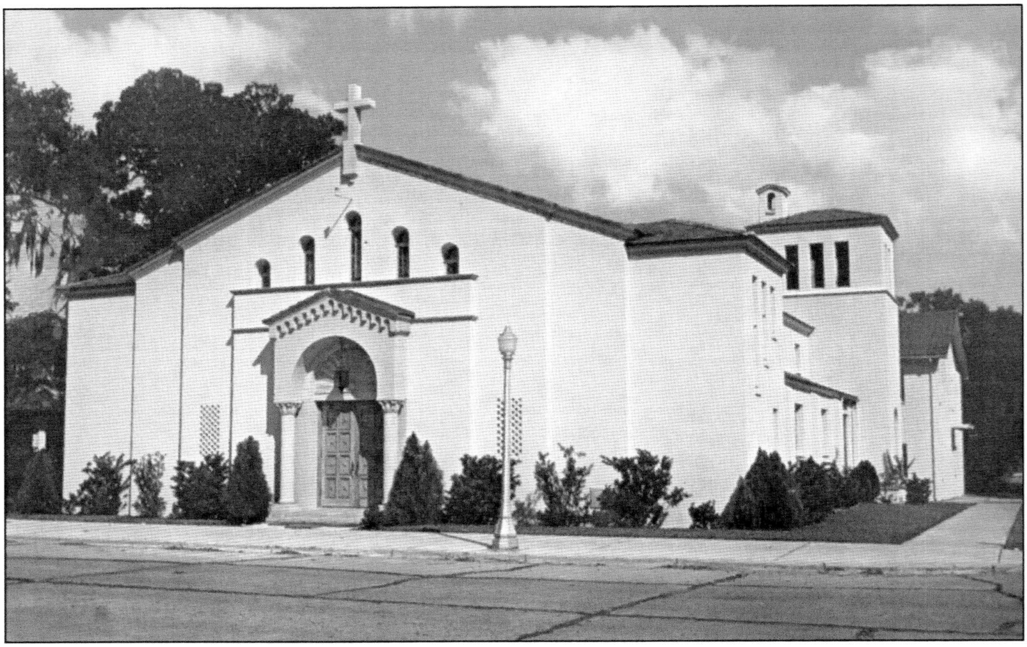

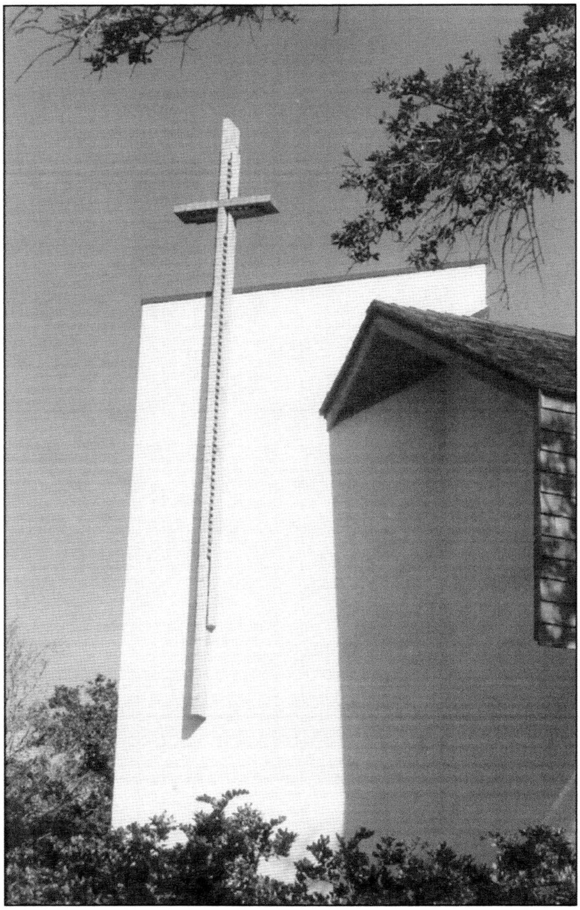

First United Methodist Church. Located on the corner of Palmetto and Douglas Streets in the heart of the historic district, the First United Methodist Church lives by the motto "Loving God, Sharing Love, Making Disciples." This congregation is an active community participant, helping to sponsor a hot meal program three days a week, providing a clothing ministry to those in need, and hosting an annual Thanksgiving dinner that is attended by more than 500 residents.

Coronado Community United Methodist Church. Serving an average attendance of 500 worshipers, the Coronado Community United Methodist Church has come a long way from its small beginnings in 1904. The current sanctuary was constructed in the 1980s. Through prudent land acquisition, the church is a hive of activity with day school programs, support groups, a thrift store, youth groups, small groups, community ministry, dinners, and of course, worship services.

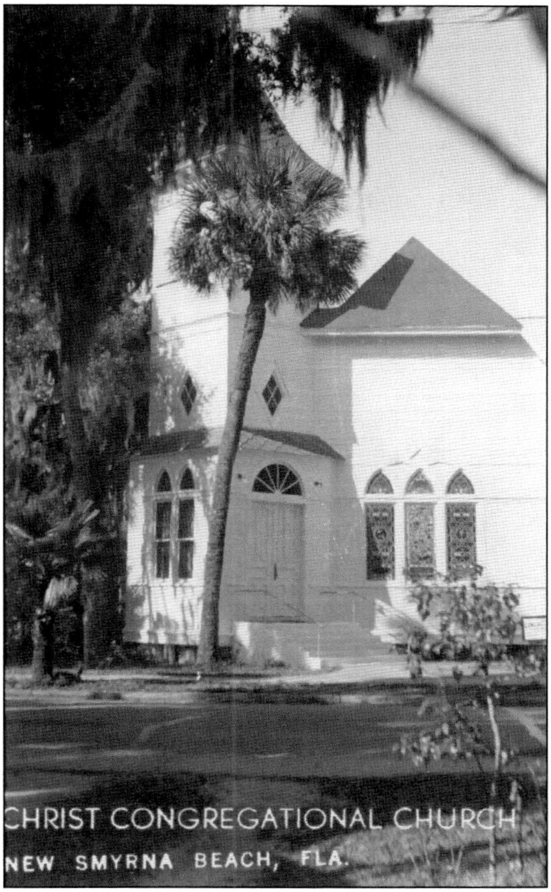

Christ Congregational Church. Led by the Reverend Charles Selleck in 1875, a group of 16 devoted followers laid the foundation for the Christ Congregational Church. The first service was held in the newly completed sanctuary in November 1889. The city library was originally housed here when Washington E. Connor donated 300 books for a free library. Quickly outgrowing this space, the library's collection was moved to an outbuilding. Connor donated the library to the city after officials agreed to purchase his toll bridge for the sum of $32,500. Years later, the Connor Library building was moved to Old Fort Park, where it served as home to the New Smyrna Museum of History before being returned to use as office space for city employees. (Right, courtesy Dorothy Moore.)

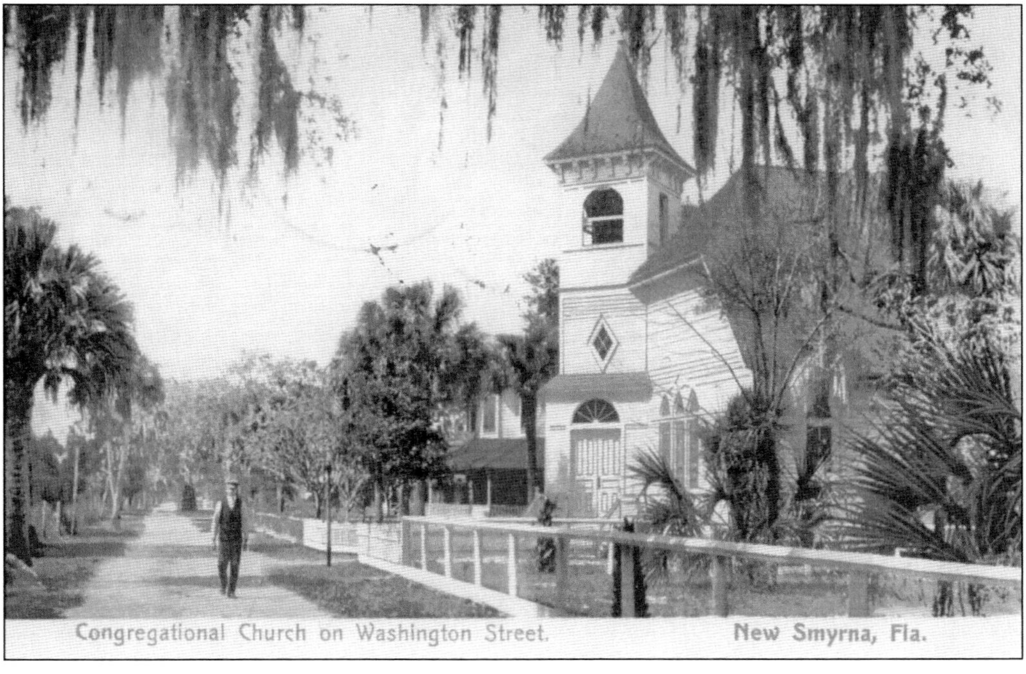

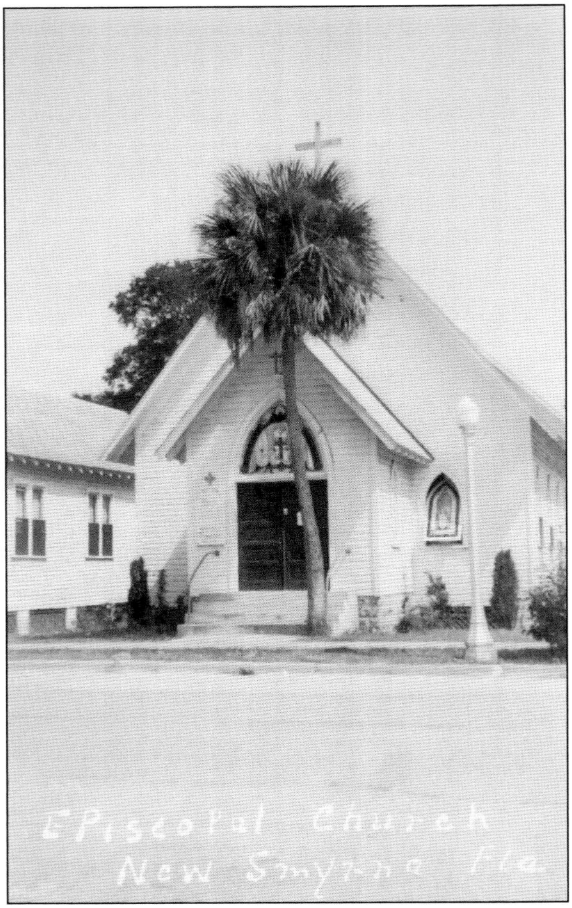

St. Paul's Episcopal Church. St. Paul's Episcopal Church traces its origins to an Anglican church founded during the Turnbull settlement era. The current church building, originally located at the corner of Palmetto and Downing Streets, dates to 1907. The current name was bestowed on the church by Rt. Rev. Cameron Mann in 1922. St. Paul's was named to parish status in 1952. In 1977, the church building was moved to its present location on Live Oak Street. (Courtesy Dorothy Moore.)

Sacred Heart Catholic Church. The original Sacred Heart Catholic Church building was constructed around the turn of the 20th century, and Fr. Joseph Downey took over leadership of the church in 1926. The building was originally located on Faulkner Street but was moved in 1956 to serve the growing African American Catholic population. That building is now home to the Mary S. Harrell Black Heritage Museum. Today, Sacred Heart, which is part of the Orlando diocese, fronts US 1.

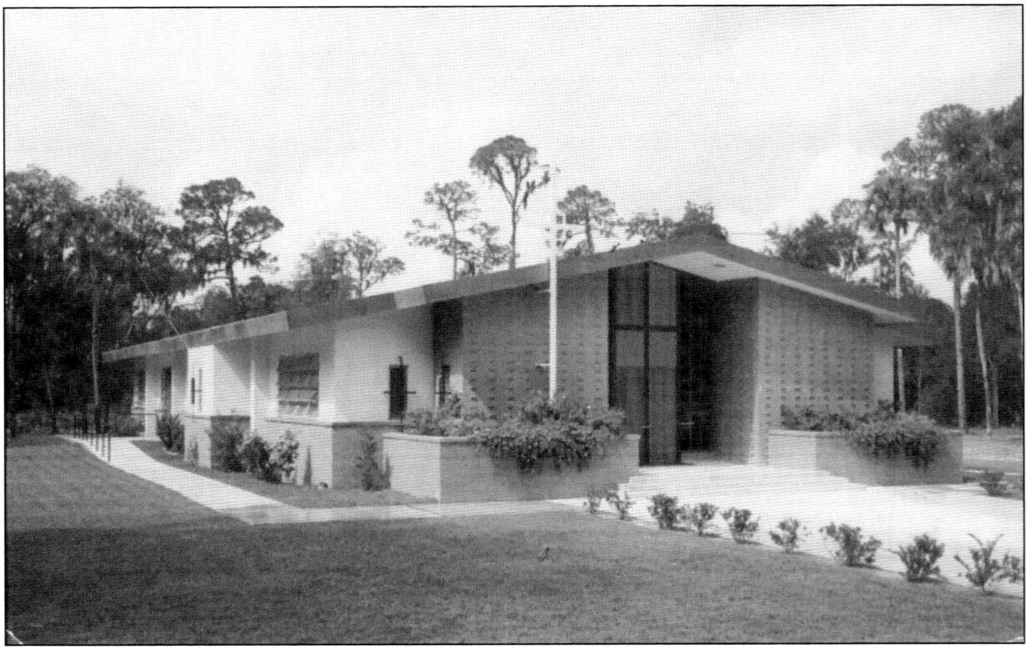

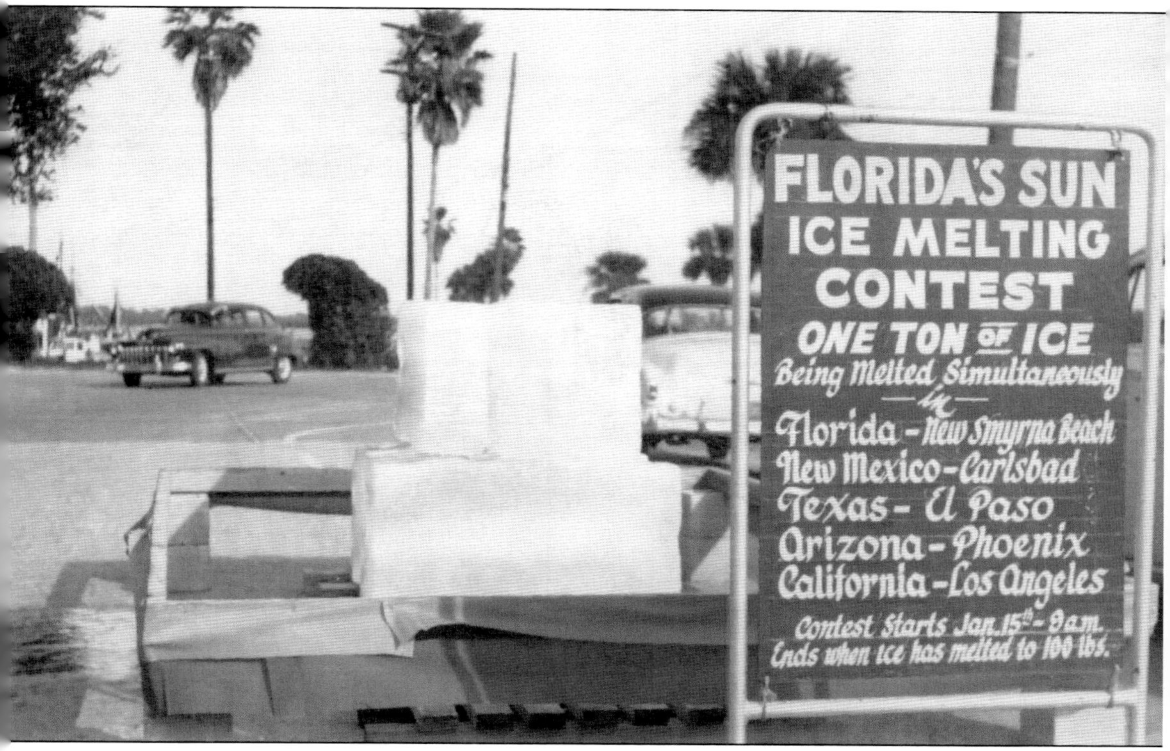

ICE-MELTING CONTEST. New Smyrna Beach was an unofficial entrant into this 1952 ice-melting contest that featured cities from the southwest United States. Royal Palm Ice Co. donated the blocks of ice used locally. The official winner was El Paso, Texas, with a time of 36 hours, 41 minutes, and 52 seconds needed to melt their ice to the required weight. Los Angeles was disqualified when rain helped wash away their ice. In a show of good sportsmanship, New Smyrna Beach sent a key to the city to the El Paso Chamber of Commerce. According to the local newspaper, the ice in New Smyrna melted in only 32 hours. (Courtesy Norm Shepard.)

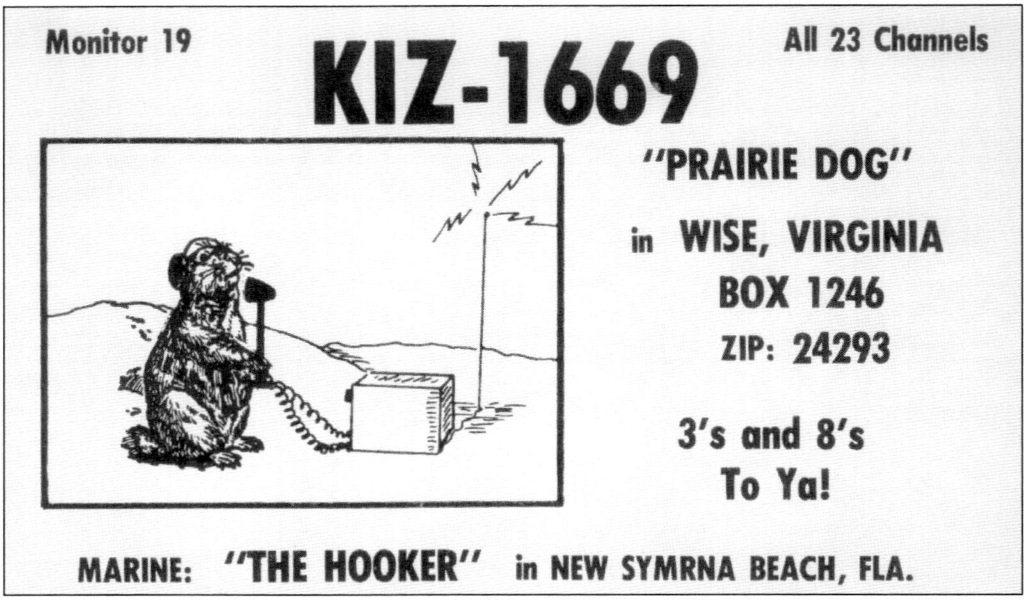

KIZ-1669. The world of citizen band (CB) radio was a popular one in the 1970s, and this appears to have been a calling card of sorts for a user who resided in both Wise, Virginia, and New Smyrna Beach, Florida. On land, his handle seems to have been "Prairie Dog," and on the water, he was known as "The Hooker," most likely a fishing reference. The phrase "3's and 8's to ya!" is a sign-off in CB lingo meaning "best wishes."

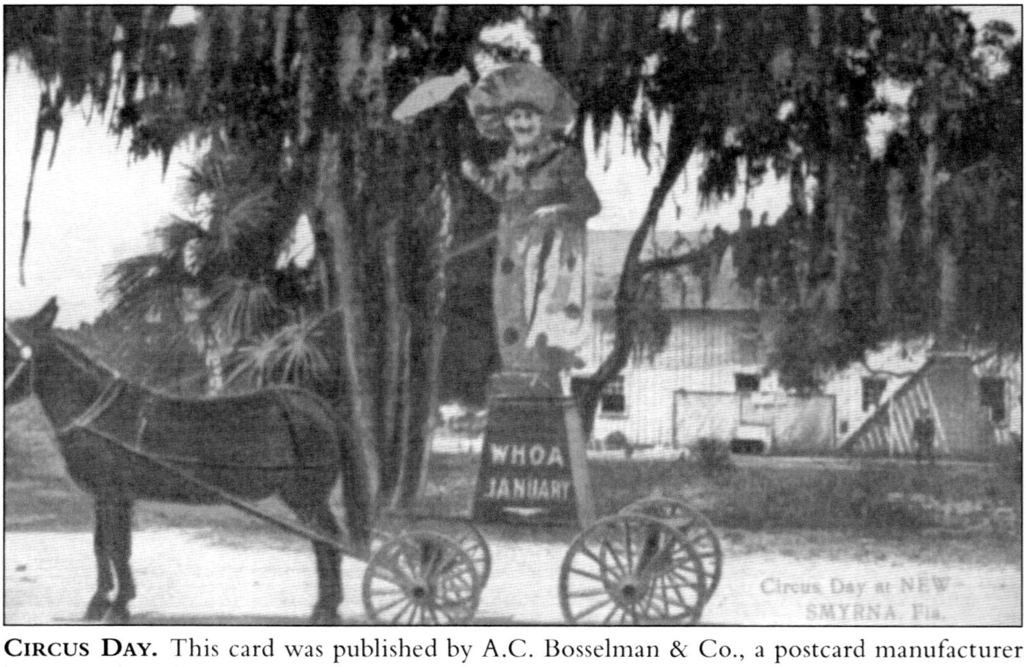

Circus Day. This card was published by A.C. Bosselman & Co., a postcard manufacturer known to have been in business from 1905 to 1914. While not certain, this card might date to 1913. On July 25, 1913, the *New Smyrna Daily News* ran an article outlining an entertaining circus that youngsters had held the prior week as a fundraiser for the volunteer fire department. In the article is mention of the Honorable Alan Smith, who stood upon the seat of his buggy encouraging locals to attend.

JUNGLE ROAD. Perhaps named for the dense brush that used to cover the area, Jungle Road is now a prime development area. Thanks to the efforts of Jim Humphrey and other preservationists, a parcel of just over 40 acres at the corner of Jungle Road and Highway 44 has been preserved. This area contains the remains of Turnbull-era canals, and Humphrey had hoped to one day see a public park opened on the land.

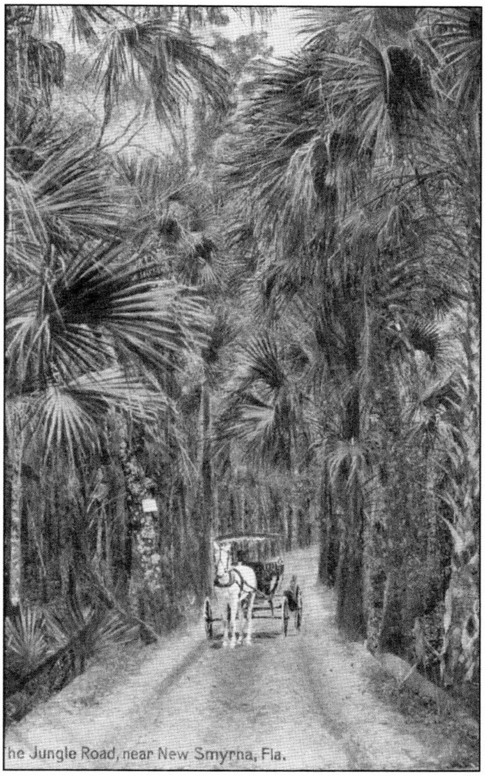

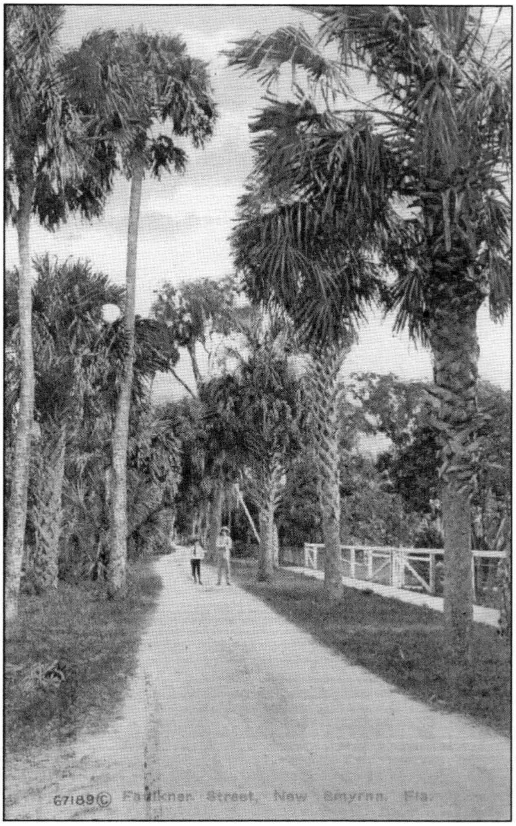

FAULKNER STREET. The dirt road in this image shows the tranquil nature that is still characteristic of much of Faulkner Street. Faulkner is generally a residential street that runs north of busy Canal Street. At one time, a fire station was located on the street, just a block off Canal. The Faulkner Street School, which remained open for 70 years, was perhaps the largest intrusion into the peacefulness of the area.

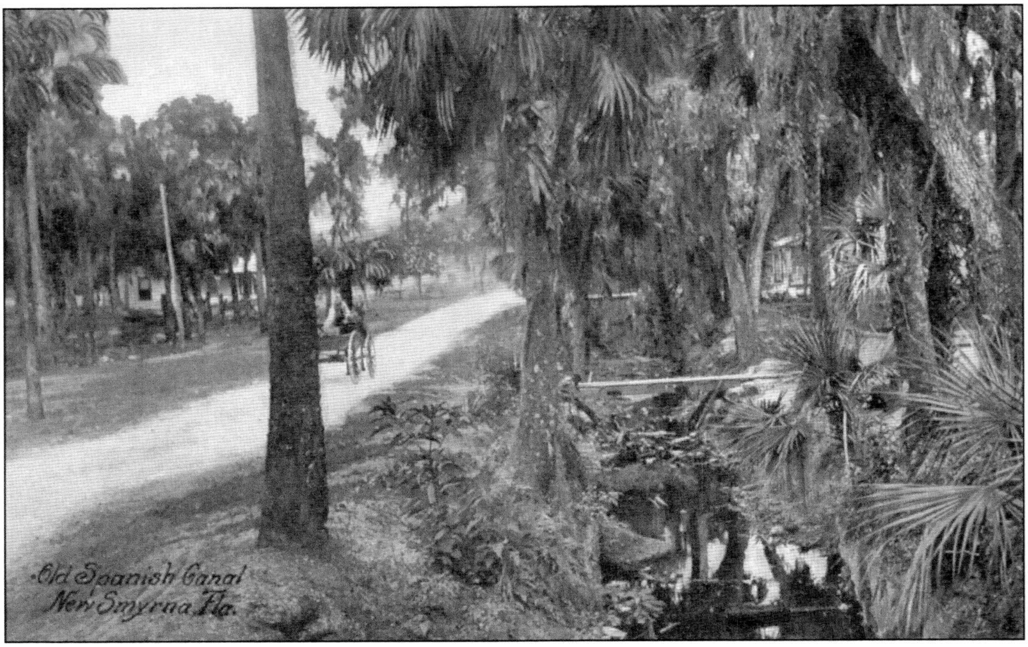

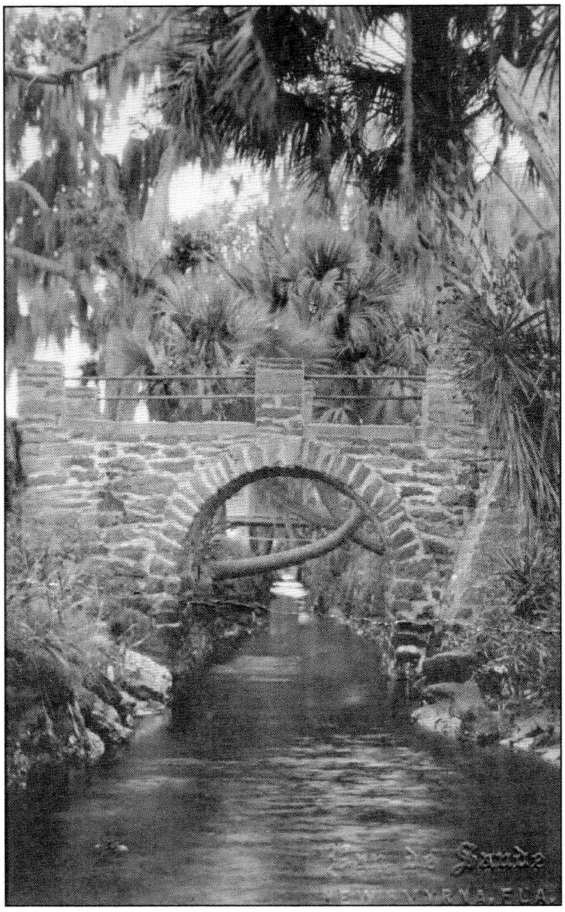

TURNBULL-ERA CANALS. While not a street in the traditional sense, these canals were used for the transport of crops from the fields to the wharf area, located on what is now Riverside Drive. The card above shows what appears to be the canal on the western end of Canal Street. Note the narrow, rickety-looking planks that property owners had to traverse to reach their homes. A much more solid bridge, which led to the Ocean House, is shown in the image at left. It is said the photographer, Theo van de Sande, had to stand in the canal to take this series of shots.

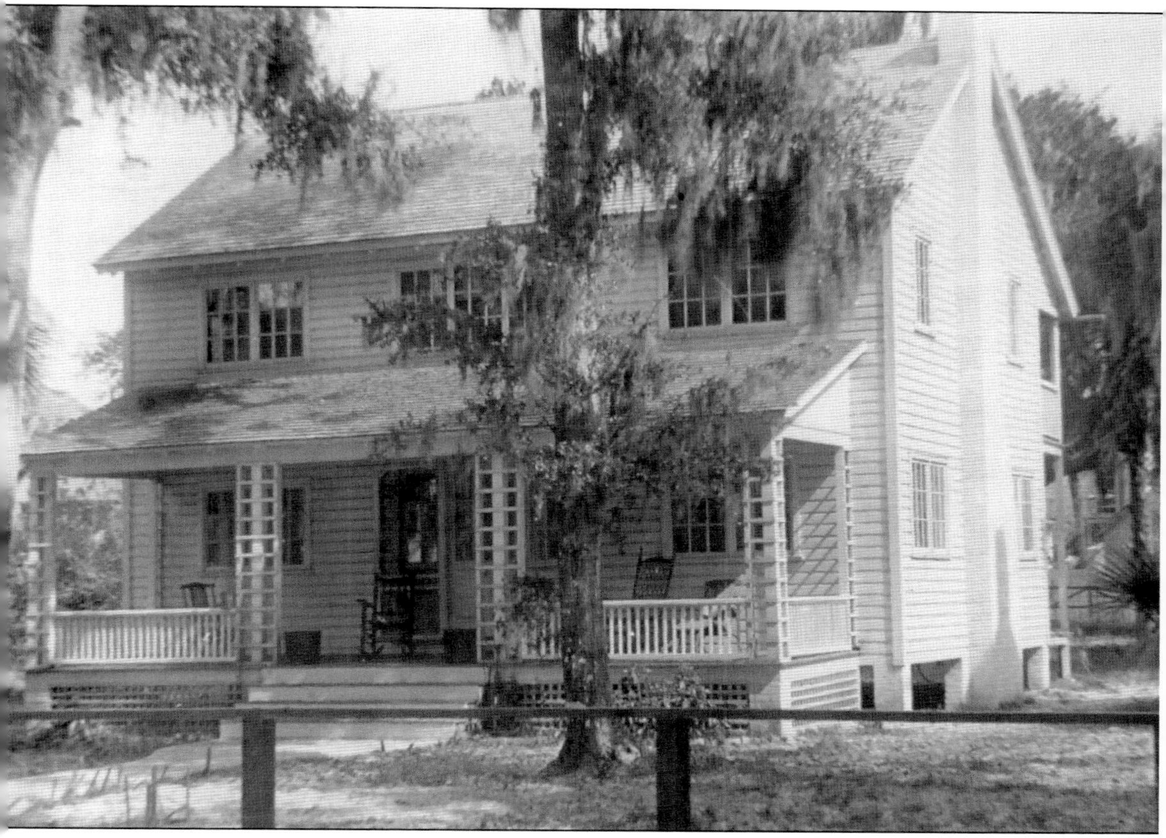

WHITE HOUSE. While the location of this house is still unknown, the date of the image and the identity of the photographer are known. The card was created in 1911, and the back is marked as being photographed by Harry Conrad. He and his wife, Maude, wintered in New Smyrna, where he would set up a photography business each year. His business, shown in period photographs, was often called Conrad's Kodak Place. (Courtesy Dorothy Moore.)

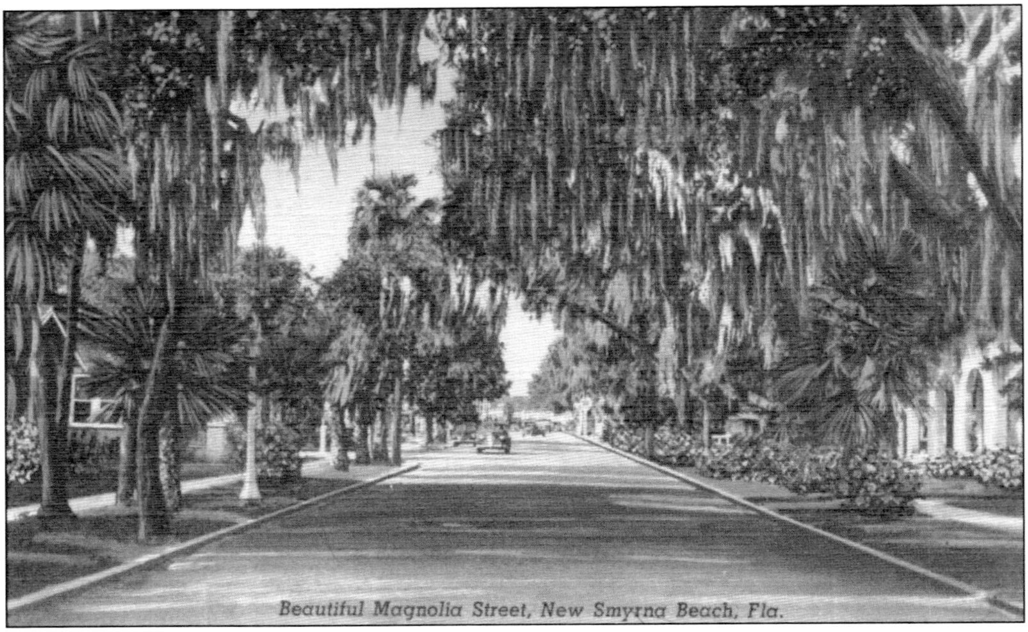

MAGNOLIA STREET. This view is looking north toward downtown and Canal Street. On the right side is the Woman's Club of New Smyrna. This can be determined by the multiple arches that are showing. Magnolia Street is similar in appearance today, with many beautiful live oak trees providing shade from the hot summer sun.

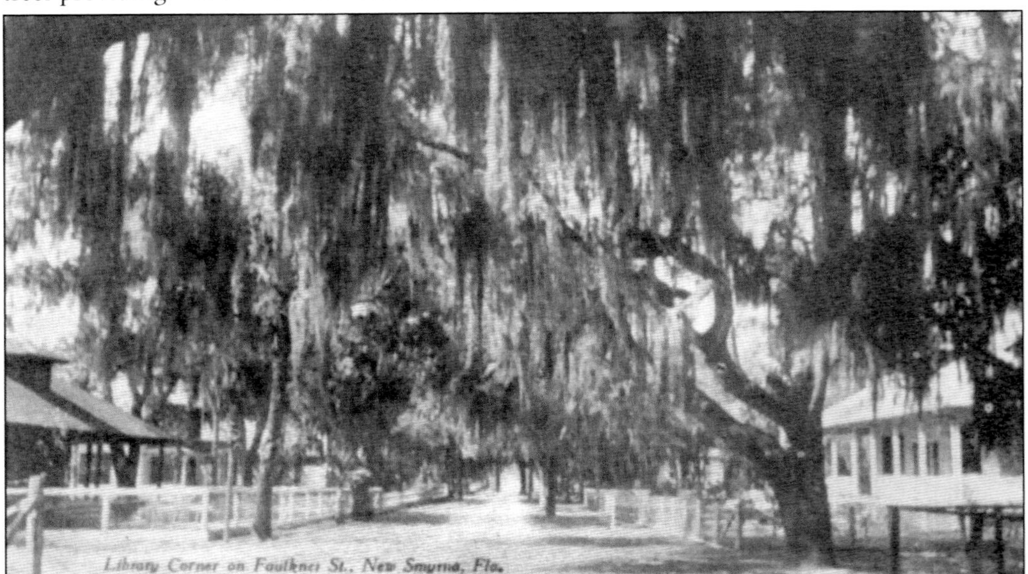

LIBRARY CORNER ON FAULKNER STREET. Thanks to Washington E. Connor, New Smyrna had a free lending library that was housed in a building on the corner of Faulkner and Washington Streets. Long after the library had been moved, serious discussions were undertaken as to what to do with the crumbling building. Eventually, the building, still called the Connor Library, was moved to its current home in Old Fort Park in 1991. Its move and rehabilitation cost more than $120,000. The city is now using the building for office space. There is a small historical marker at the corner where the library originally resided.

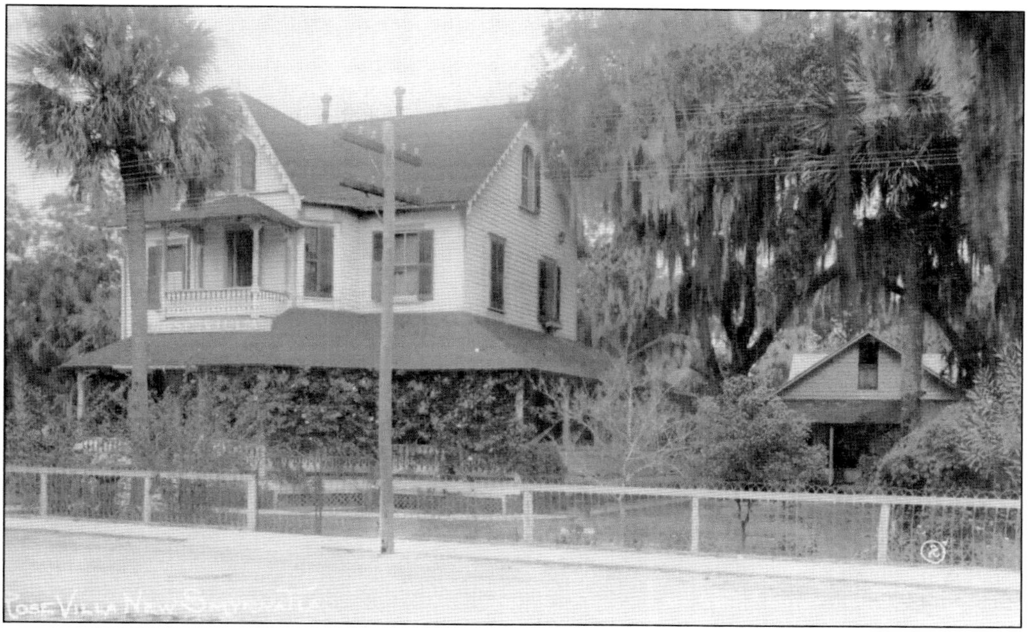

TWO-STORY HOMES. The real-photo postcards shown here highlight the beauty and tranquility that New Smyrna Beach is often known for. While the exact location of the image below is still unknown, the photograph above is identified as Rose Villa. Most recently, this building was home to Nuns and Roses B&B Suites. Neighborhoods like these helped contribute to an approximately 100-acre section of town being recognized by the National Register of Historic Places in 1990. This area is now known as the New Smyrna Beach Historic District and features 313 contributing structures.

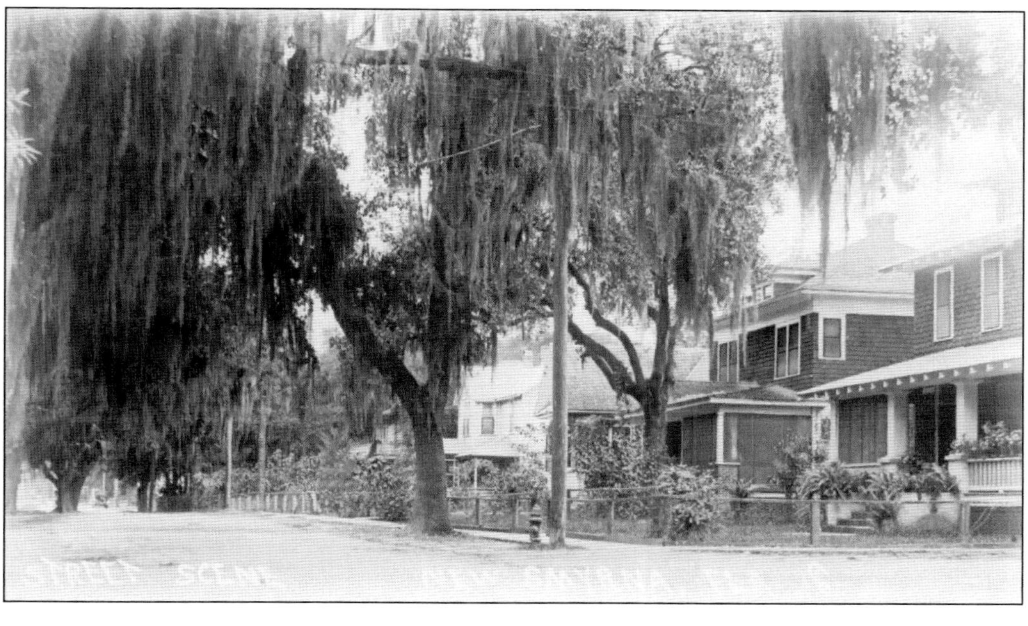

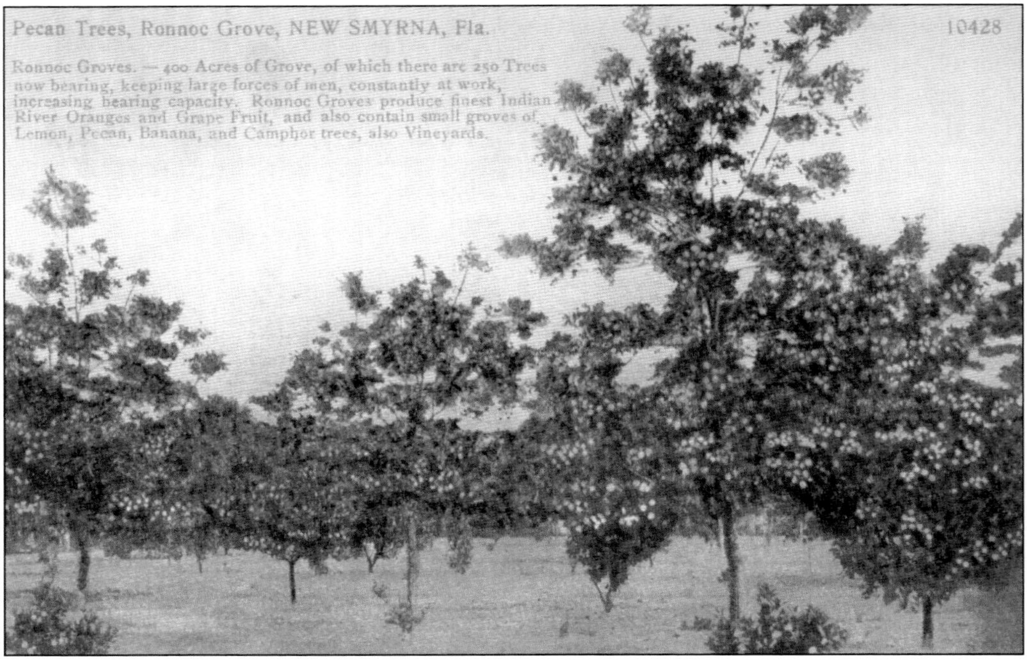

RONNOC GROVE. Ronnoc Grove, owned by wealthy New York financier Washington E. Connor, contained 400 acres and included 250 active pecan trees. Also in the grove were oranges, grapefruit, lemons, bananas, and a vineyard. (Courtesy Dorothy Moore.)

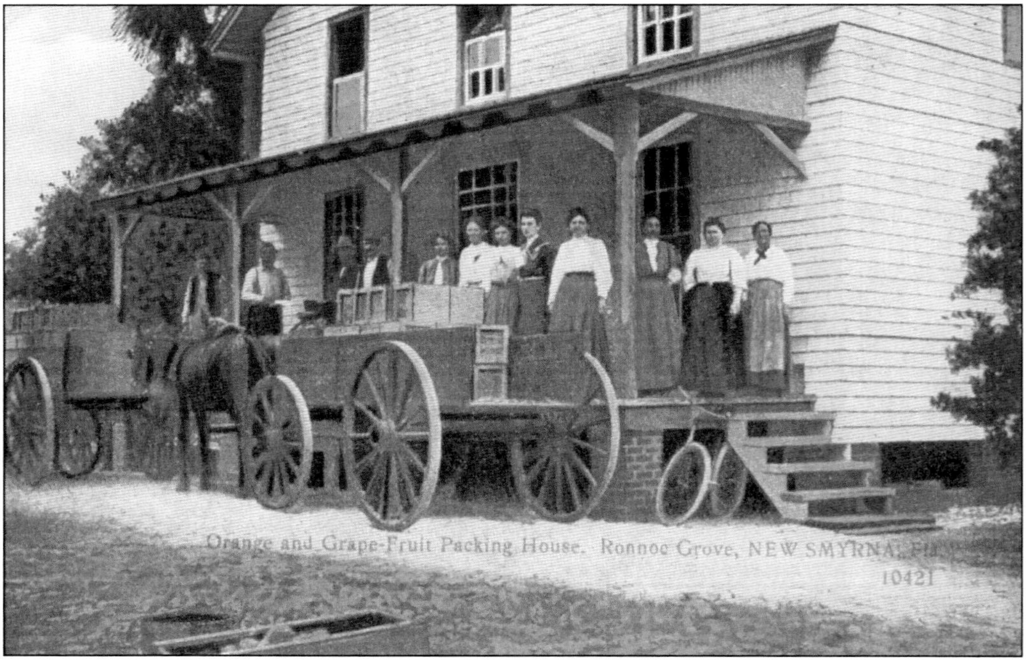

ORANGE AND GRAPEFRUIT PACKINGHOUSE. Located in Ronnoc Grove near the railroad, the Ronnoc Grove packinghouse was kept busy by the large variety of fruits, vegetables, and nuts produced on the farm. The harvests would be cleaned, packed, and then shipped by rail to awaiting markets.

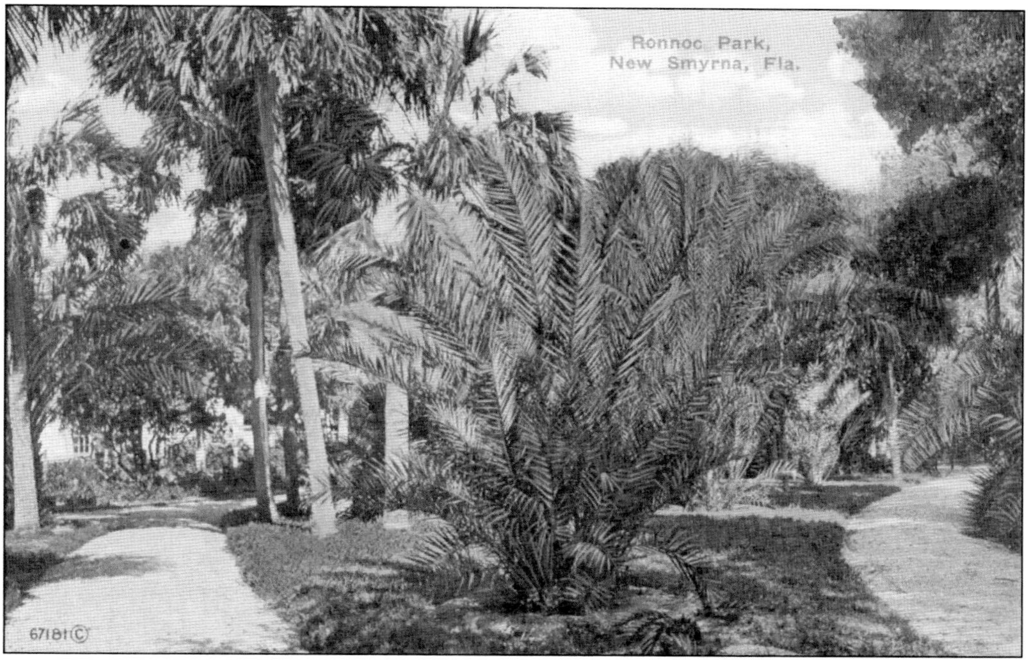

Ronnoc Park. The Washington E. Connor name is synonymous with the early days of New Smyrna. Connor was a New York stockbroker who first visited New Smyrna in 1884 and stayed at the luxurious Ocean House. Liking what he saw, he acquired 3,000 acres of prime real estate. Connor founded the first library in town and also built a toll bridge, helping to connect New Smyrna and Coronado Beach. Later, he purchased the land containing the ruins of the sugar mill, eventually giving them to his second wife, historian Jeannette Thurber Connor. Ronnoc Lane, as shown at right, is named for him. (Both, courtesy Susan Bergert.)

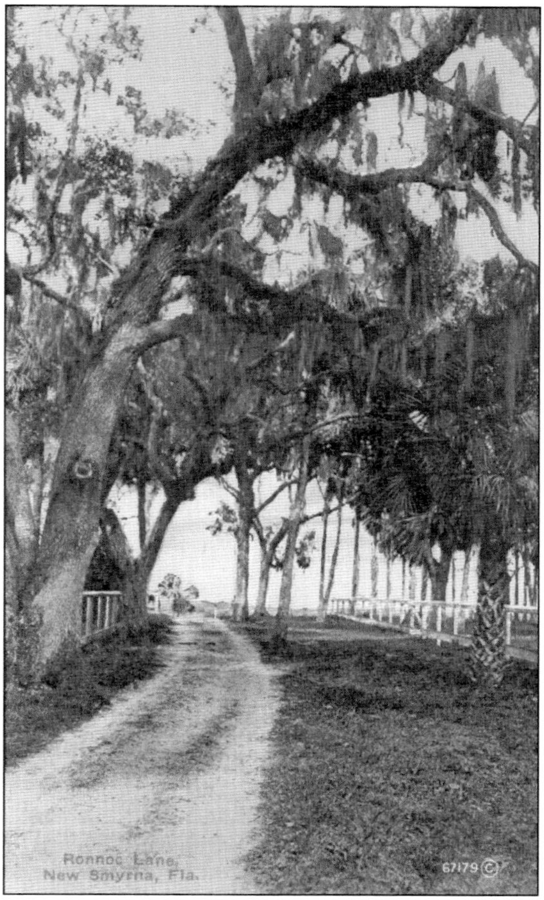

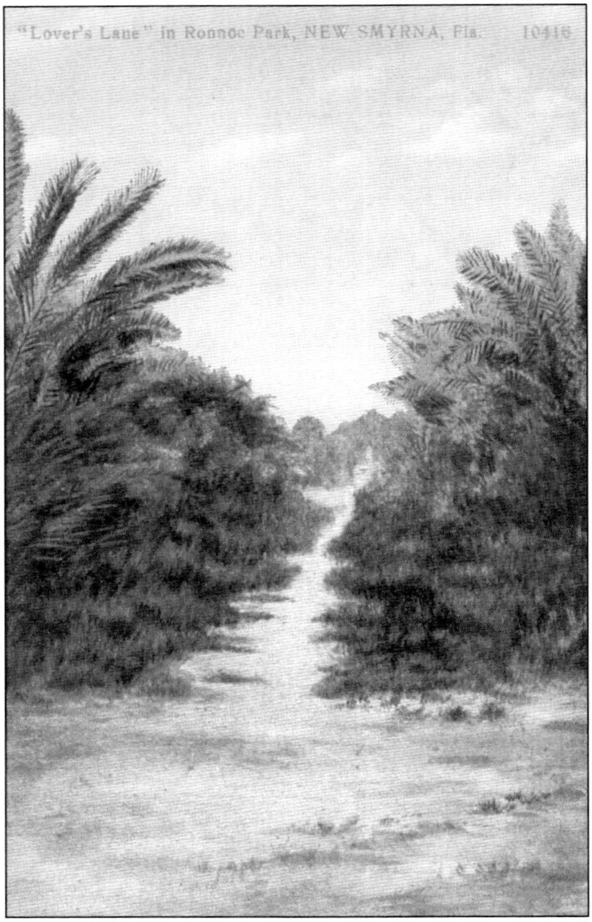

ROADS THROUGH RONNOC PROPERTY. These cards show just two of the many roads through the massive Ronnoc property. Palmetto Row was obviously named for the large palmetto palms lining the road. On the right side of the road are several carts that could have been used to haul crops to the packinghouse for shipment to faraway destinations.

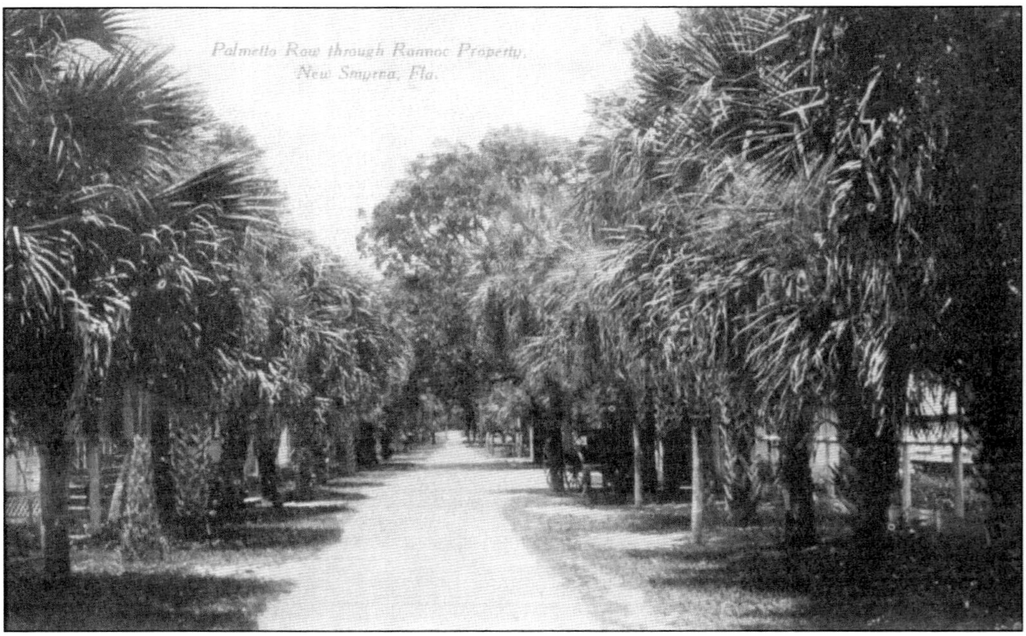

Three

TIME TO ENJOY LIFE

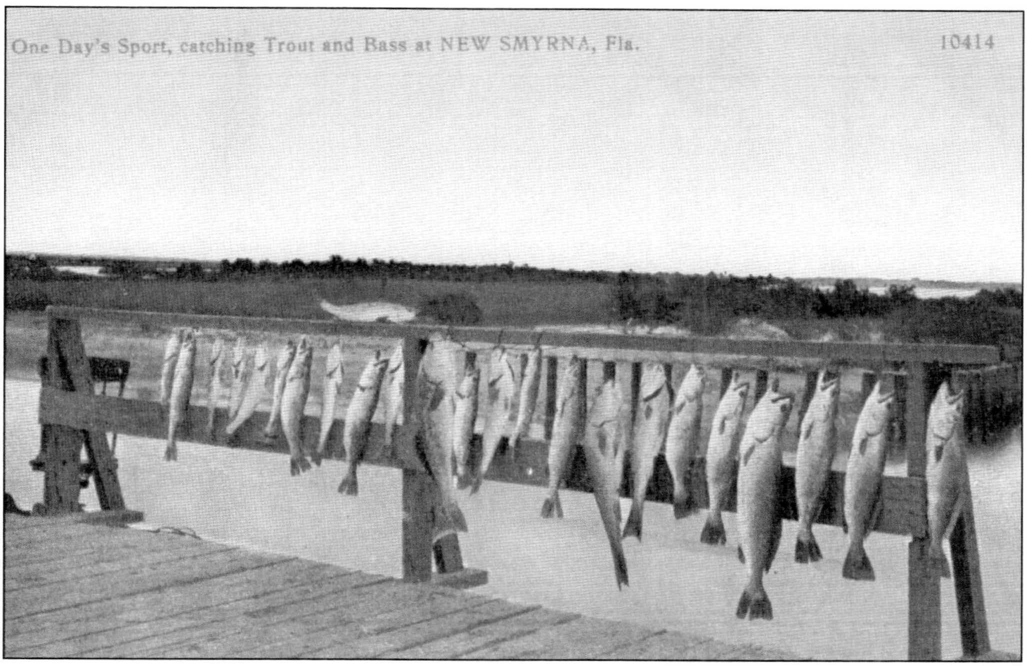

ONE DAY'S SPORT. Fishing has been both a pastime and a way of life for those in New Smyrna Beach since its founding. While the industry has declined, fishing for personal enjoyment is still as popular as it was in this 1910 postcard. While catches of this size and quantity are no longer as common, folks can still be found fishing in the Indian River every day. The most popular fish now caught in the river are sea trout and redfish.

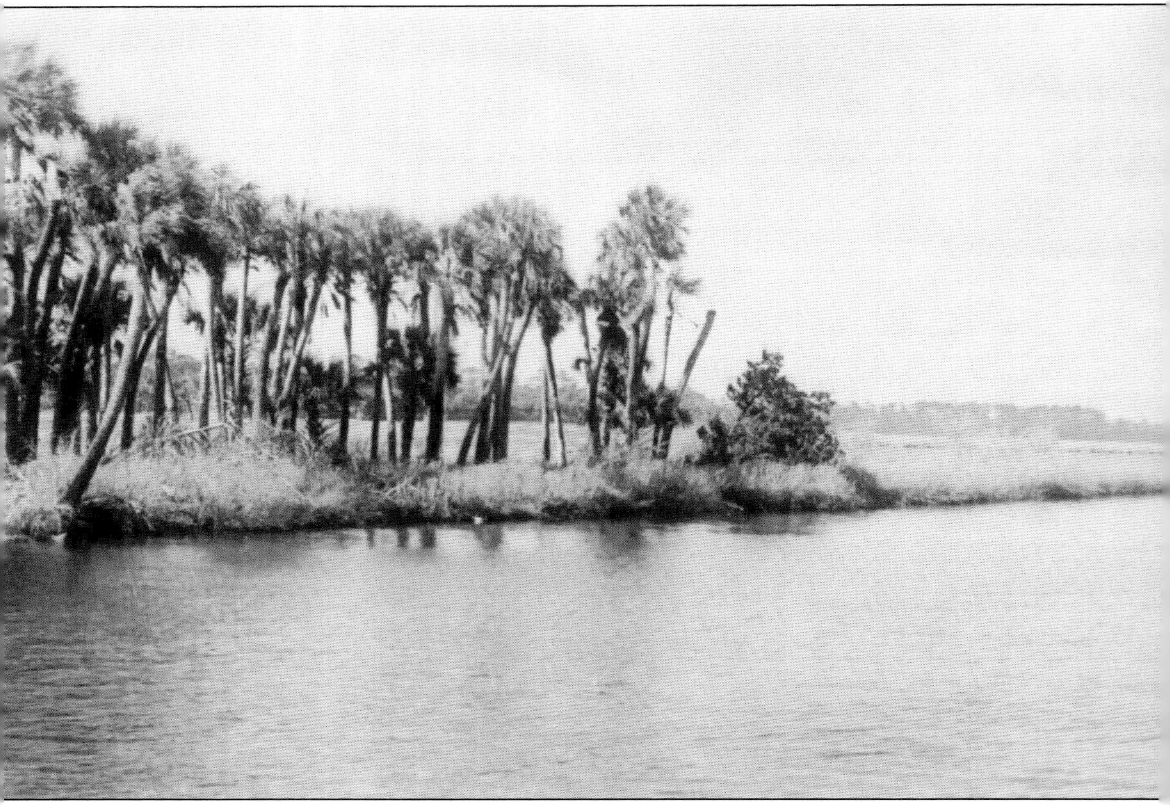

INDIAN RIVER. This double-wide, real-photo postcard showing the Indian River at New Smyrna, Florida, was mailed to Attica, New York, in February 1924. This beautiful view, little changed in almost 100 years, can still be found at the Doris Leeper Spruce Creek Preserve, located

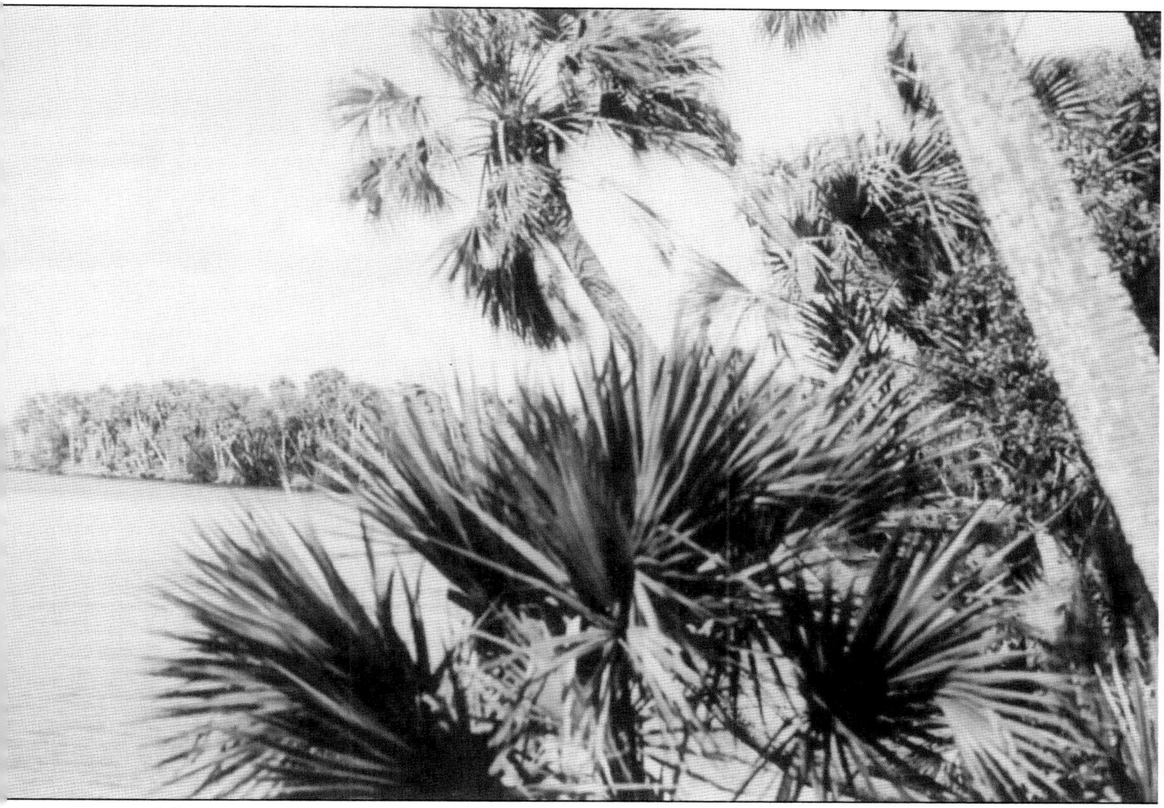

just north of the city. This 2,500-acre preserve is a popular destination for picnics, boating and canoeing, fishing, hiking, and sightseeing. It is not uncommon to see dolphin swimming in the brackish waters of the preserve. (Courtesy Dorothy Moore.)

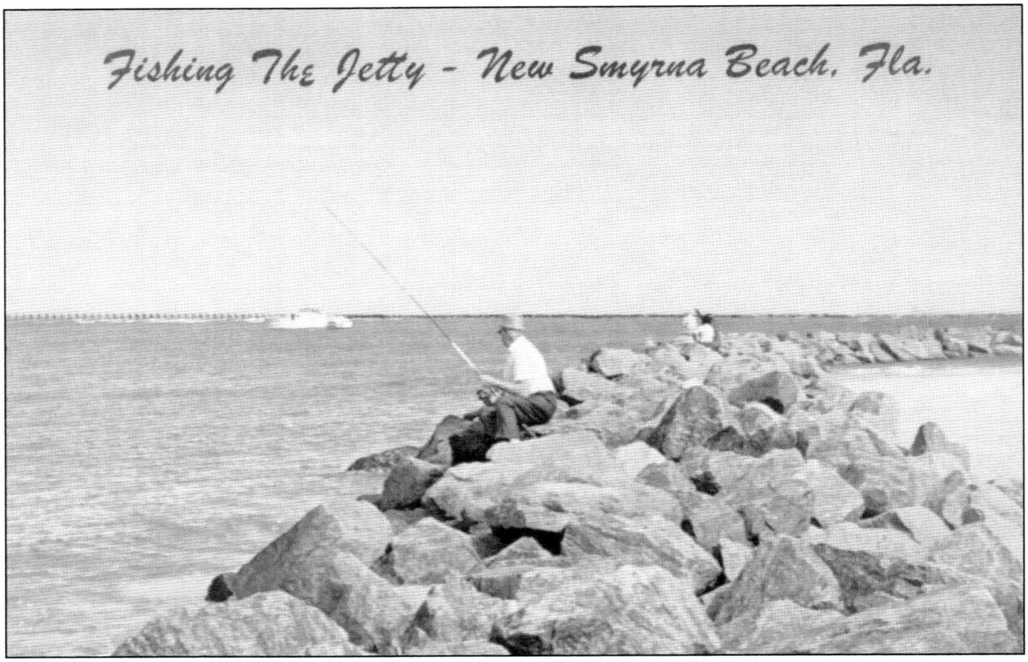

FISHING THE JETTY. This man-made outcropping into the Atlantic Ocean is a popular spot not just for fishing, but for surfing as well. The jetty is paved for approximately half its length, making for easy access. If this gentleman were to look straight ahead from where he is sitting, he would easily see the Ponce Inlet lighthouse.

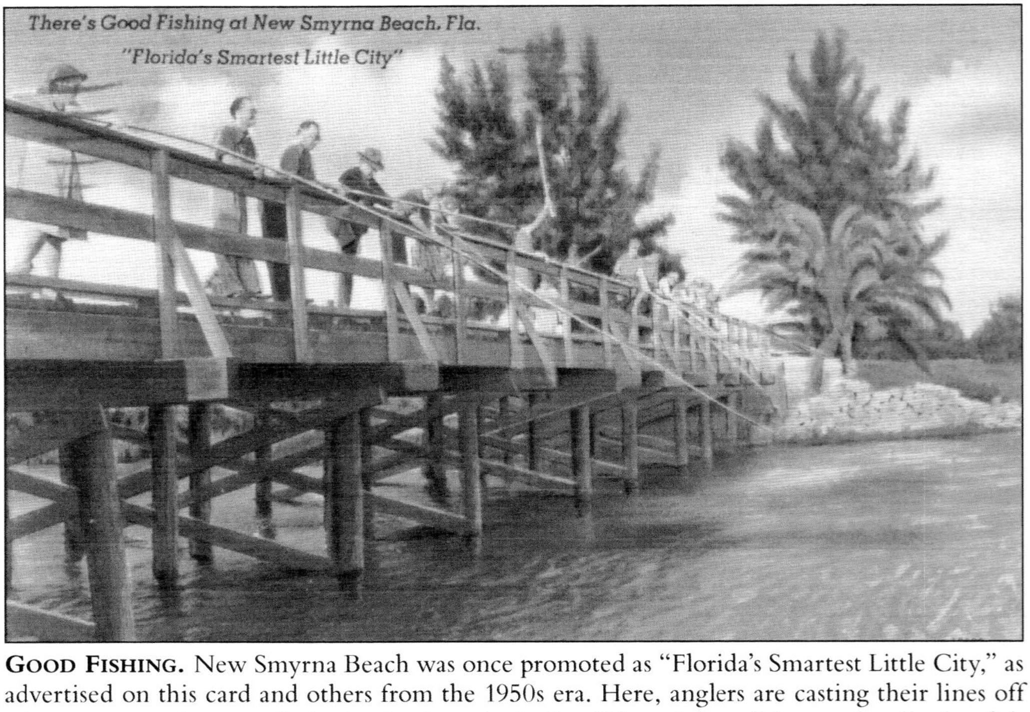

GOOD FISHING. New Smyrna Beach was once promoted as "Florida's Smartest Little City," as advertised on this card and others from the 1950s era. Here, anglers are casting their lines off what appears to be a small pier jutting into the Indian River. It is well known locally that fish often congregate in such areas.

Landing 25 Pounders. Pulling large fish from the river has been a tradition in New Smyrna Beach since its founding. This card estimates the fish being handled by the two men to be 25 pounds each. Prior research dates this card to after 1902, based on the presence of the telephone pole. It was postmarked in 1911. The area now known as Old Fort Park is located in the rear of the view.

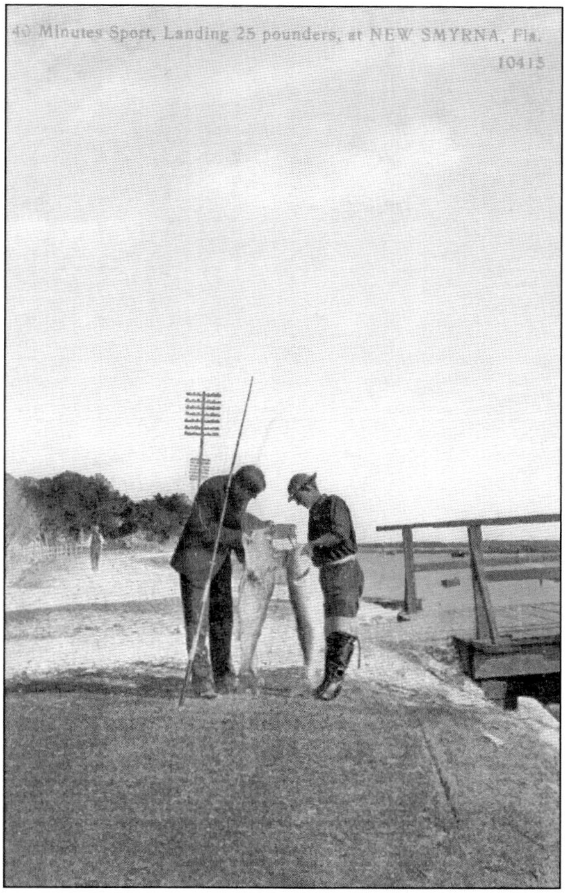

A Good Catch. The men in the boat have had a successful day of fishing in the Indian River—not the India River, as labeled on the card. Shown in the background is the Ocean House, one of the grandest hotels in the city. Also shown is the end of the canal that ran through town, giving Canal Street its name. The canal still empties into the river but is covered by a sidewalk through downtown. Note the people standing on the bridge over the canal. (Courtesy Dorothy Moore.)

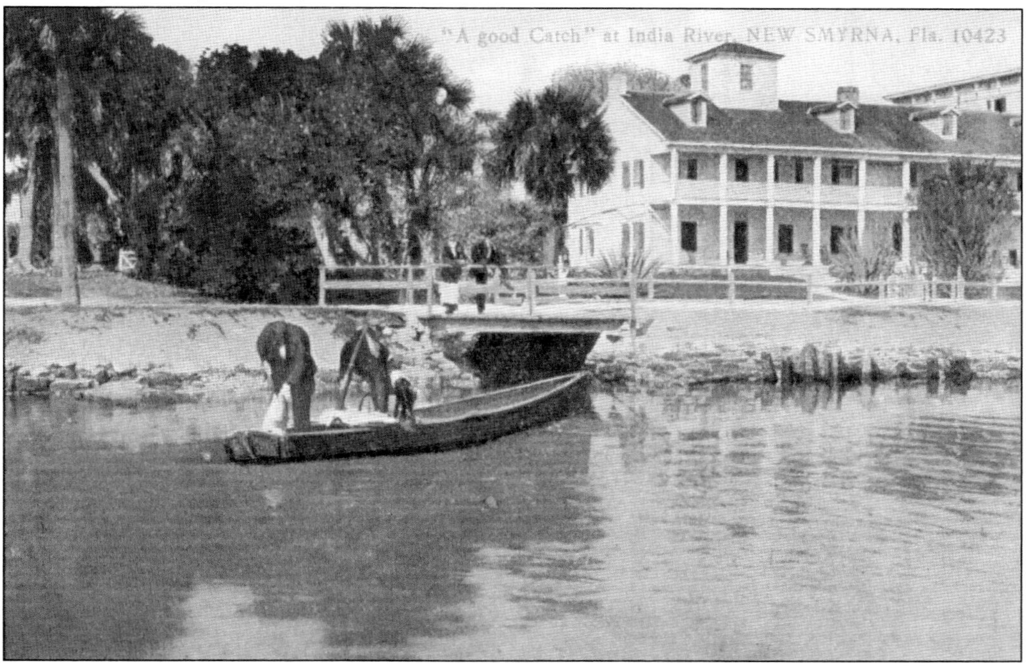

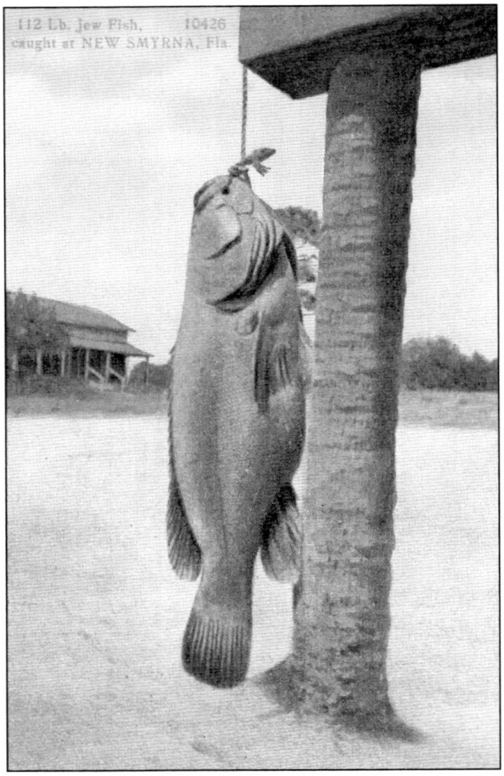

JEWFISH CATCH. The jewfish, or Goliath grouper, as they are more commonly called today, was a common catch in the waters around New Smyrna. This specimen, at just over 100 pounds, would have been young, as mature adults weigh in around 400 pounds and are known to reach to over 700 pounds and a length of eight feet. Young Goliath grouper tend to be found in brackish waters, oyster beds, and canals, making New Smyrna a prime home for them. Declining numbers of the fish led to its protected status in the United States in 1990.

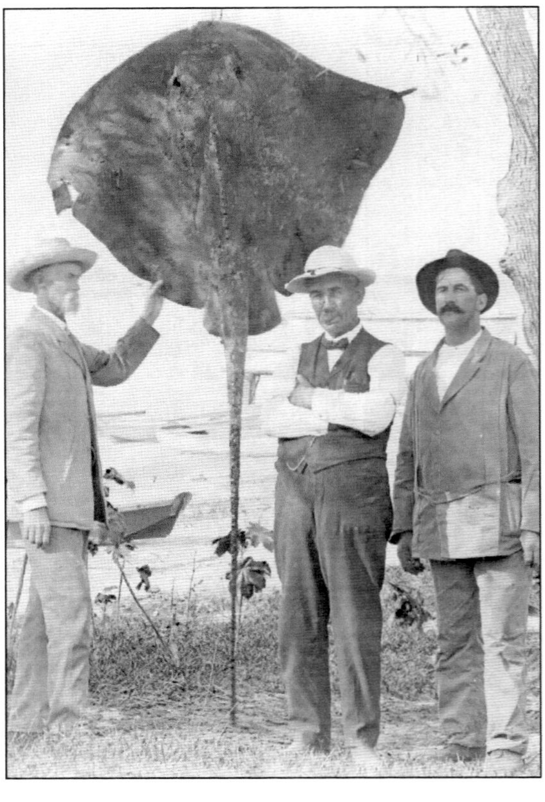

GIANT STINGRAY. The three unidentified men here seem happy with their catch. This catch looks to be at least eight feet long. The ray family is related to sharks in that both are cartilaginous fish. Stingrays are edible, and the wings, or flaps, are the favored part. It is highly likely that this specimen ended up on the dinner table. (Courtesy Zelia V. Sweett.)

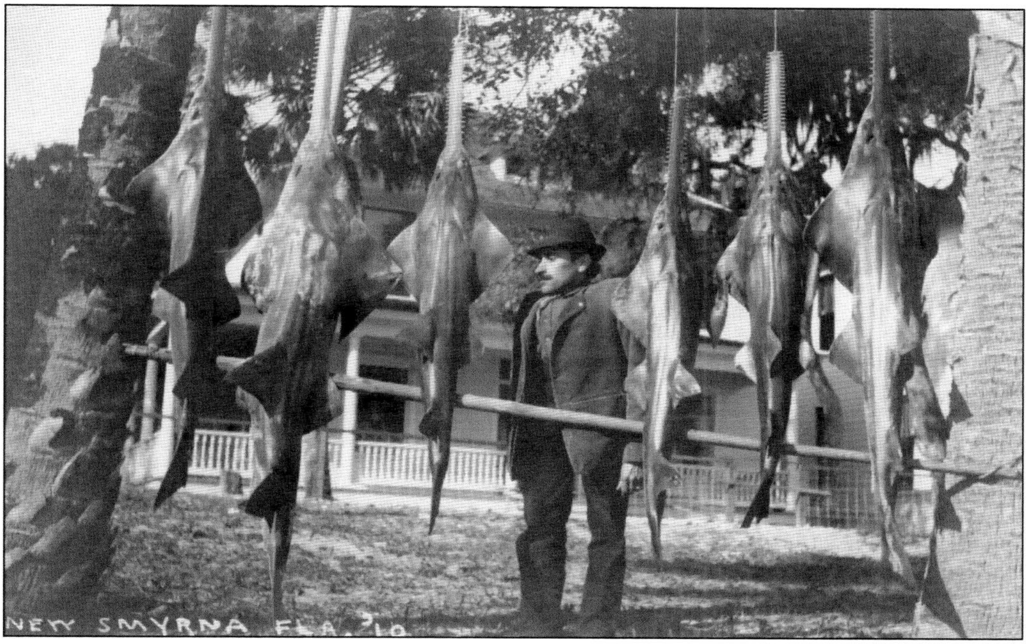

LARGE FISH. The Atlantic Ocean around Mosquito (now Ponce) Inlet and the Indian River has long been known for the size and quantity of a catch that can be taken. The gentleman in the image above shows off his catch of six sawfish. These appear to be young sawfish due to their smaller size. Perhaps this is a tourist, as the photograph seems to have been taken in front of the Ocean House. Today, sawfish are considered an endangered species due to habitat loss and overfishing. While an exaggeration, the image below could be used to show friends back home the type of fishing that could be done at Coronado Beach and New Smyrna. Actual photographs from the era when this card was mailed in 1912 attest to the size of fish that could be pulled from the river. (Both, courtesy Norm Shepard.)

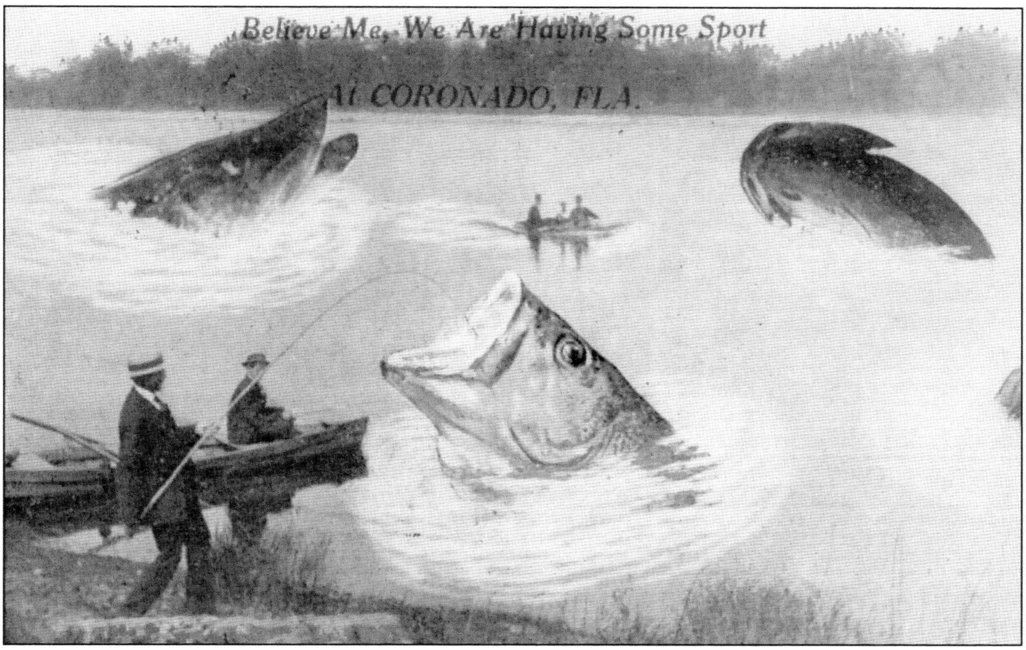

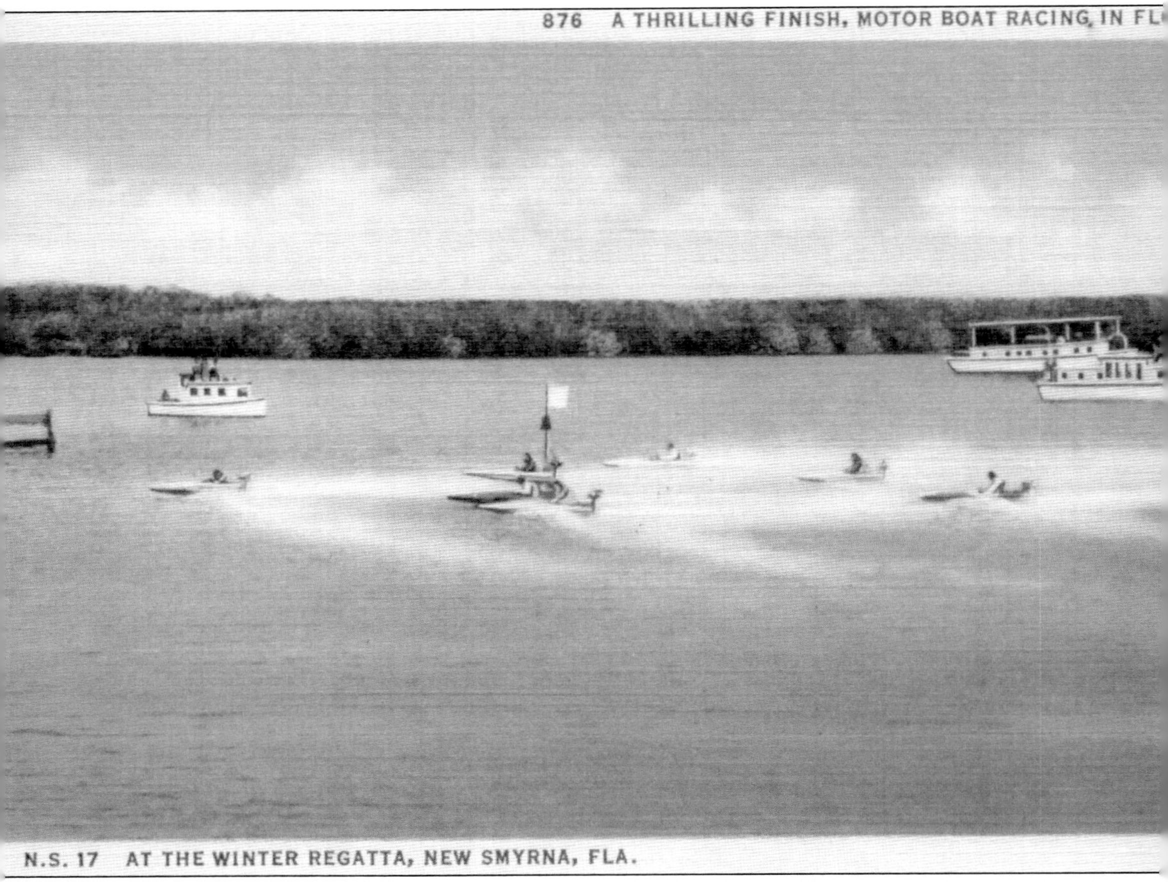

MOTORBOAT RACING. The Smyrna Yacht Club has been offering powerboat racing since its inaugural race in 1928. These races were held on Armistice Day through 1931. The races shifted to George Washington's birthday in 1932. In 1933, New Smyrna participated with the city of Miami in a series of races sponsored by the American Power Boat Association featuring international talent. Four separate 10-mile races were held in each city. The eight winners were slated to compete head-to-head in a single 10-mile heat to be held in Miami. The first commodore of the Smyrna Yacht Club, Russ J. Christy, was later elected as commodore for the American Power Boat Association. (Courtesy Norm Shepard.)

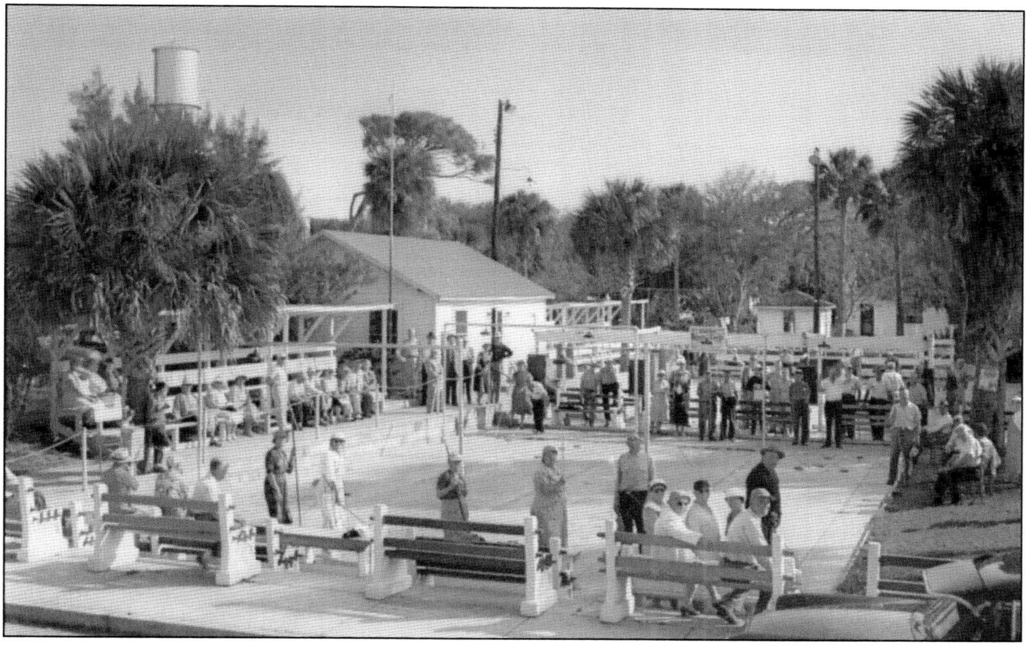

CORONADO BEACH SHUFFLEBOARD CLUB. Dating to 1937, these courts on Flagler Avenue are the lone remaining shuffleboard club in New Smyrna Beach. With the renewed interest in the game, the courts are often full. It is important to note the water tower in the upper left corner. A platform just below this tower was used by members of the Aircraft Warning Service during World War II to watch for enemy planes and submarines.

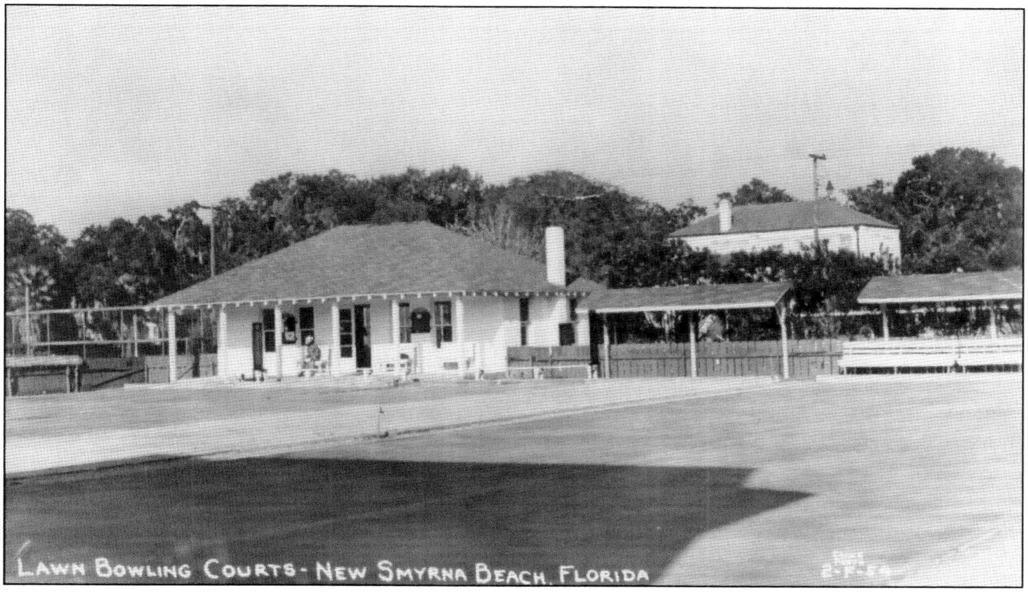

MAINLAND SHUFFLEBOARD CLUB. Seen in this real-photo postcard is the Mainland Shuffleboard Club that was located at the corner of Sams Avenue and Julia Street. The city has sold this land for development as Tabby House, a potential mix of residential and commercial property that will be overseen by a homeowners association. The shadow in the foreground is the former post office building, which is now home to the New Smyrna Museum of History. Also note the city hall building in the distance at right.

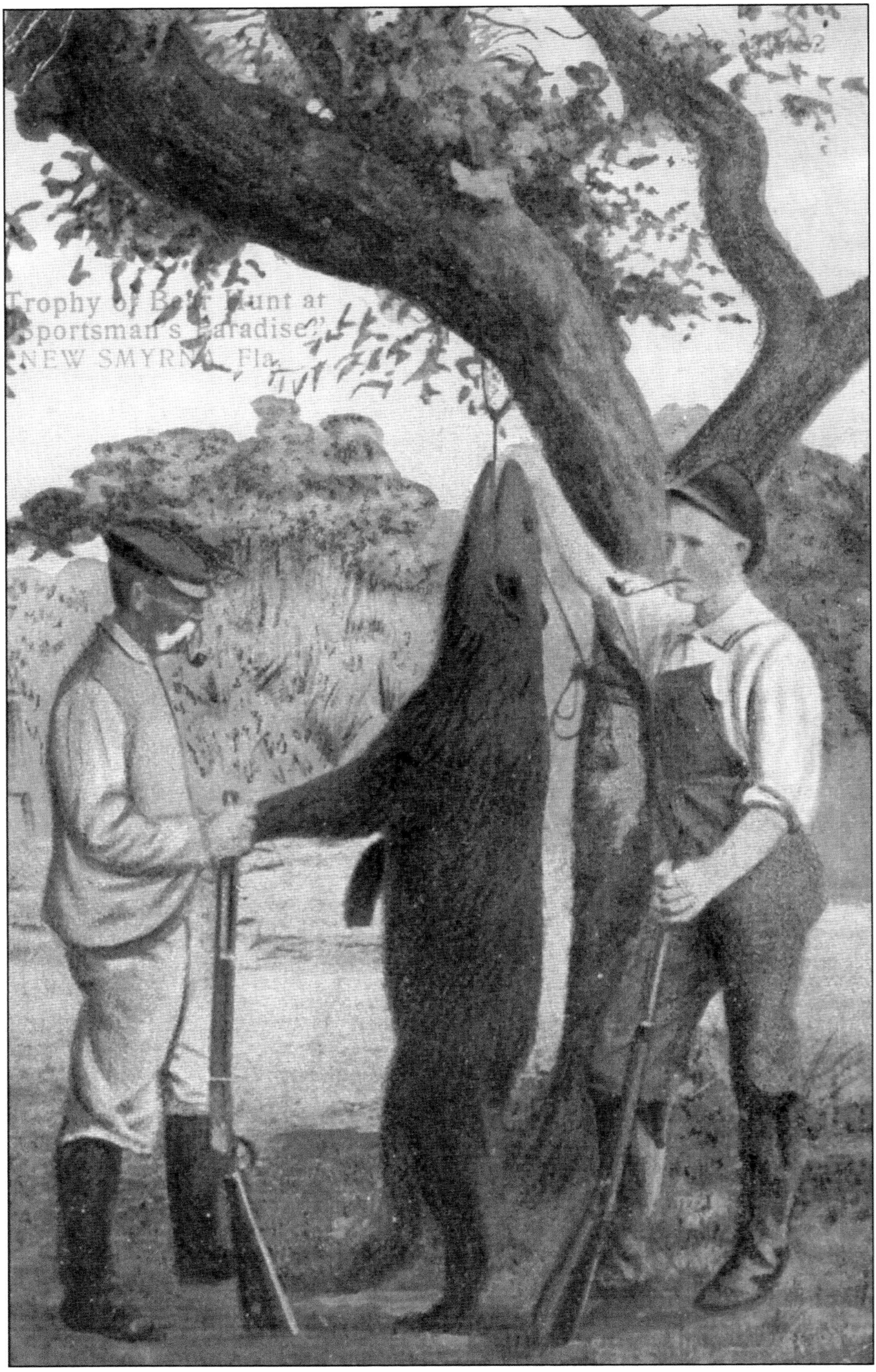

Trophy Bear Hunt. These two men are shown celebrating their hunting success by smoking pipes. It appears the man on the left is examining the bear's left paw. A recent state-authorized bear hunt in Florida makes this card especially relevant today. The card was posted to Dutchess County, New York, in September 1909. The sender writes of having purchased an incandescent lamp and says it is "like gas and a great help in reading & lighting up the room."

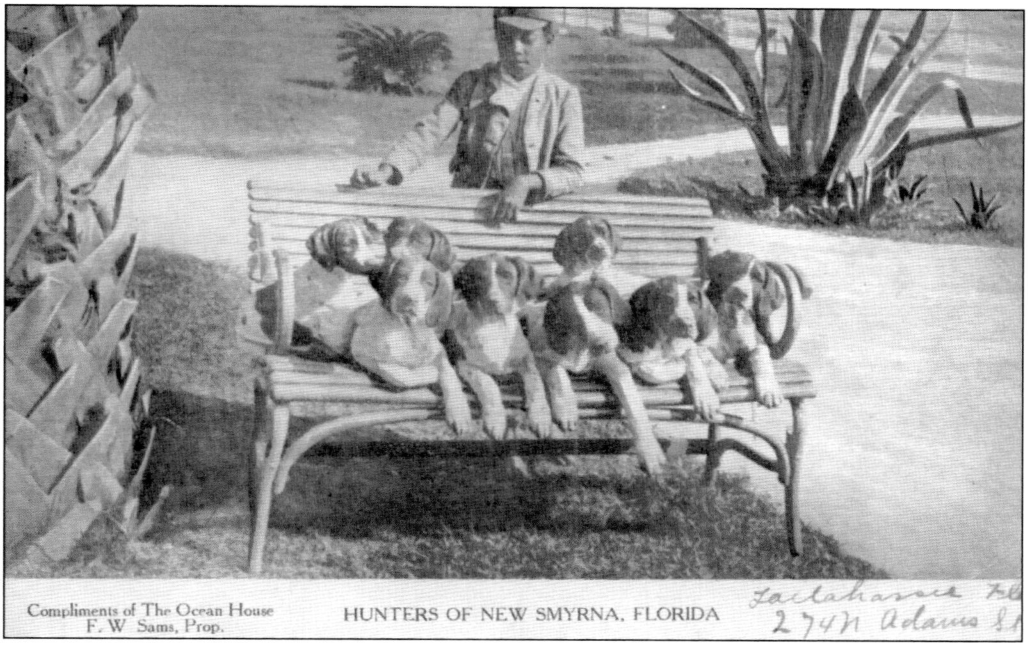

HUNTERS OF NEW SMYRNA. These playful puppies are under the watchful eye of a young caretaker who was employed by Frank W. Sams, owner of the Ocean House. Based on the card's caption, it would appear these dogs were being trained as hunting dogs and would no doubt have been available for rent by men staying at the hotel. In fact, the image below may be showing some of the same dogs out on a successful deer hunt.

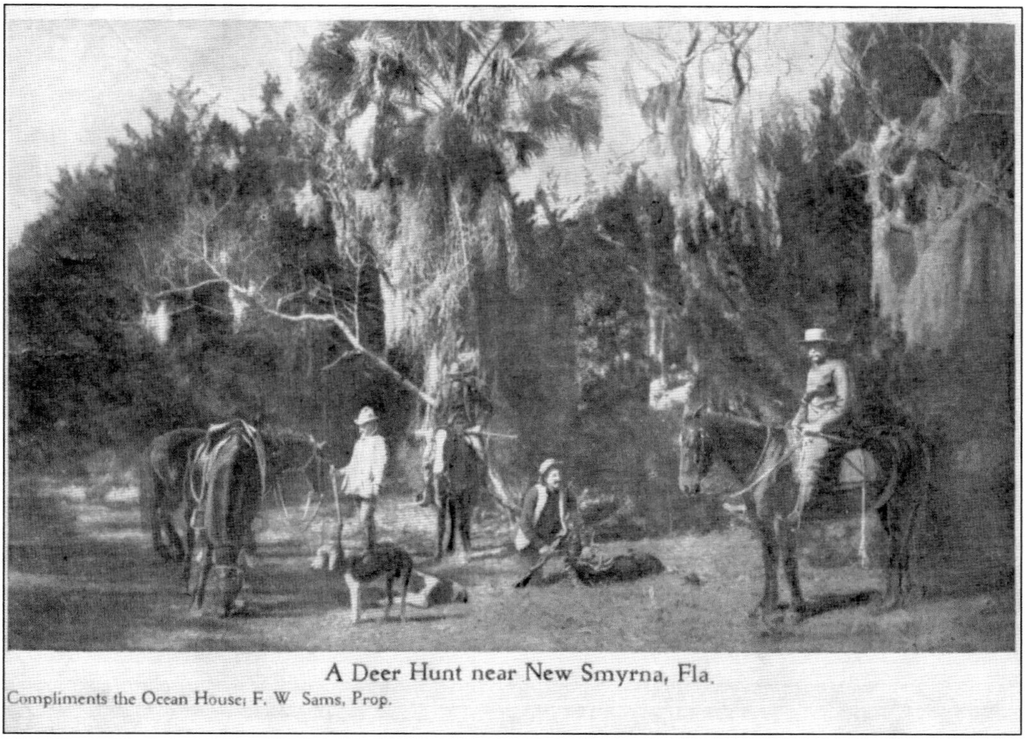

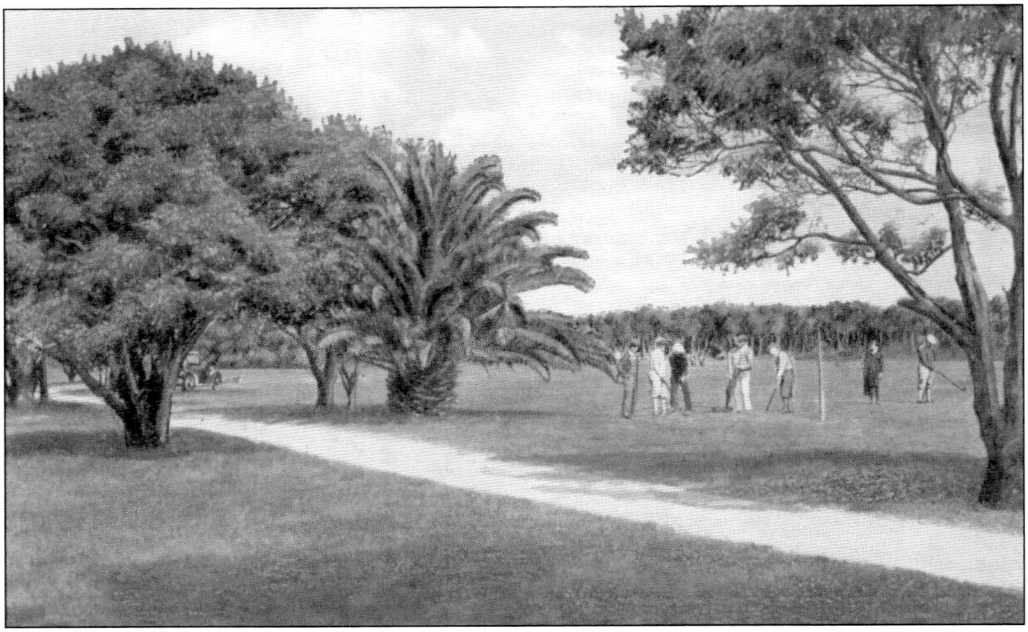

NEW SMYRNA BEACH GOLF & COUNTRY CLUB. Designed by Donald Ross, this 18-hole course is owned by the city. A challenging 6,200-yard course and reasonably priced greens fees make this the choice of many locals and visitors. Modern facilities include a pro shop and putting green, and lessons are available as well. On-site is the popular Italian restaurant Tiano's, owned by Vittoria and Caterina Tiano. Here, golfers can enjoy a drink with friends after a round or return for dinner and entertainment from local musicians.

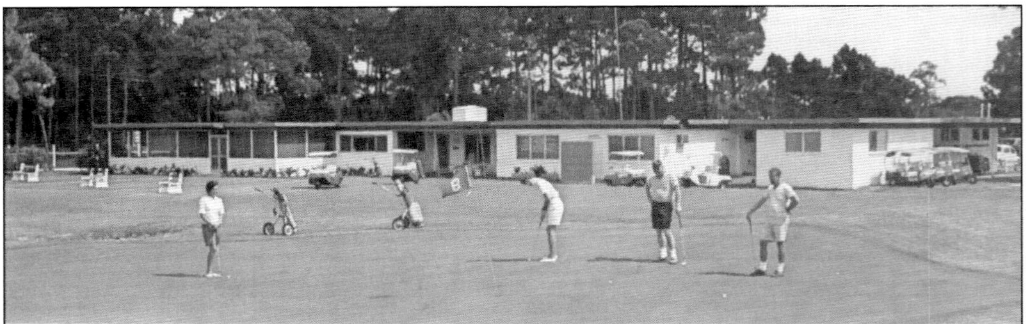

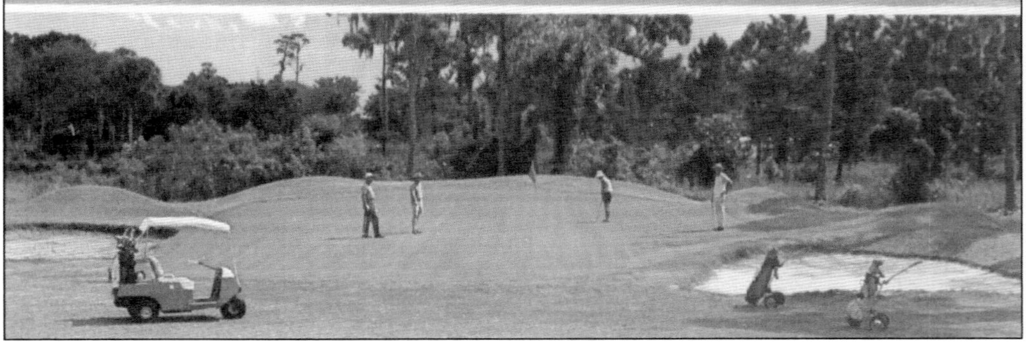

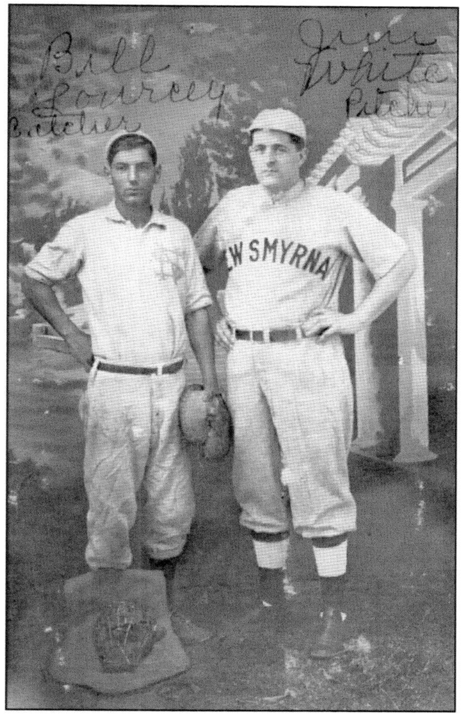

Baseball Players. Shown in this real-photo postcard are catcher Bill Lourcey (left) and pitcher Jim White (right), according to the notes written on the card. Note the antique catchers gear on the ground in front of Lourcey. There is no indication of the date the photograph was taken. Lourcey and White were lifelong residents of the city. Both men were employed by the Florida East Coast Railway and were members of the Free and Accepted Masons. White left employment with the FEC in order to be appointed chief of police, a position he held until his untimely death in 1938 at the age of 43 due to a heart attack suffered after a hunting trip. Lourcey served as an engineer for FEC and passed away in 1953. Both men are buried in the Edgewater–New Smyrna Cemetery.

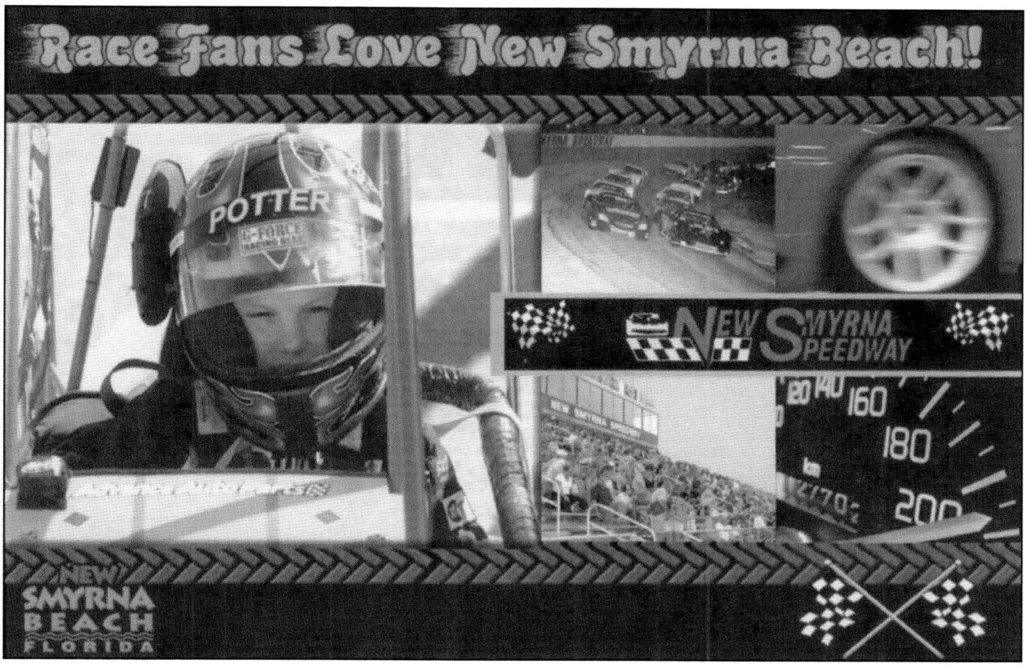

New Smyrna Speedway. For more than 45 years, the New Smyrna Speedway has brought the thrill of weekly races to local enthusiasts. The speedway plays host to all kinds of racing, including go-karts, super late models, modifieds, sportsmen series, and more. The track is a half mile long and contains high banking. During Daytona Speedweeks, it is not uncommon to find NASCAR drivers, such as Tony Stewart, Ryan Newman, or Kyle Busch, trying their luck at this local legend.

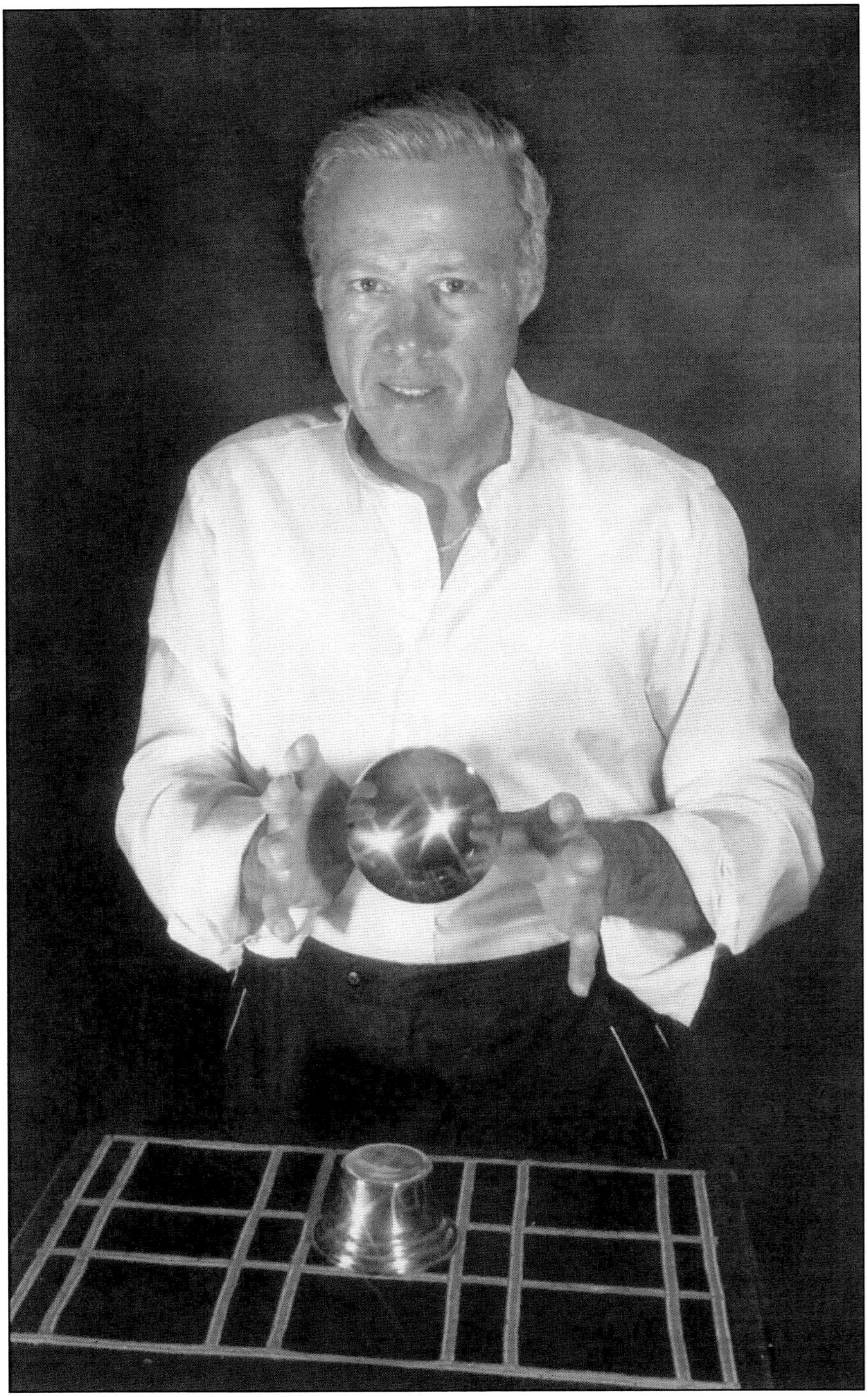

MAGIC BY MIEDER. One can make entertainment problems disappear with Magic by William Mieder. Mieder was a former television star, having been on *Captain Noah and his Magical Ark* in the Philadelphia area. He also appeared on *The Ed Sullivan Show* and *The Tonight Show* with Johnny Carson. During the late 1970s through mid-1980s, he owned the Magic Ice Cream Parlor in Maryland before moving to New Smyrna Beach, where he continued to entertain audiences.

Four

A Place to Fill Your Stomach and Rest Your Head

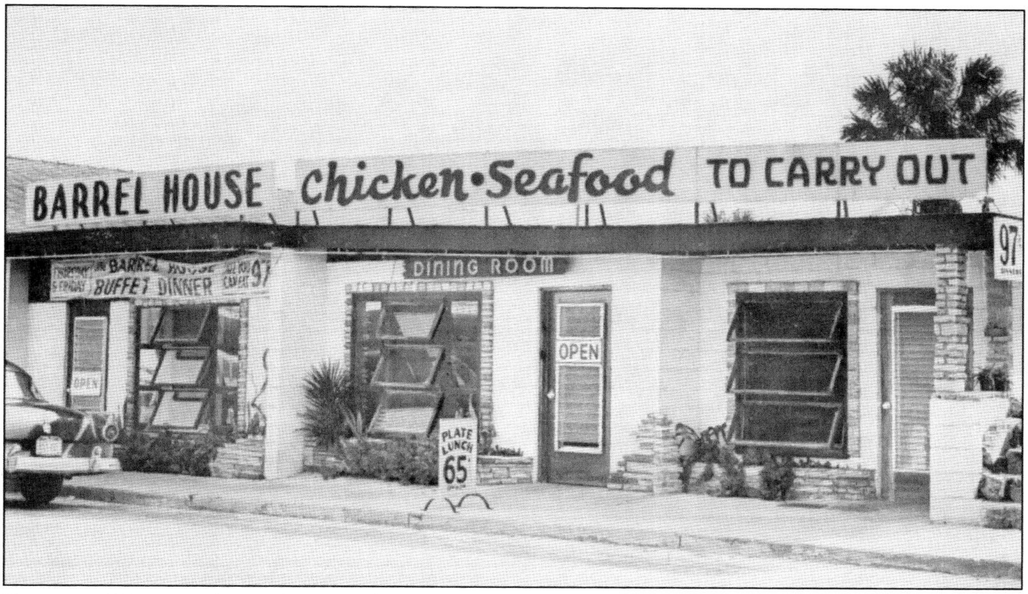

Barrel House. According to the reverse side of this card, the Barrel House was home to fresh seafoods, chicken, and western steaks. Hungry patrons could have lunch between noon and 2:00 p.m. for as little as 65¢. A dinner buffet on Thursday and Friday cost only 97¢. A gift shop is now located at 407 Flagler Avenue, the former site of the Barrel House.

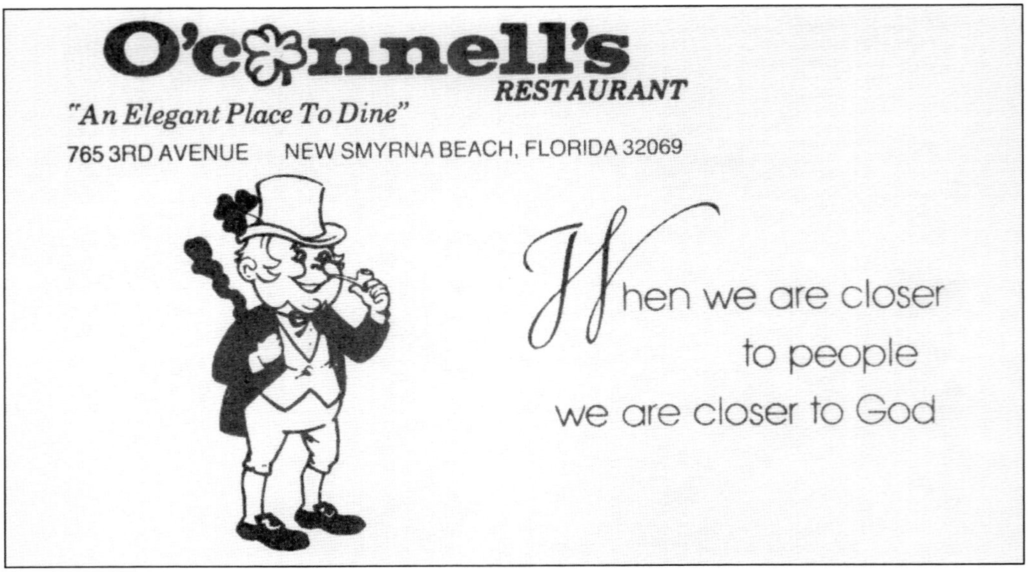

O'Connell's Restaurant. This family-run business was located just over the south bridge at 765 East Third Avenue, a busy thoroughfare traveled by beachgoers and residents alike. At its peak, the restaurant sat 165 and served popular fare, such as meatloaf, corned beef and cabbage, sandwiches, and more. Opened in the mid-1970s, the restaurant closed in 1989.

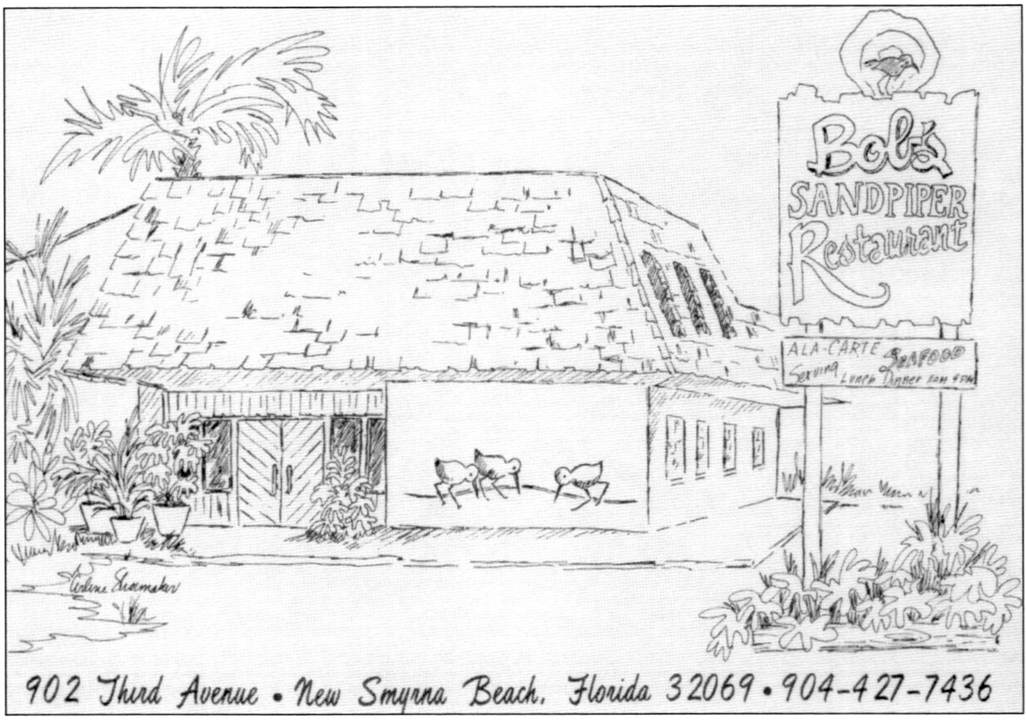

Bob's Sandpiper Restaurant. A popular restaurant known for its seafood during the 1970s, Bob's was located at 902 Third Avenue. On June 23, 1980, a fire started in a dumbwaiter and gutted the building, causing over $200,000 worth of damage. Luckily, there were no major injuries, though five firefighters were treated on-site for smoke inhalation. The site was later home to the Liquor Locker.

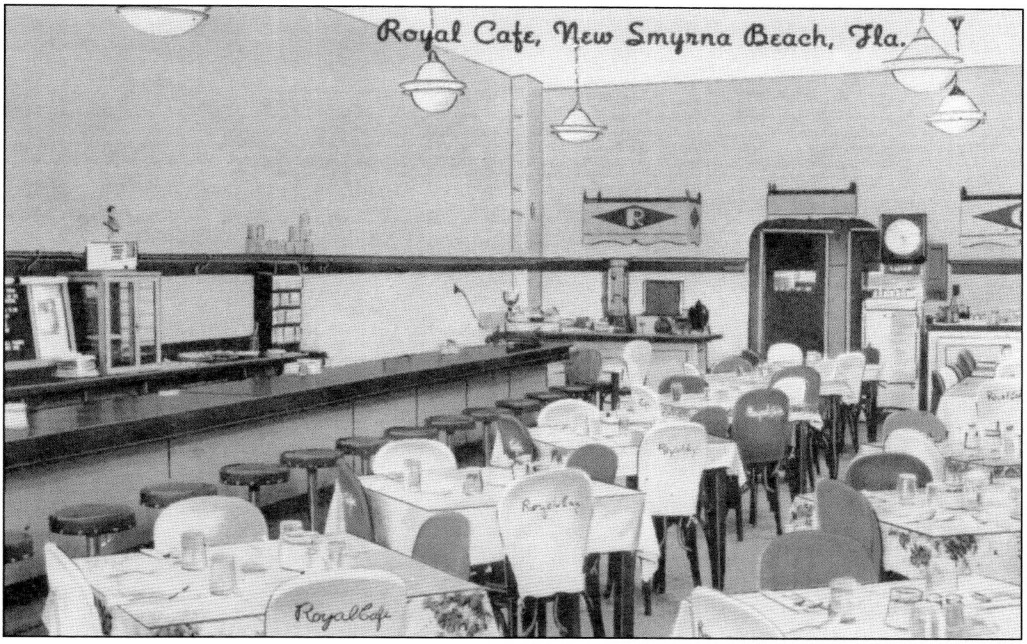

Royal Café. Michael and Dorothy Jacobine owned the Royal Café, located on Canal Street near the Bank of New Smyrna. The Royal Café was billed as New Smyrna Beach's finest restaurant, specializing in seafood, steaks, and chops, all served in a modern dining room.

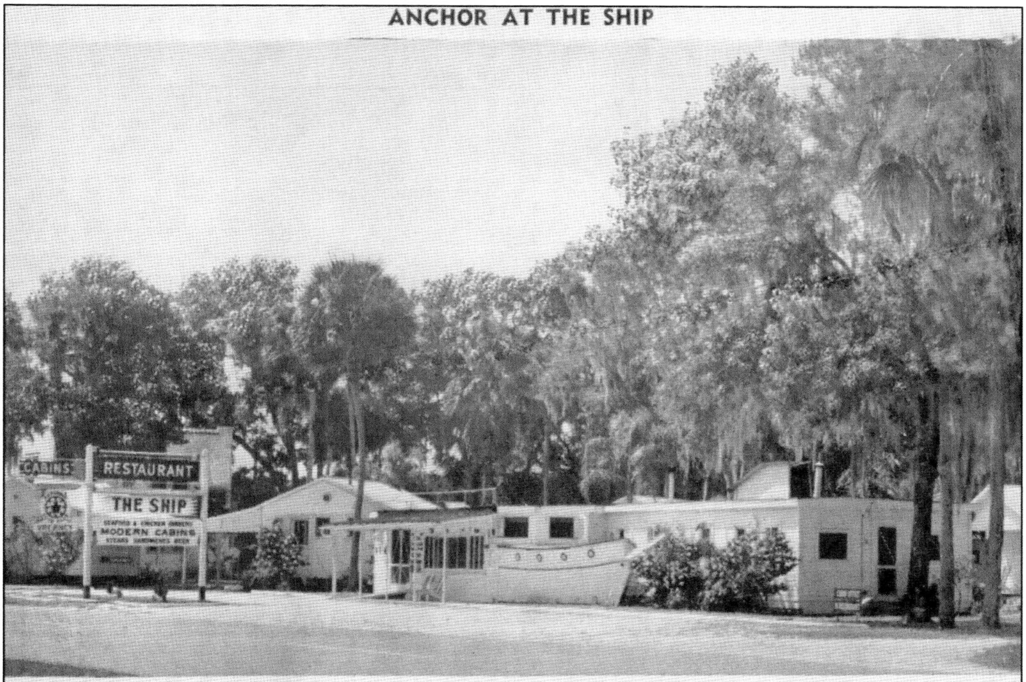

Anchor at the Ship. Located just south of New Smyrna Beach on US 1, the major north and south road of the time, the Ship restaurant prided itself on offering seafood and chicken dinners, steaks, sandwiches, and beer. For the weary traveler, modern cabins with covered automobile parking were available.

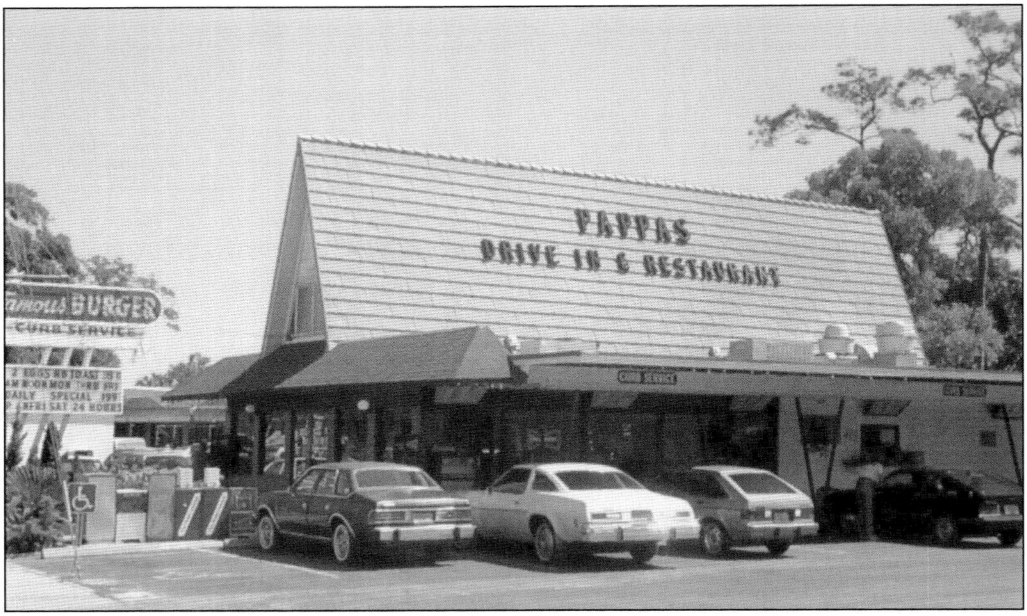

Pappas Drive-In & Restaurant. For more than 50 years, the family-operated Pappas Drive-In & Restaurant has been a New Smyrna Beach tradition. The reverse side of this card advertises the six-way service available at Pappas: car service, window service, curb service, phone service, counter service, and table service. As the sign shows, Pappas is known for its burgers.

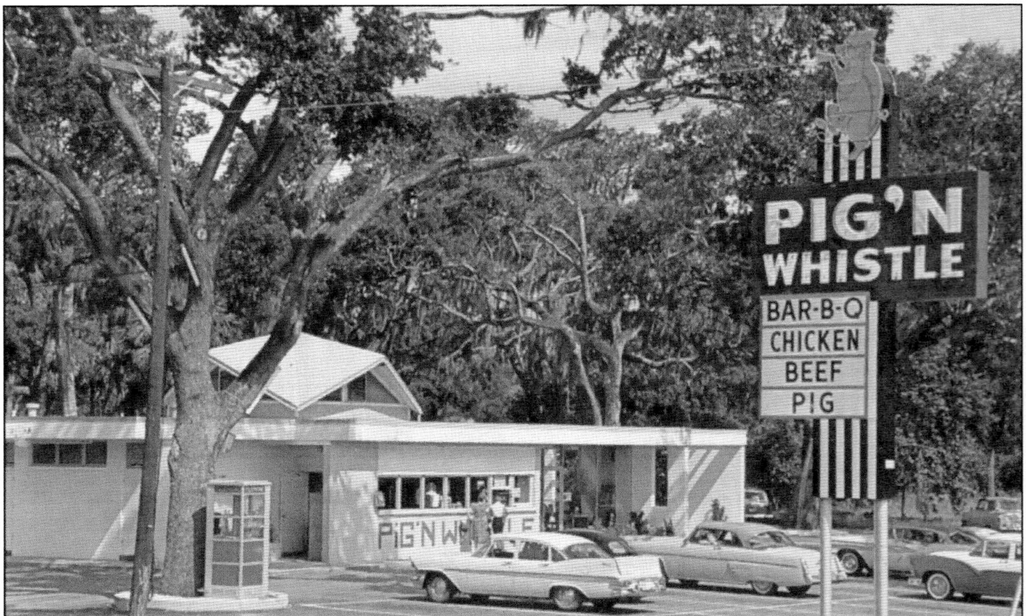

Pig 'N Whistle. The Pig 'N Whistle was a favorite for many, not just because of the food, but because of the hours. Conveniently located at the corner of Wayne Avenue and US 1, the restaurant was open from 6:00 a.m. until midnight—in an era when this was not the norm. The Pig 'N Whistle building was incorporated into a larger structure and has since served as a local community college, then a shopping center, and after sitting nearly vacant for many years, it is currently being remodeled into an assisted-living facility. (Courtesy Dorothy Moore.)

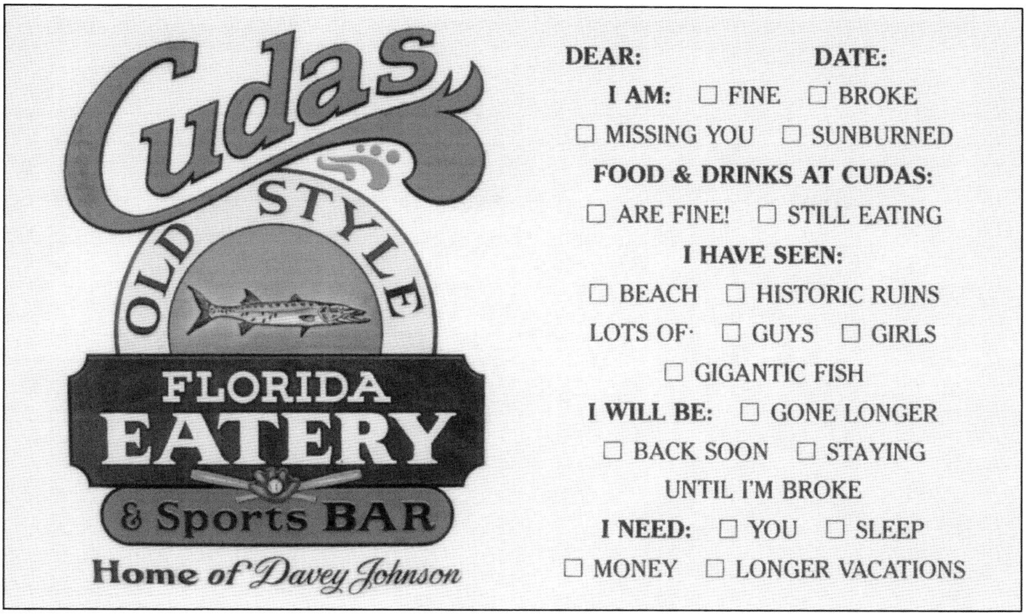

CUDAS OLD-STYLE FLORIDA EATERY. Professional baseball player and manager Davey Johnson owned this restaurant and sports bar, which is now closed. Johnson played for 13 seasons and compiled a career batting average of .261, earned four all-star game nominations, and participated in four World Series. Short for the Barracudas mascot, "Cudas" is the nickname of New Smyrna Beach High School. Cudas was located at 540 Dixie Freeway, which is now home to Labosco's Pawn Kings & Pickers Barn.

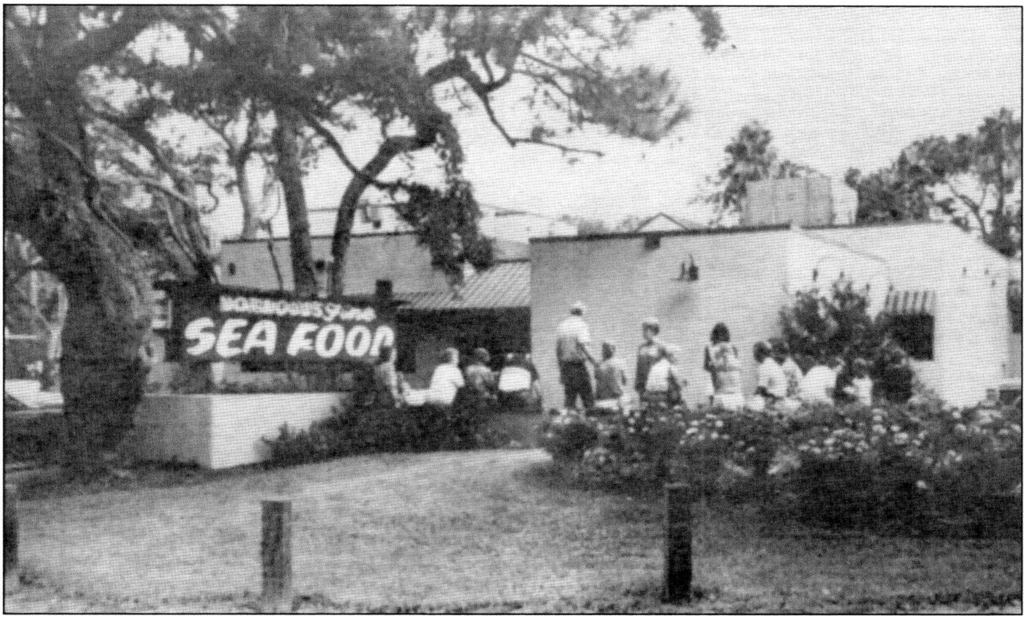

NORWOOD'S FINE SEAFOOD. Norwood's has been a favorite among locals and visitors since 1946, when Earl Norwood bought the building and opened a restaurant. While no longer in the Norwood family, the restaurant continues old traditions paired with modern changes. The recently opened "tree house," an outdoor bar and eating area located above the restaurant, and more than 30,000 bottles of wine help set Norwood's apart and keep guests returning.

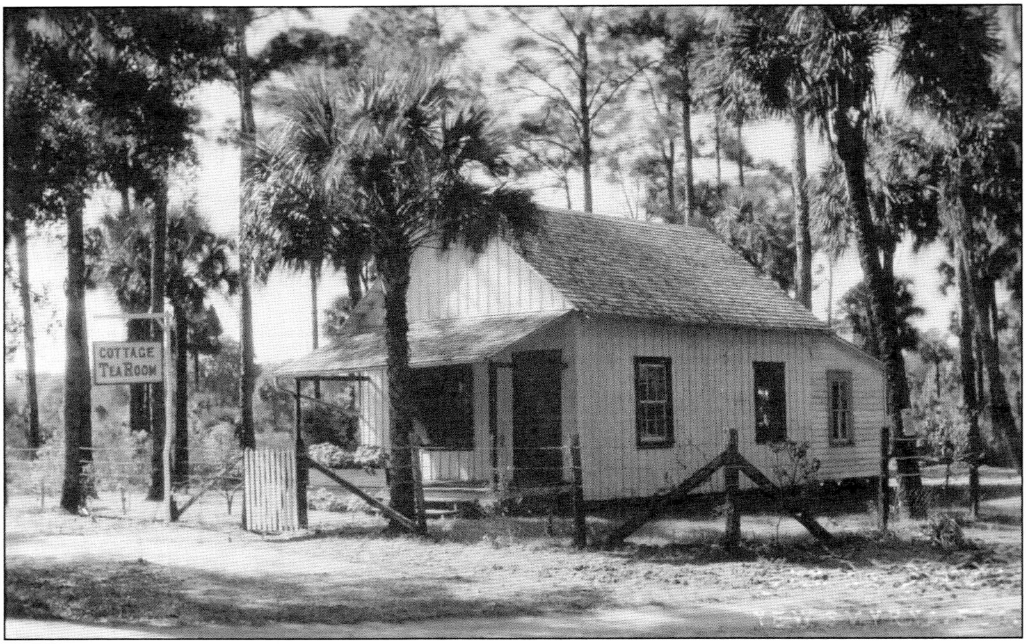

COTTAGE TEA ROOM. These real-photo postcards were produced by local photographer Theo van de Sande. According to New Smyrna's 1917 city directory, the Cottage Tea Room was located at the corner of Wayne and Orange Avenues, an area that was a part of Ronnoc Grove. The owner Martha Connor was the wife of Wayne Everett Connor, president of Ronnoc Grove Company and son of Washington Everett Connor. The Connors had three children: Holden, Barbara, and Martha. In 1939, Martha and Wayne were divorced. Martha passed away in 1969.

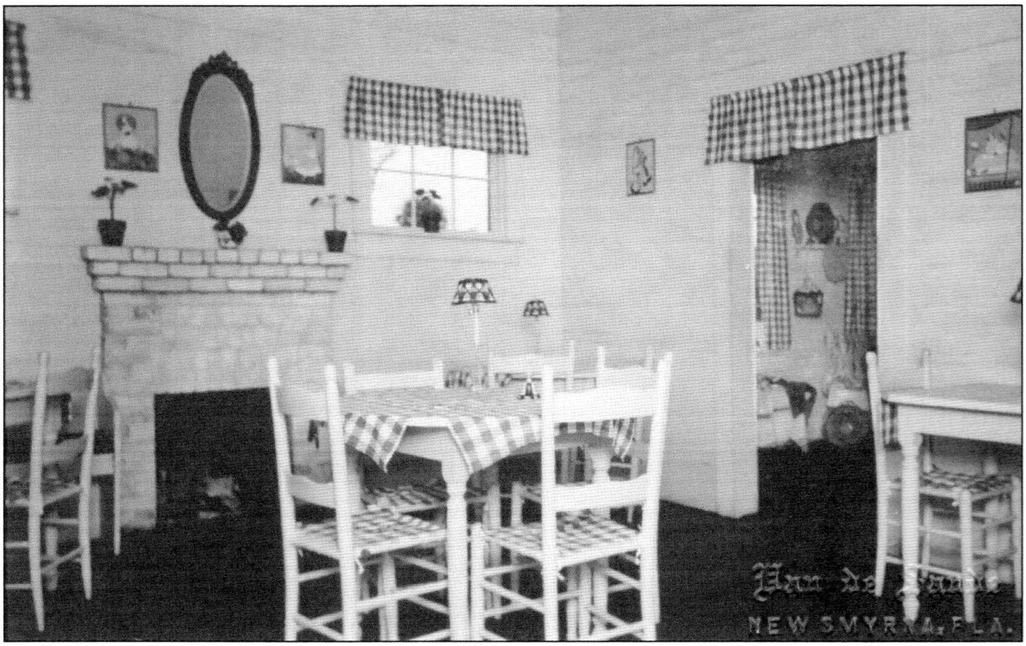

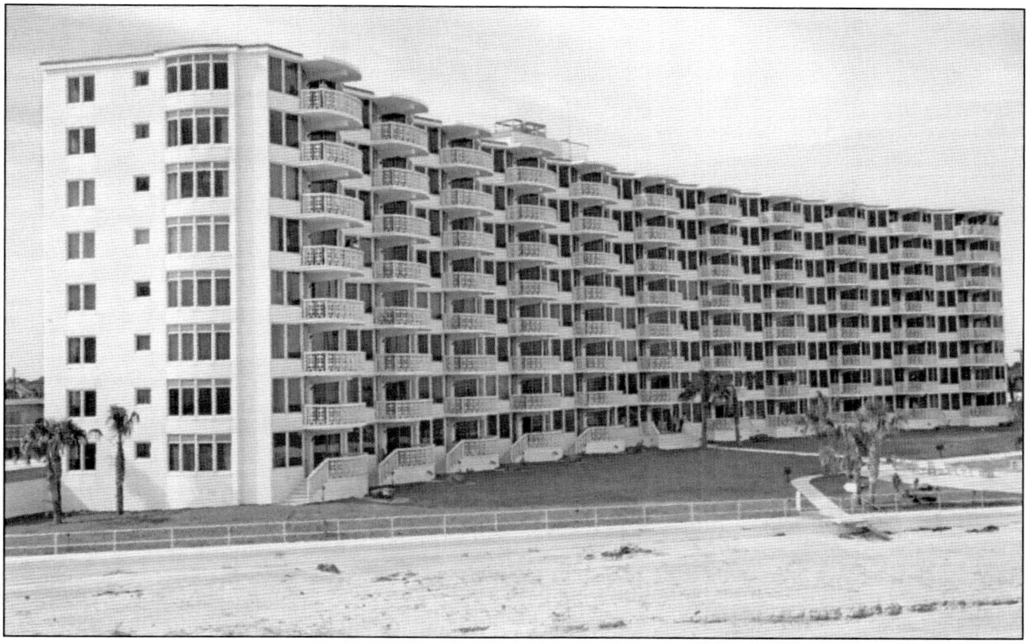

GOLDEN ARMS CONDOMINIUMS. Located directly on the beach, the Golden Arms condominiums are available for ownership or rental. At just over 1,200 square feet each, along with a 250-square-foot balcony, each of the 88 units feature two bedrooms, two baths, a full kitchen, and garage parking. As their promotional material says, "Just bring your suntan lotion, sunglasses, and beach towels and enjoy New Smyrna Beach!"

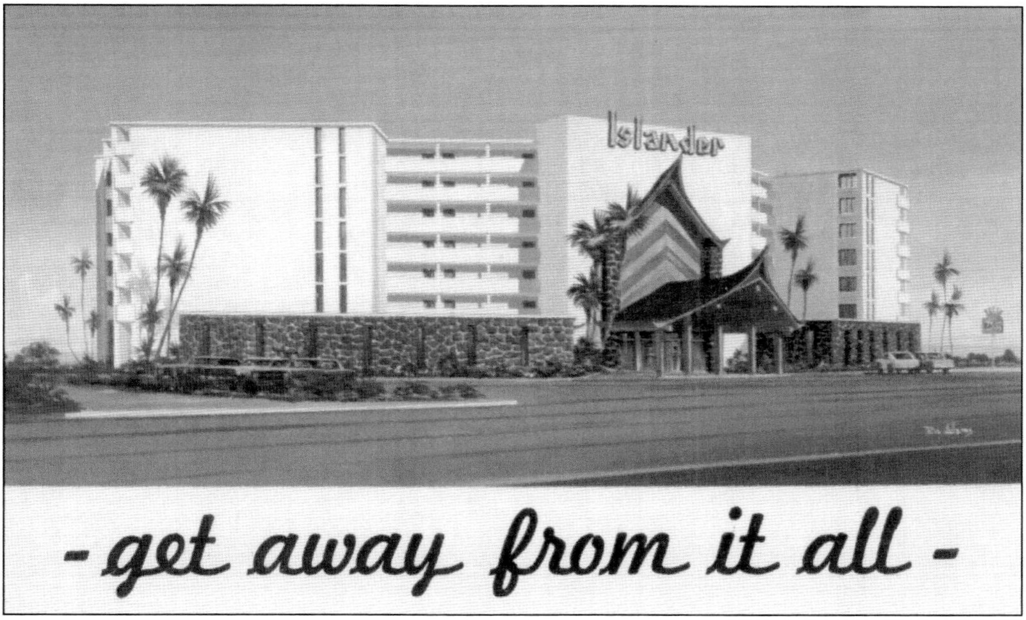

GET AWAY FROM IT ALL. The Islander Beach Resort, located at 1601 South Atlantic Avenue, has been a favorite of visitors and winter residents for years. The Polynesian theme shown in this image has been replaced with a clean blue-and-white motif that is more modern and inviting. The Islander features 114 units, from studios to two-bedroom suites. All include a full kitchen, and laundry facilities are available on-site.

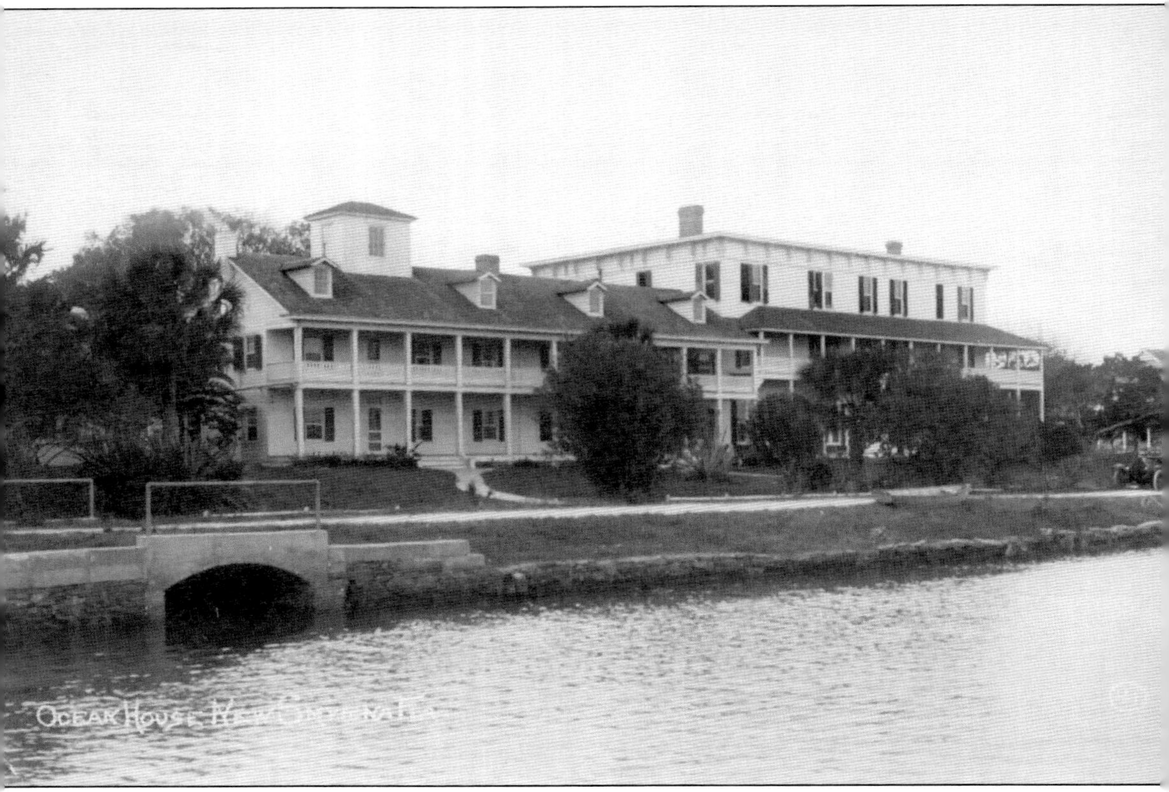

Ocean House. Originally built by E.K. Lowd in 1866, the Ocean House served as the major guest house in town for nearly a century. Lowd later sold the property to his brother-in-law Frank Sams, who enlarged the hotel by adding the section on the right of the building. Sams Avenue, the block behind Riverside Drive where the hotel was located, is named for Frank. This card was postmarked in 1916 and was sent to Maryland. It is important to note on the left side of this view are the remains of a Turnbull-era canal that flowed through downtown. To the right, note the car, which might have been used to transport visitors to the beach or to and from the railroad station. The hotel burned to the ground in the 1940s, and the county operates offices where it used to stand.

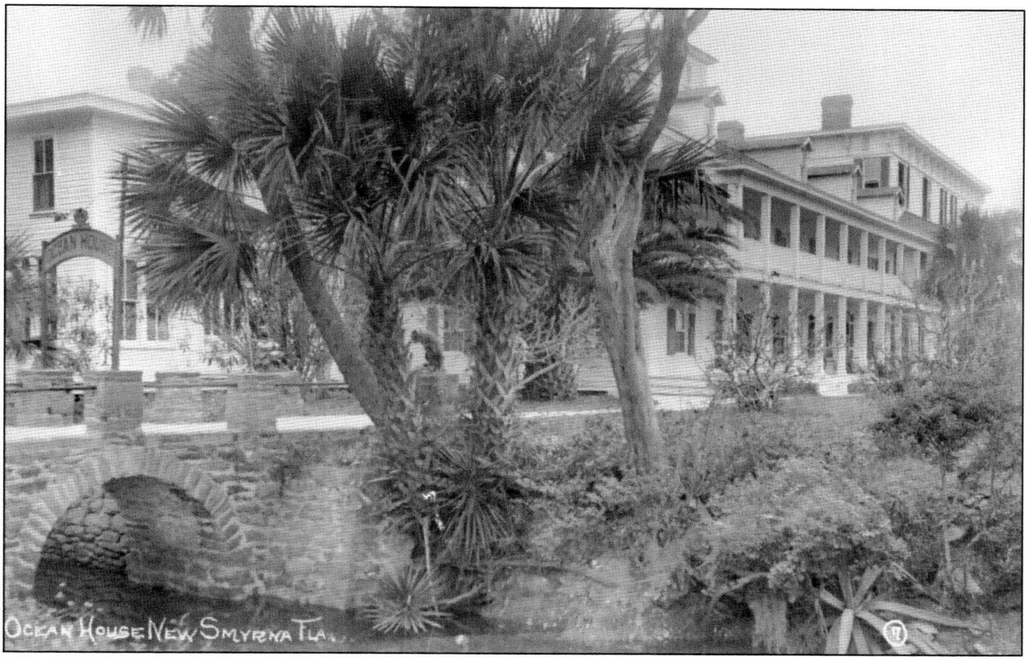

OCEAN HOUSE. Located a stone's throw from the Indian River, the Ocean House offered hospitality aplenty to visitors. Beautiful views of the river, fishing, transportation, and other amenities were available. Above, the Turnbull-era canal is shown in the lower left. This canal still runs underneath sidewalks along Canal Street. Just above the canal, note the highly decorative sign welcoming visitors. To the right of the sign are statues of a fox and a hare. These were of European make and were gifts to the owners. Murray Sams gave these to the president of Rollins College. Since 1956, the fox has made an annual appearance at the school to signify a spring day deemed "too pretty to have class." (Both, courtesy Susan Bergert.)

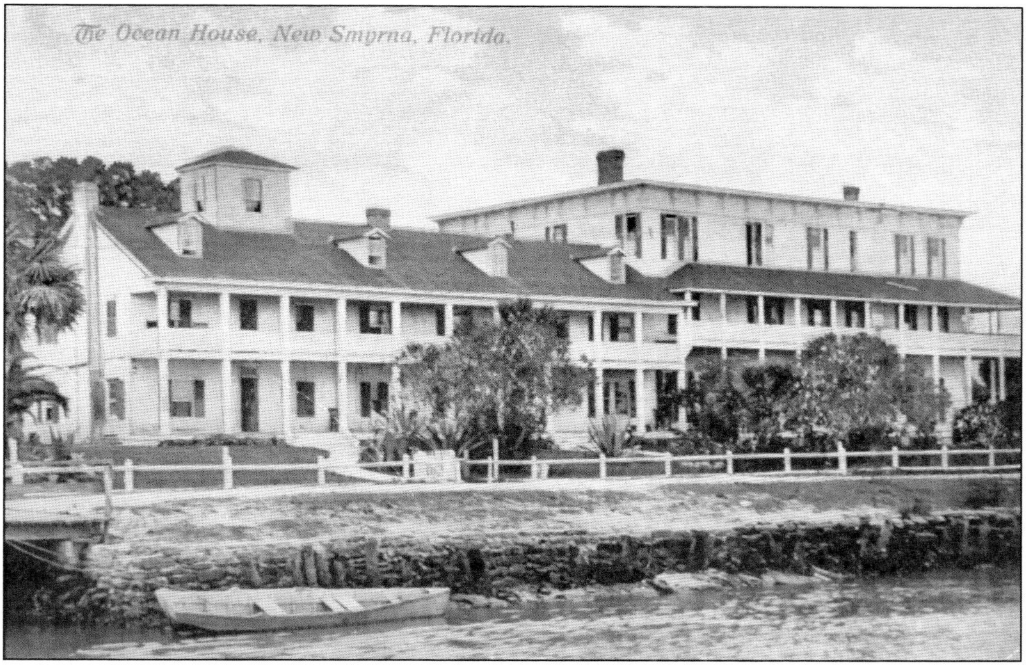

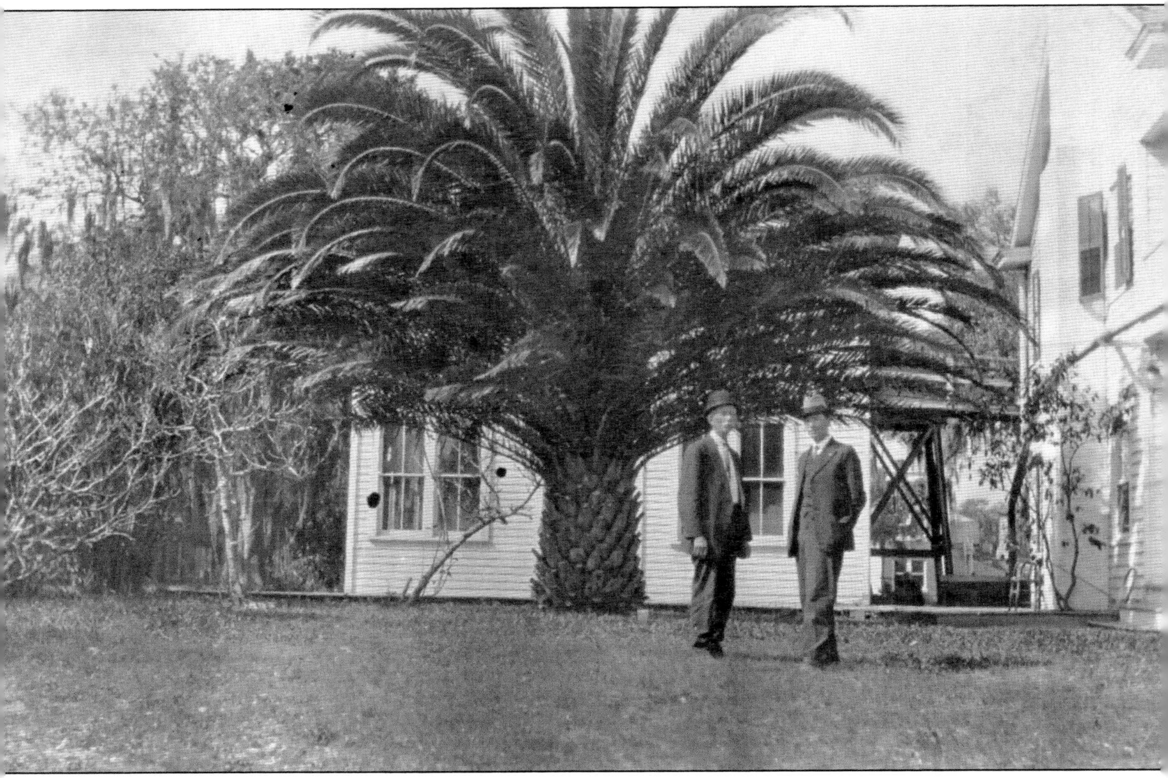

SIDE OF THE OCEAN HOUSE. This image is dated 1916 and shows two unidentified men standing at the edge of the Ocean House looking east toward the Indian River. The Ocean House stood for almost 100 years before burning to the ground in the 1940s. County offices are currently located where these well-dressed men were standing. (Courtesy Zelia V. Sweett.)

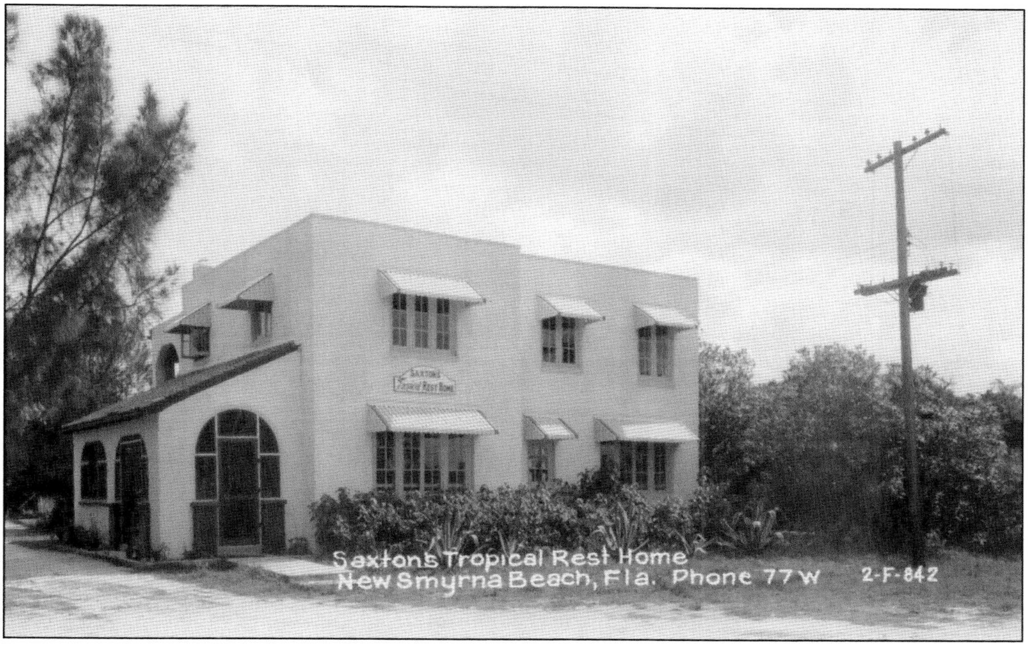

SAXTON'S TROPICAL REST HOME. Saxton's Tropical Rest Home was located beachside along what is now Third Avenue. Descendants of the owners state that it stood approximately where the Shell gas station is now situated. These cards give excellent insight into what 1940s beachside properties were like. (Above, courtesy Carlton Hudgins; below, courtesy Dorothy Moore.)

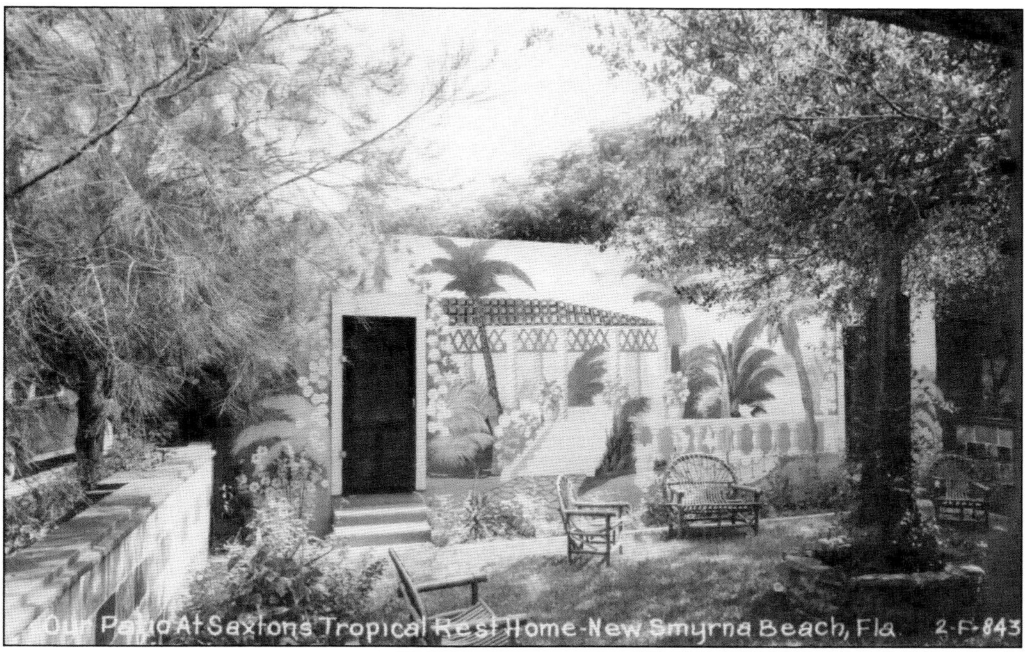

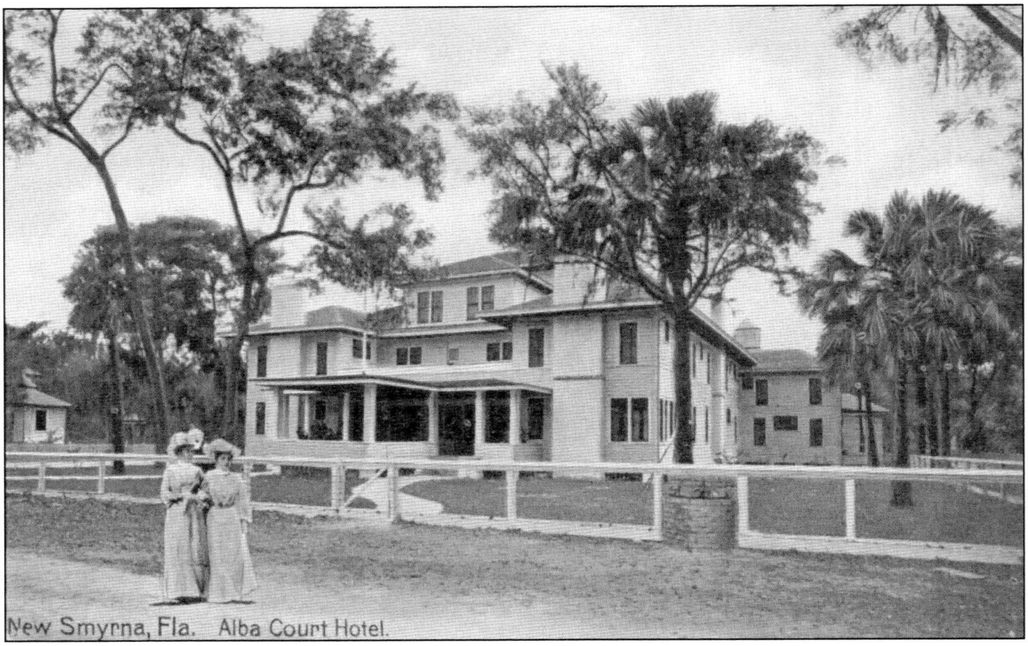

ALBA COURT. Alba Court was one of the grand hotels that housed winter visitors in New Smyrna Beach. The hotel was built in 1905 and 1906, opening its doors to guests in the fall season of 1906. There were originally 26 rooms situated around a large lobby. By 1917, upgrades had been made, including the addition of private baths to some rooms. As tastes changed, however, the owners of Alba Court could no longer afford to make all the needed upgrades. The property eventually became home to many low-income seniors. The property was sold in 2006, and in 2007, it fell victim to the wrecking ball. Currently, the land sits vacant.

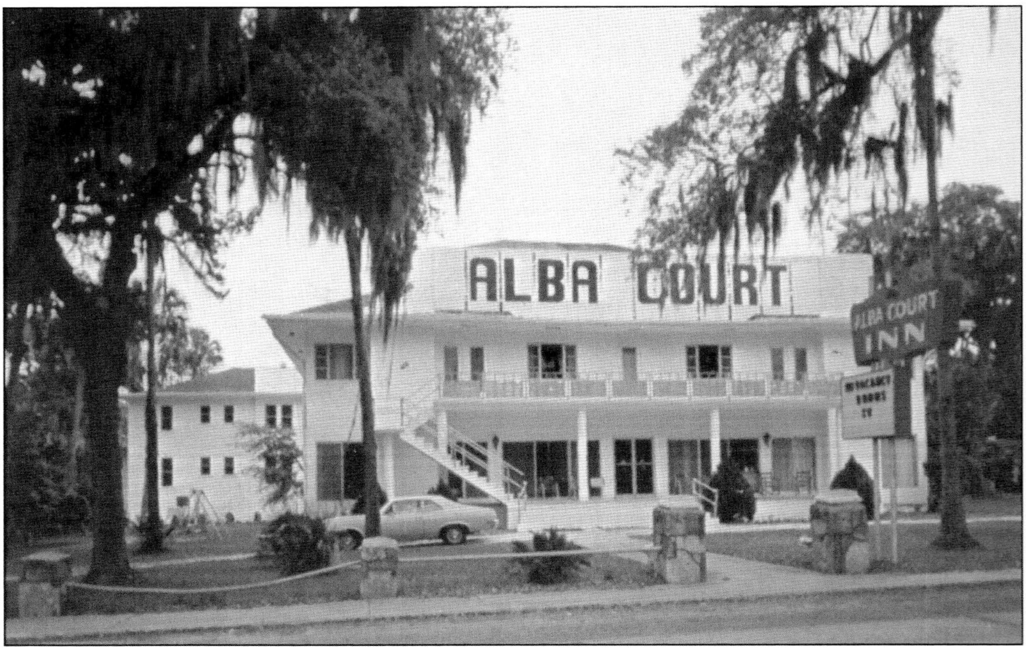

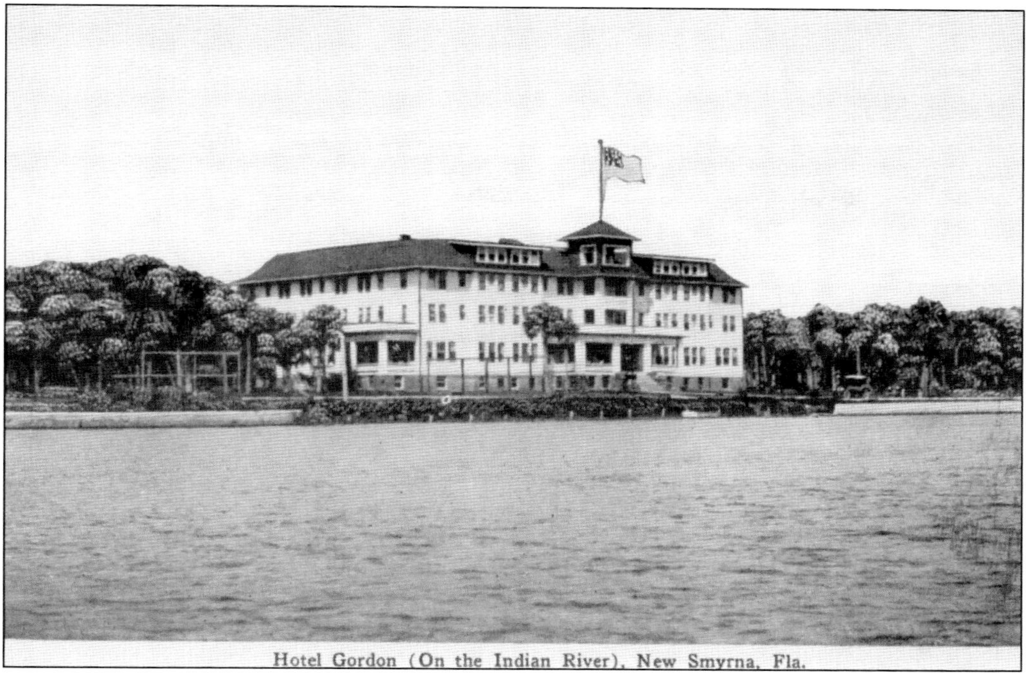

NEW SMYRNA HOTEL. Whether named Rio Vista, New Smyrna Hotel, Hotel Gordon, Indian River Inn, or Indian River Lodge, this imposing structure offered tremendous views of the Indian River. According to the card below, which was postmarked in 1951, the hotel offered a European plan with no meals for $3 to $6 single occupancy or $4.50 to $7.50 double occupancy. For the American plan, which included three excellent meals per day, the charge was an additional $3 per person. The structure was demolished in 2005 once it was determined no buyer was willing to make the needed repairs.

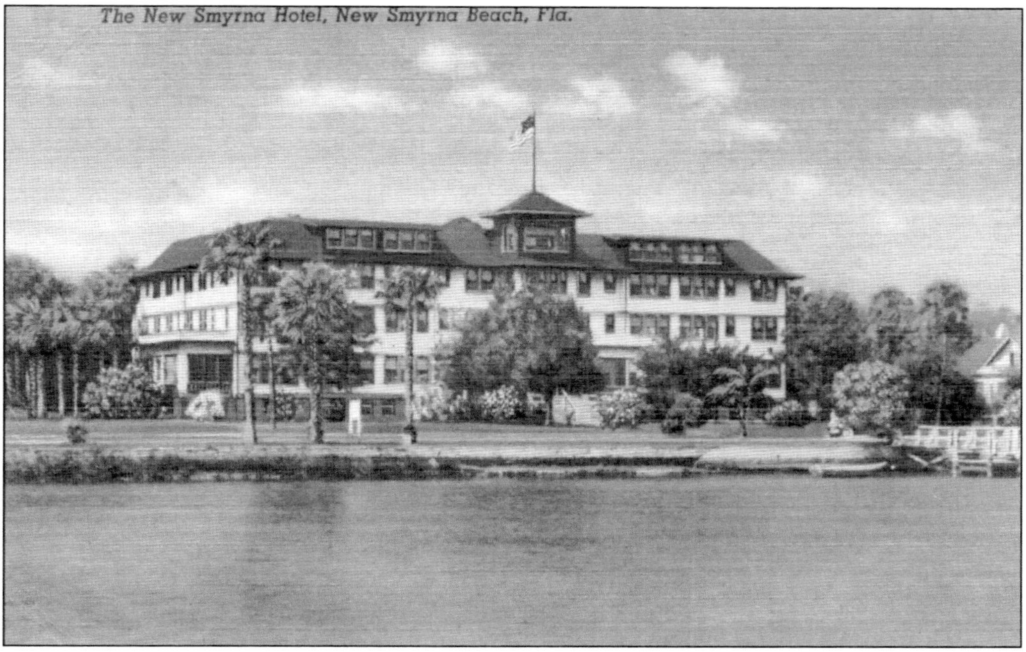

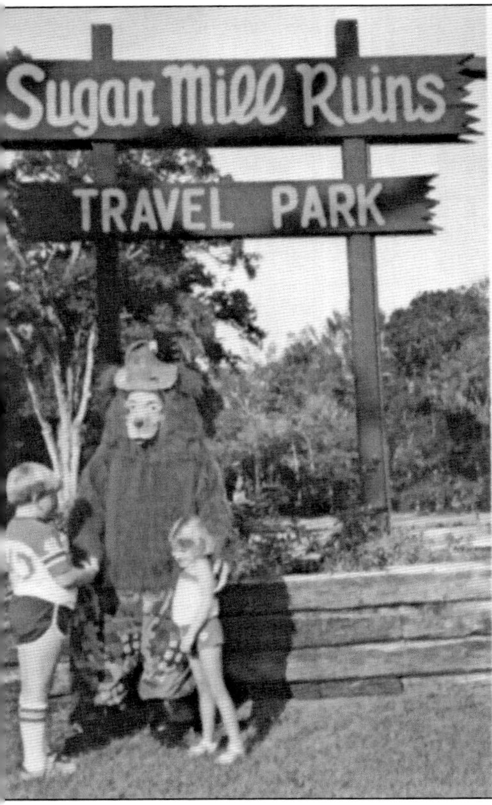

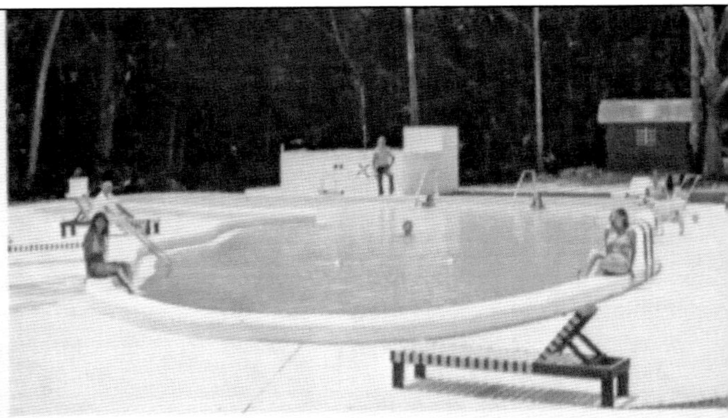

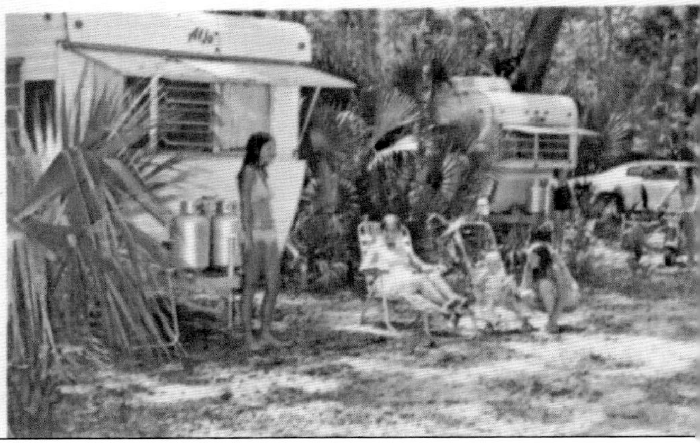

SUGAR MILL RUINS TRAVEL PARK. Appropriately located on Old Mission Road, the Sugar Mill Ruins Travel Park has been a favorite of campers, RVers, and those looking for an economical place to stay while traveling. While being close to the city, the travel park is isolated enough to offer a peaceful location to those staying there. Activities include fishing, basketball, volleyball, hayrides, a swimming pool, and more.

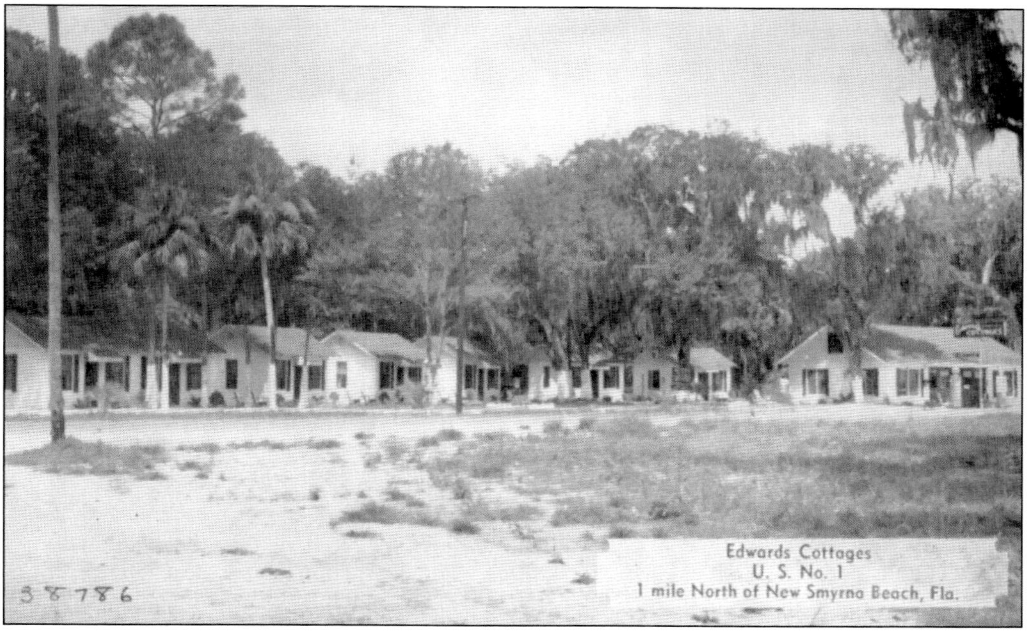

EDWARDS COTTAGES. Owned by Olin Schottler, the nine units at Edwards Cottages could sleep two to four people each. All included private tile showers, continuous hot water, innerspring mattresses, cross ventilation, and comfortable furnishings. The cottages were located at 1200 Orange Avenue. This property appears to be part of the land that was home to Mullinax Ford until the dealership moved.

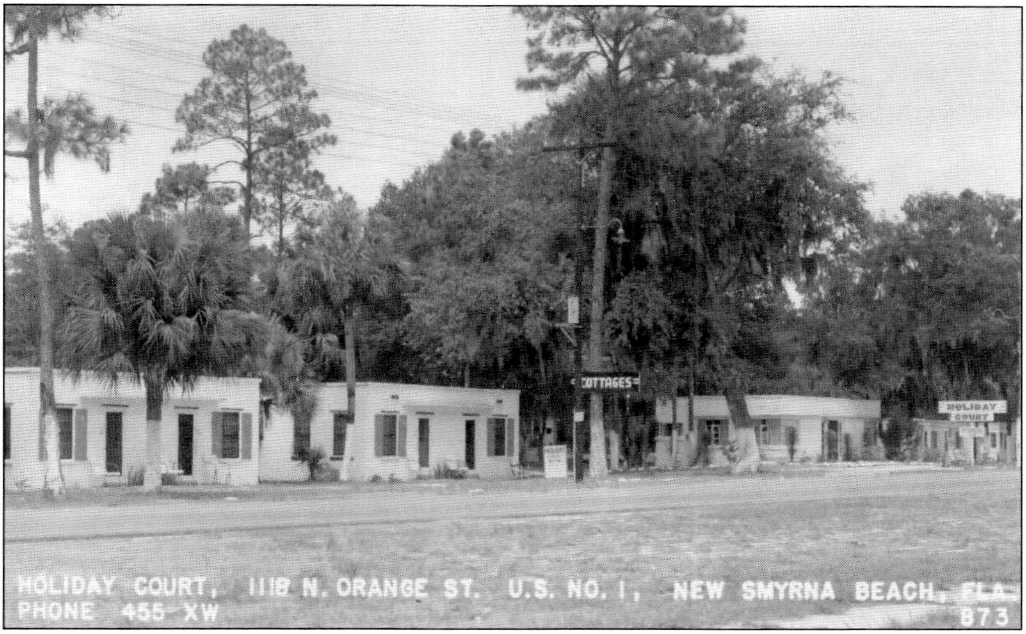

HOLIDAY COURT. The Holiday Court was yet another of the many small family-owned hotels that dotted US 1 in the days before the interstate system. Postmarked in 1951, this card brags about the excellent fishing in Turnbull Bay, which was only two miles away. The Connecticut recipients of this card were also left to imagine the beauty of the two sides of the bay, as the sender described.

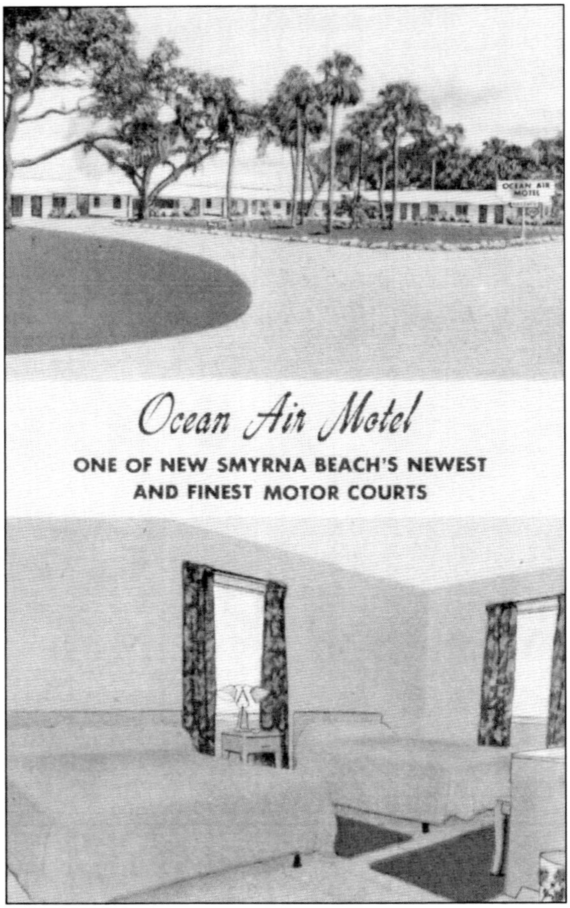

OCEAN AIR MOTEL. Mr. and Mrs. David Shade were the owners of the Ocean Air Motel when these cards were issued. The back of the card details what guests could expect, including air-conditioning, forced-air heat, Beautyrest beds, ceramic tile baths, and moderate rates. The Ocean Air Motel is still in business and is now owned by Fred and Sharon Vincent. The motel prides itself on cleanliness and convenience, while being pet friendly.

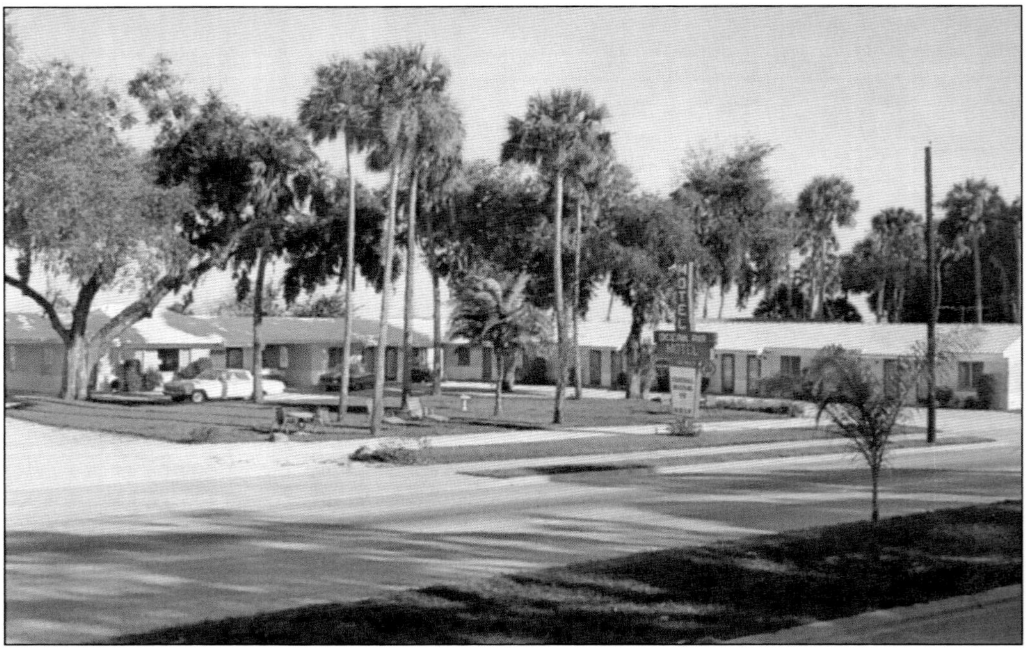

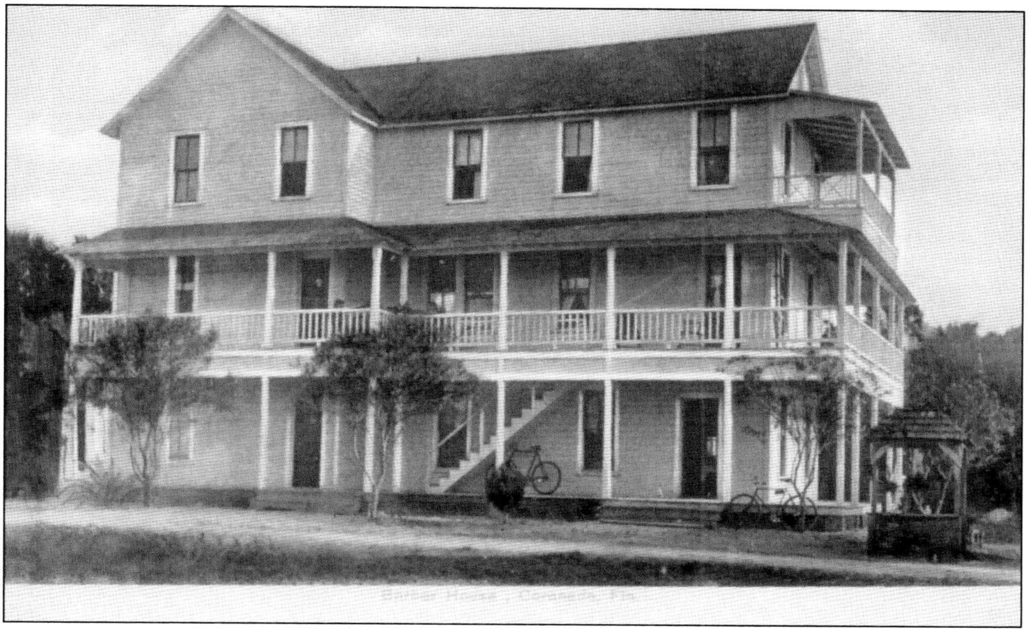

Barber House and Riverview Hotel. Built by Samuel Barber in 1885, the hotel originally had only two stories. Around 1905, Barber hired contractors to add a third story. They did this by jacking up the entire structure and building a new first story. In addition to owning the hotel, Barber also served as the first bridge toll taker. Fred Tyron purchased the property in 1936 and changed the name to the Riverview. Today, the property has been completely renovated into an 18-room boutique inn. (Below, courtesy Zelia V. Sweett.)

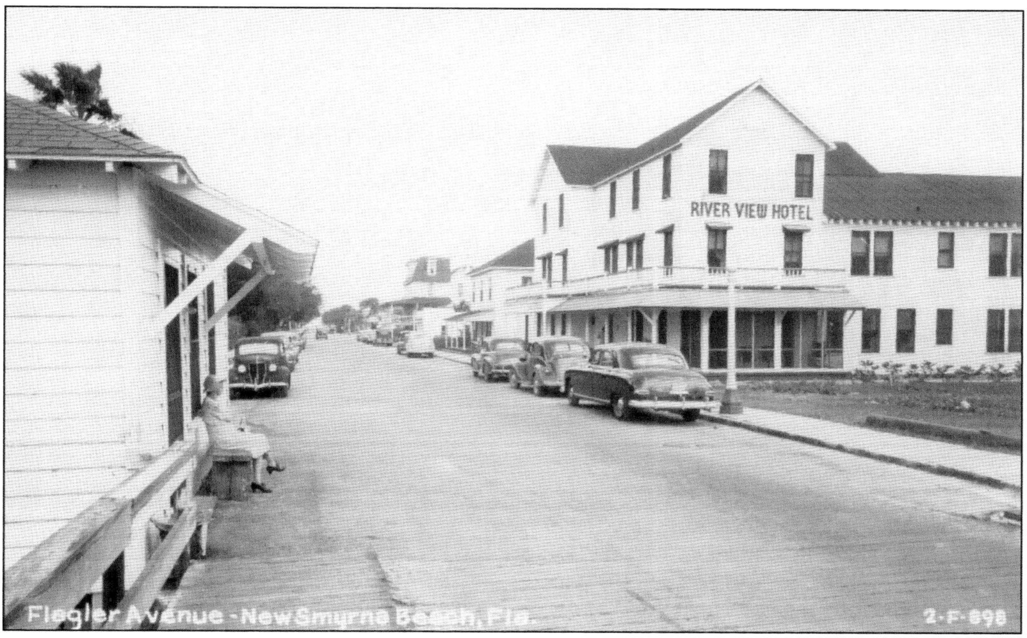

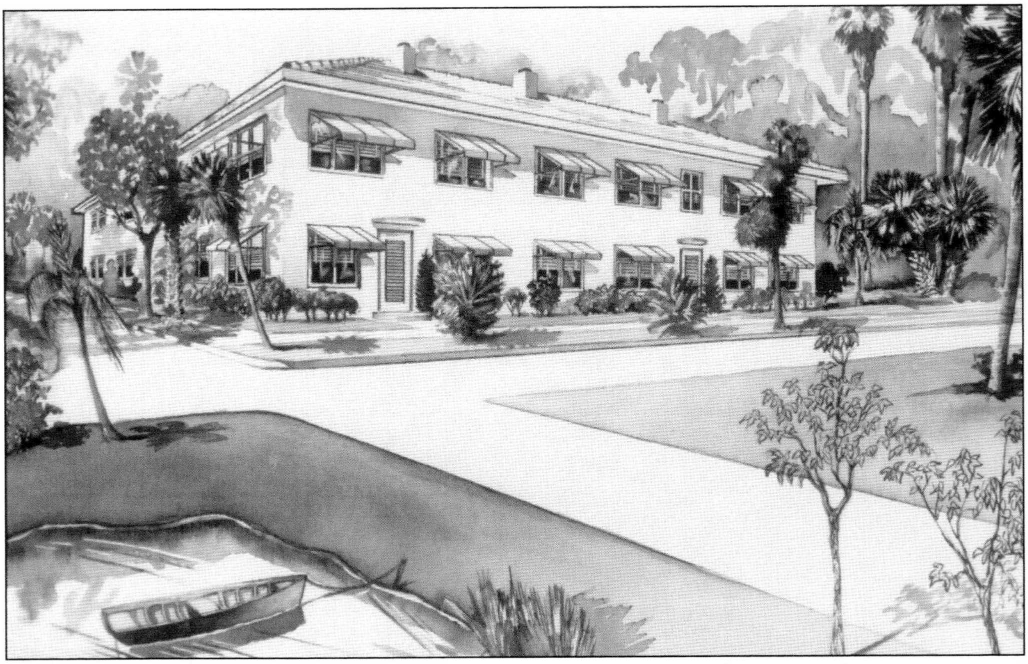

KARRER APARTMENTS. Located at 320 South Riverside Drive, the Karrer Apartments stand as a reminder of sisters Alice and Gertrude Karrer. The sisters were part of a very successful girls' high school basketball team in the 1920s, with Alice playing forward and Gertrude as a guard. Contemporary newspaper accounts stress the effort and hard play put forth by the team. The team traveled widely, including a trip to Cuba. Gertrude passed away in 1993, and Alice passed away in 1994.

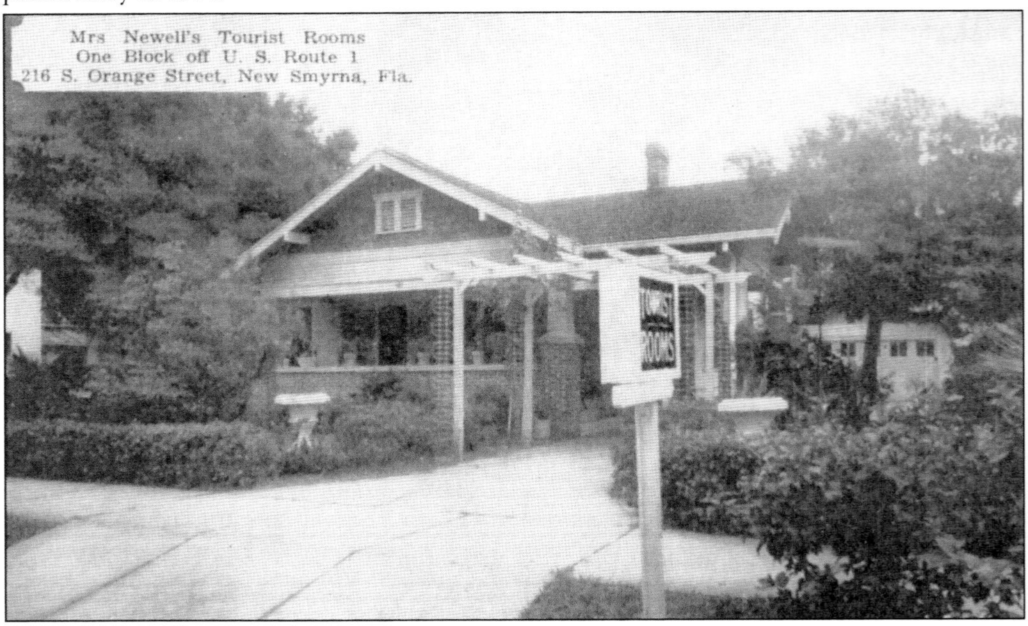

MRS. NEWELL'S TOURIST ROOMS. During the Great Depression, even prominent families were hit by the economic downturn. Annie Kendall Newell, the wife of William Harmon Newell, a former five-term mayor and former owner of the Atlantic House, rented rooms to the public in this house located at 216 South Orange Street. The home still stands today.

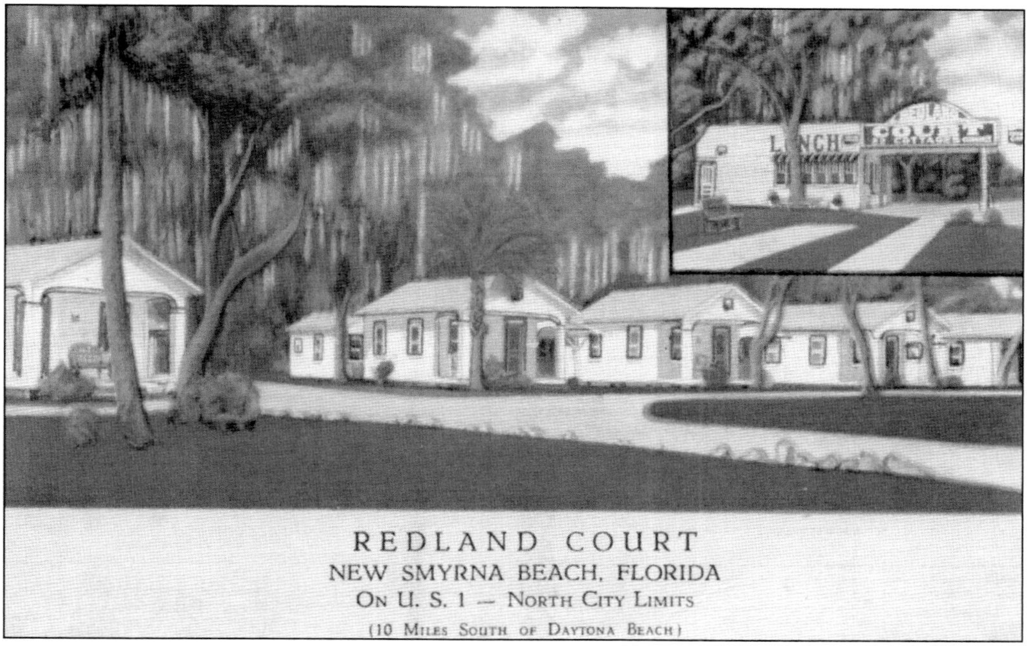

REDLAND COURT. Redland Camp/Court was located just 10 miles south of Daytona Beach and 3 miles north of New Smyrna. The card above states that there were 22 clean, comfortable cottages with private toilets, tiled showers, innerspring mattresses, kitchenettes with electric refrigeration, a dining room featuring northern cooking, and an adjacent fish camp. At the main building shown below, travelers could do everything from have a meal to buy Gulf gasoline.

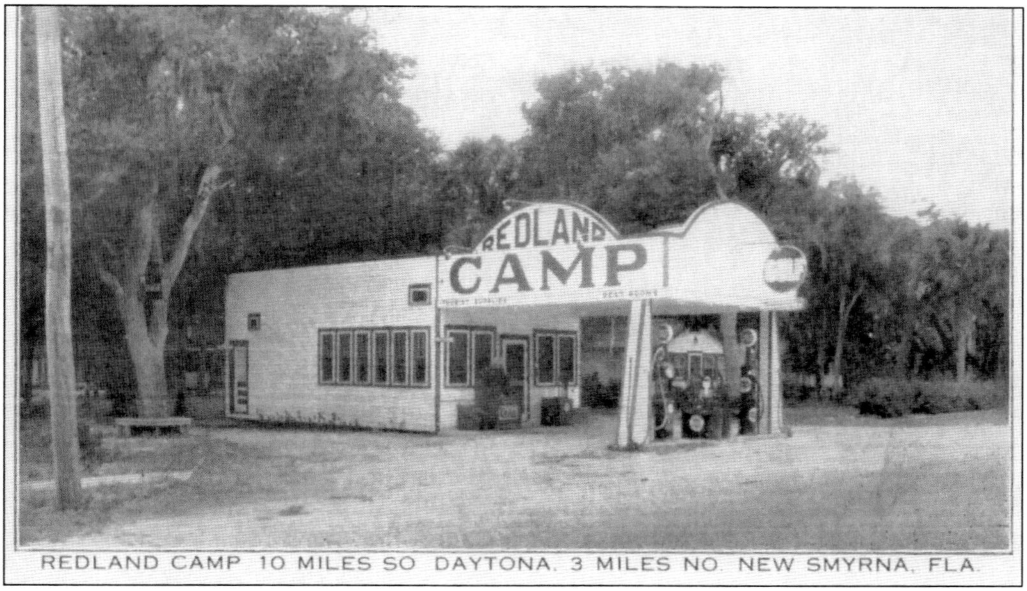

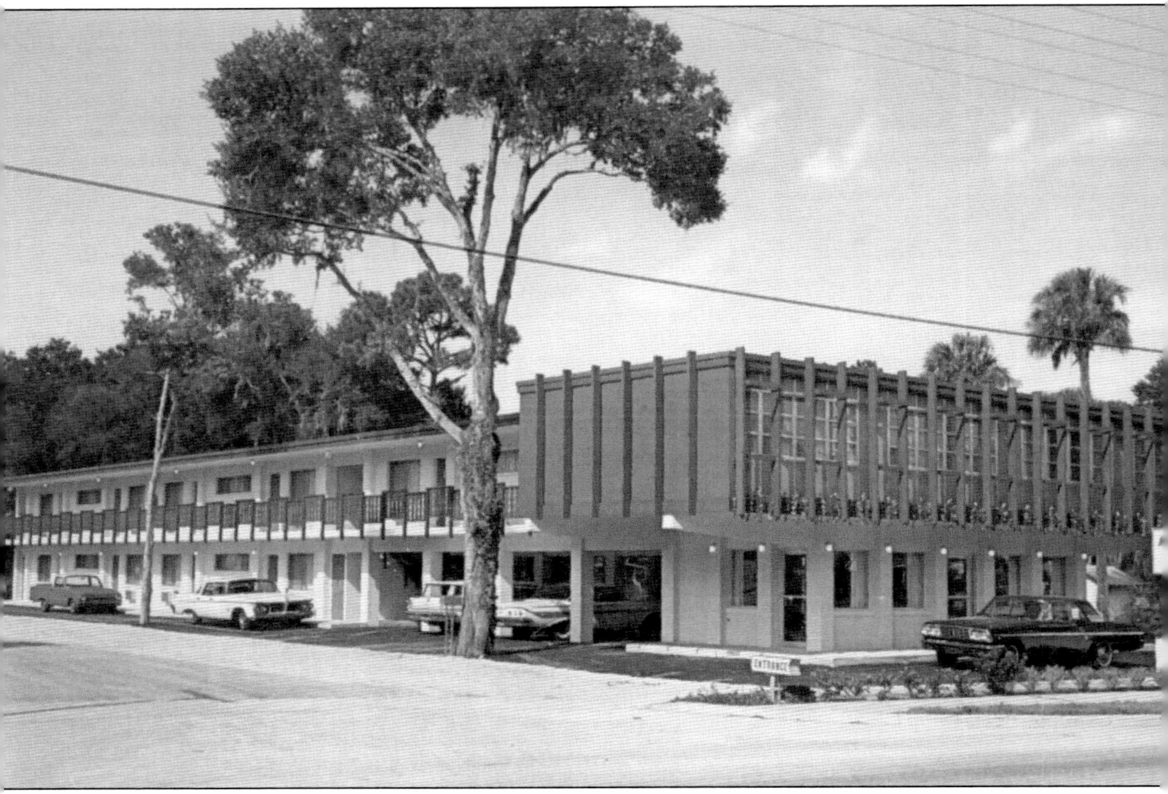

NOCTURNE MOTEL. The Nocturne name of this motel seems appropriate since most people associate a motel room with a place to stay the night. This card advertises its ultra-modern rooms with wall-to-wall carpeting, television, room phones, and individually controlled air-conditioning and heat. The Nocturne is still located at 1104 North Dixie Freeway, and while it is a throwback to the days of old in travel style, the motel has been updated and shows a much more modern appearance.

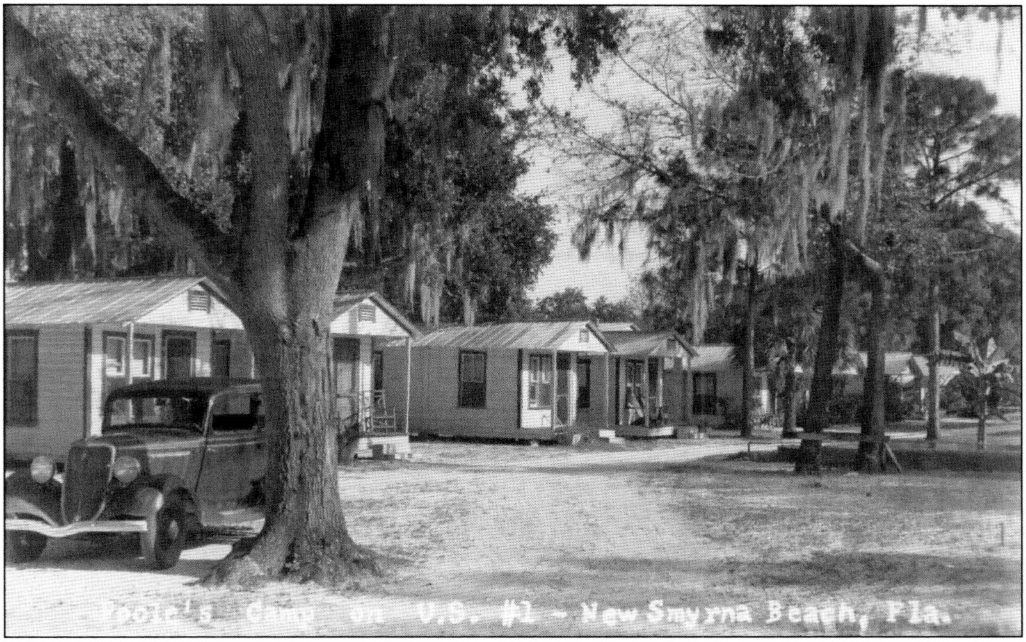

POOLE'S CAMP. In the days before the interstate and the modern chain hotel, small independently owned hotels and camps, such as Poole's, dotted US 1. Poole's Camp was located at the northeast corner of US 1 and Wayne Avenue. While these images show a rural setting, this area is now a major intersection, and the land is home to Blackbeard's Inn, a seafood restaurant. The card above was postmarked on December 11, 1946, and was sent to Rome, New York. The sender states this view is just a small part of the trailer camp where they are staying. He goes on to say that the weather is hot, but it seems good. (Below, courtesy Dorothy Moore.)

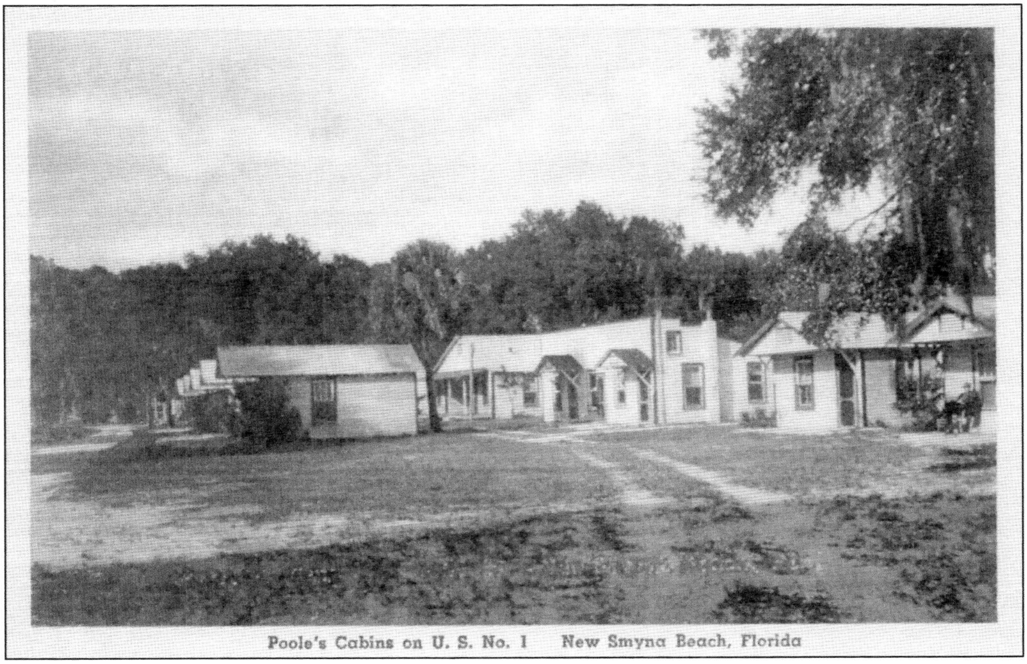

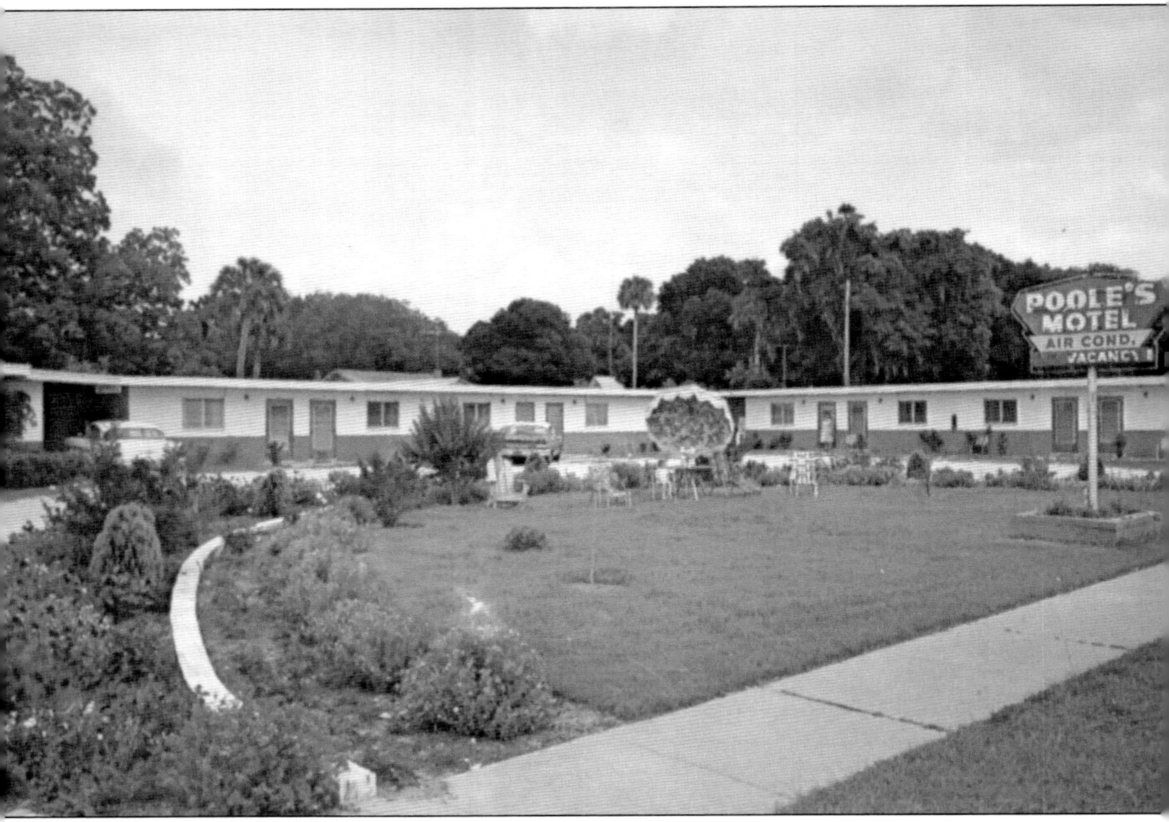

POOLE'S MOTEL. Born in Glascock County, Georgia, in 1879, Oscar M. Poole had become a resident of Volusia County, Florida, by 1930. He owned Poole's Motel, along with his second wife, Sally. Poole's Motel is located at 635 North Dixie Freeway, more commonly known as US 1. Little has changed from this postcard image to today. The sign is different, and the building has been painted, but otherwise, the view is quite similar. Oscar passed away in 1975. He is buried in the Edgewater–New Smyrna Cemetery next to his wife, Sally, who passed away in 1973.

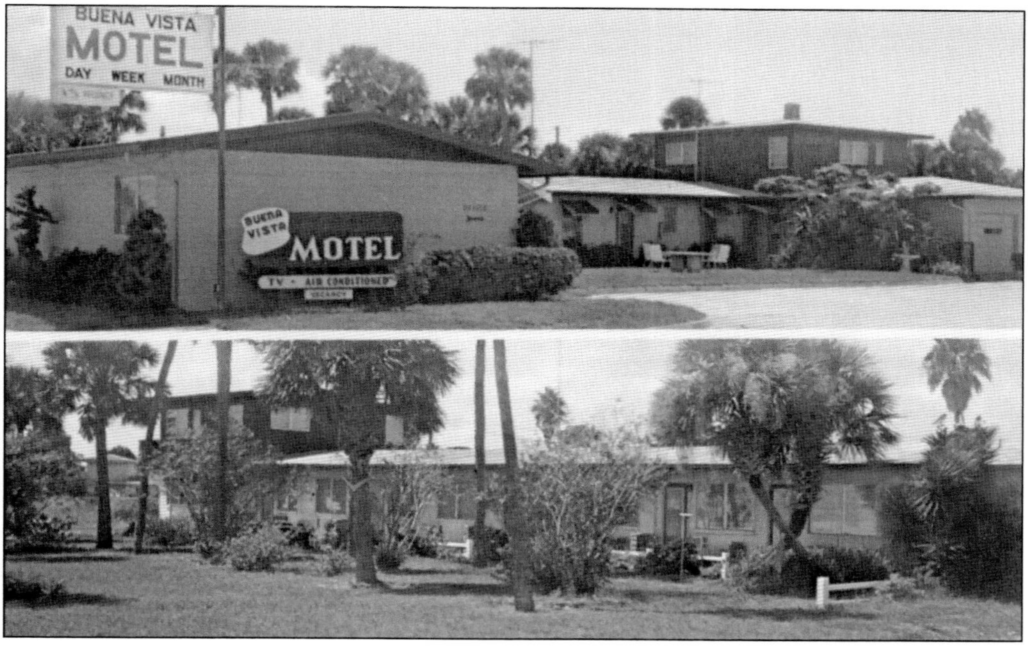

Buena Vista and Sea Vista Motels. The Buena Vista Motel is now the Buena Vista Intracoastal Inn. Open since 1955, the inn features eight guest rooms with easy access to both the mainland and the beachside. The Sea Vista Motel is now known as the Sea Vista Ocean Front Resort. Located at 1701 South Atlantic Avenue, the resort offers an on-site restaurant and tiki bar in addition to its beachfront access.

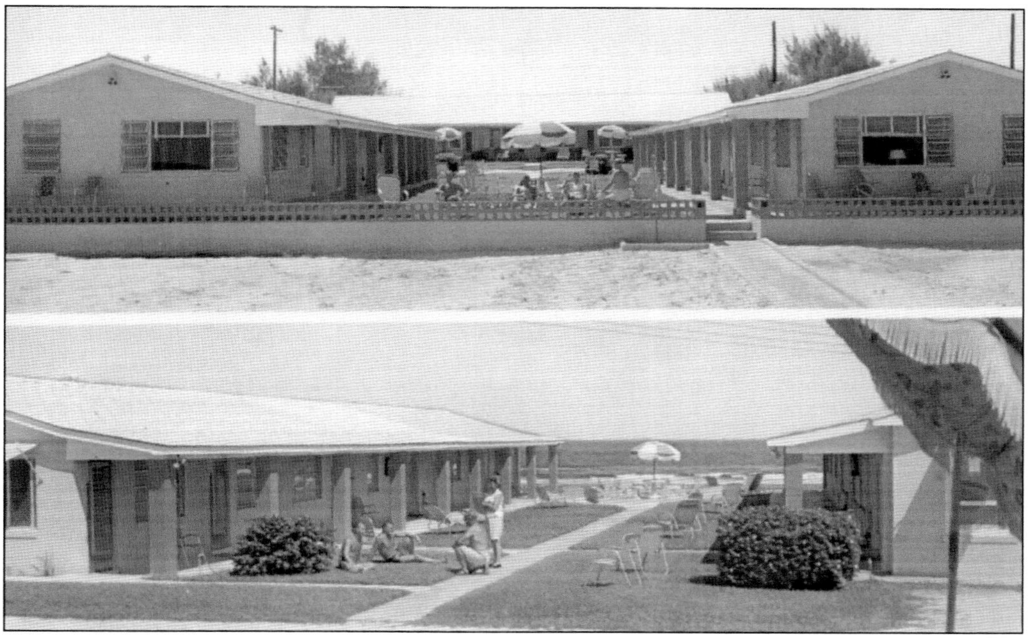

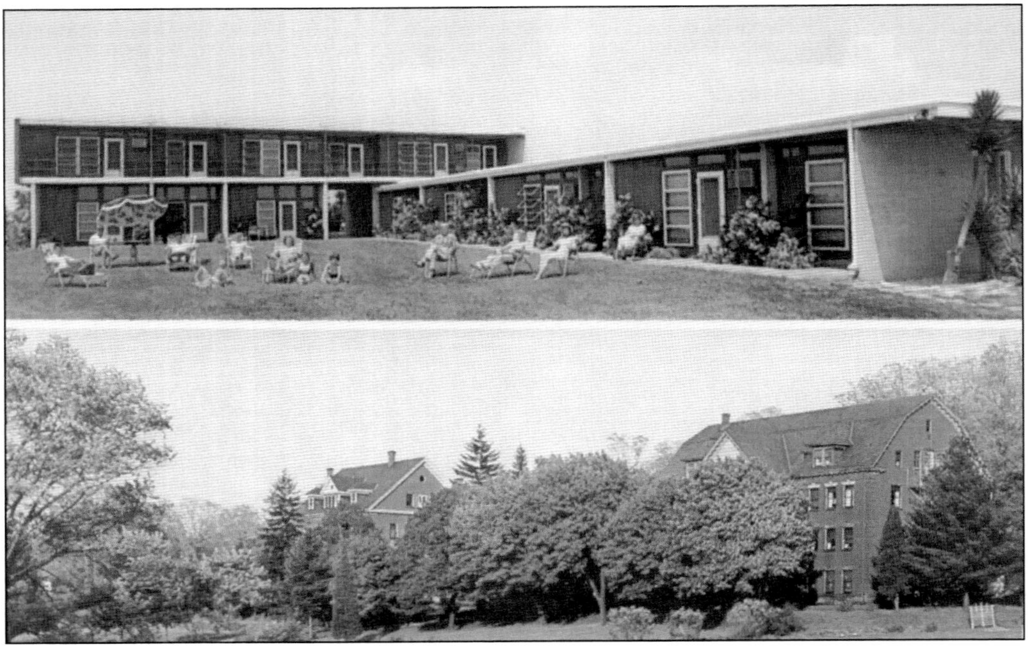

SHANNON BY THE SEA. Located a considerable way south at 3509 South Atlantic Avenue, Shannon by the Sea offered the convenience of being directly on the beach, as well as one-bedroom apartments and motel rooms. While the backs of these cards are identical, it is interesting to note the photographs. The image on the top of both cards appears to be the same, only reversed, while the bottom half of the card above is a mystery as to its location. Perhaps O'Brien Color Studios, the printer of the card, made a mistake that was later corrected in the card below. Today, the location is home to Coastal Waters Inn, a privately owned condominium hotel.

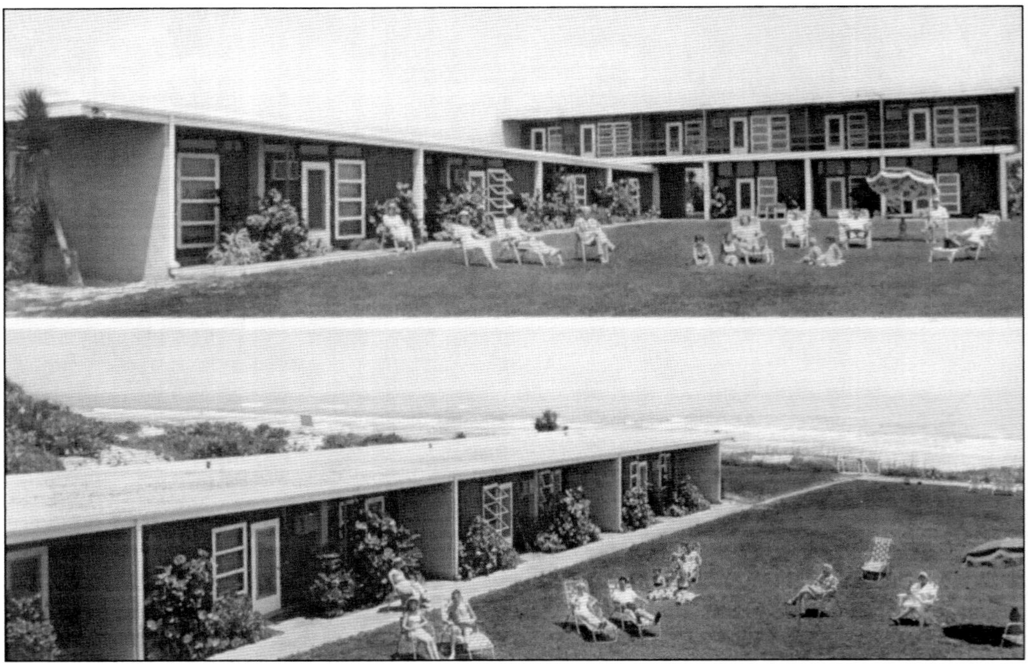

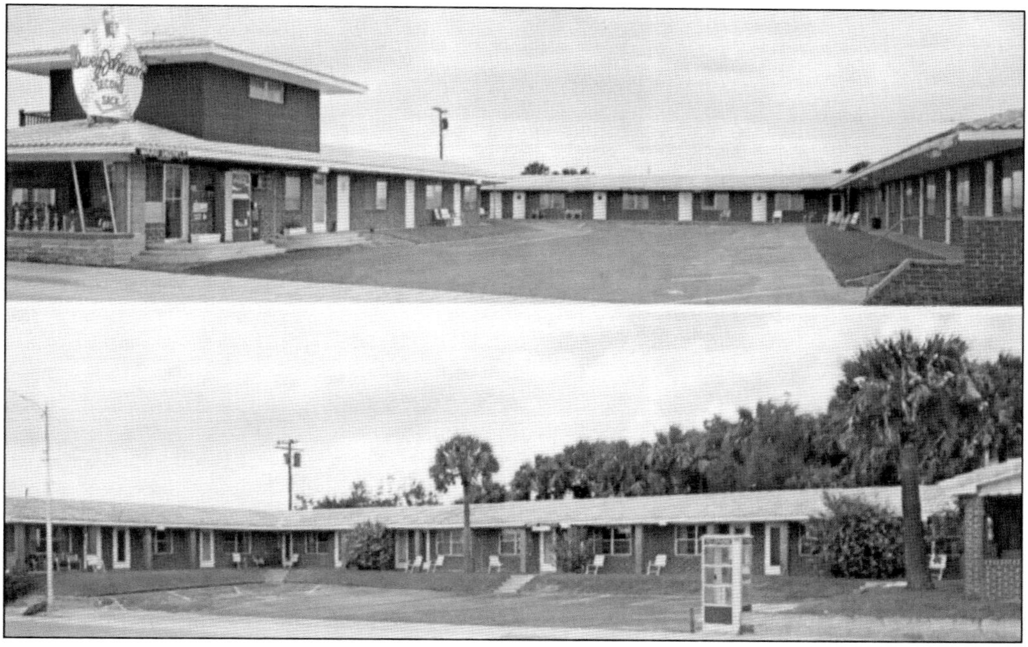

DAVEY JOHNSON SECOND SACK MOTEL. The name of this motel is a clever play on the fact that Johnson played second base for the majority of his Major League Baseball career. Note the baseball as part of the signage. While only an average player, Johnson found much more success as a manager, winning over 1,300 games. The hotel was located at 421 Flagler Avenue, an address that is now home to Peanuts Restaurant and Lounge.

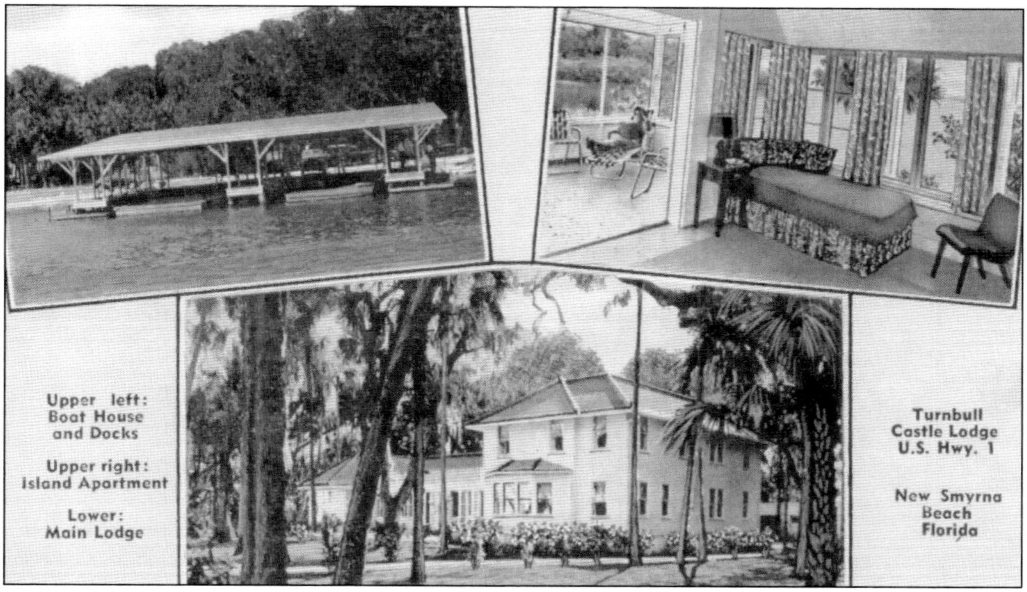

TURNBULL CASTLE LODGE. The use of the Turnbull name is prevalent throughout the area, and the Turnbull Castle Lodge is no different, alluding to the legend of the grand home where Turnbull is said to have lived. The lodge was located on US 1 at Spruce Creek, north of New Smyrna and south of Daytona Beach. Owned by Mr. and Mrs. Arthur R. Christy, the lodge boasted its location "in the royal kingdom of the fishes." Fishermen were greeted with new boats, new outboard motors, and live shrimp to use for bait. (Courtesy Dorothy Moore.)

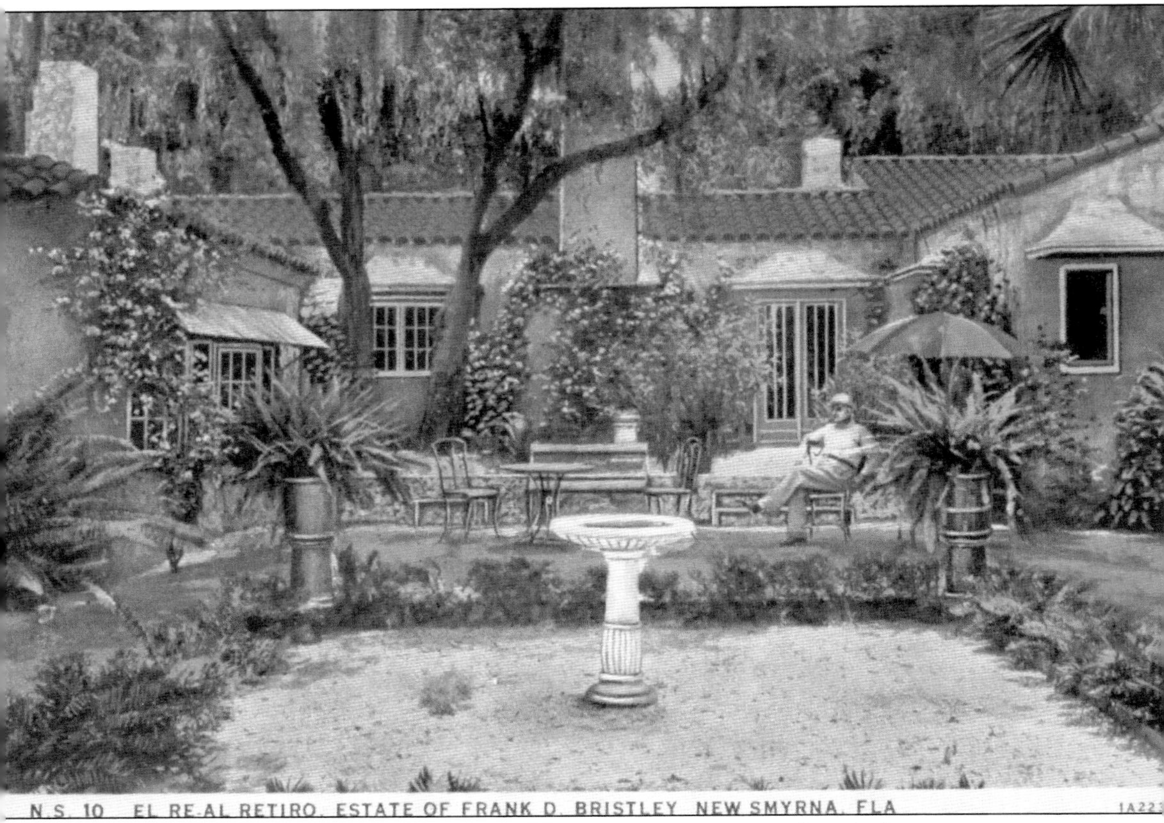

El Real Retiro. El Real Retiro is a grand property consisting of a main house, garage apartment, greenhouse, toolshed, detached carport, and detached former bathhouse. The buildings sit on approximately six-tenths of an acre, with one side facing the Indian River and the other facing Faulkner Street. The house was built in the Mediterranean Revival style, with stuccoed walls and hip and gable roofs with Spanish barrel tiles. The main structure was built by Robert Handley in 1923. The main home is also known for having murals painted by American artists Robert Lochner and Lauren Ford in the library and reception hall. With the declines in the real estate market associated with the Great Depression, Handley was forced to sell the property to local businessman Frank D. Bristley, who owned the estate from 1928 until his death in 1941, which helps date this card. Today, the property is listed in the National Register of Historic Places.

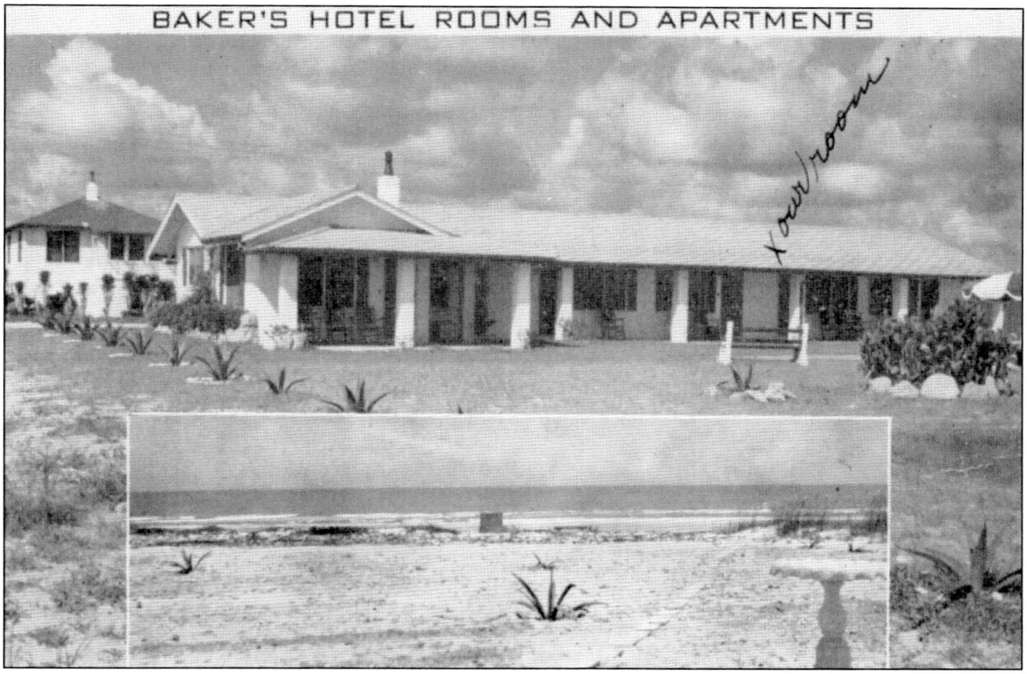

Baker's Hotel Rooms and Apartments. Baker's was one of many small family-owned hotels located beachside in New Smyrna. This card lists B. Baker as the proprietor. Amenities included a tile bath and a shuffleboard court. Rates were available by the day, week, or month. According to the sender of the card, their room was just a sleeping room, but the owner provided a small room that could be used for cooking. There, she fried bacon and eggs each morning.

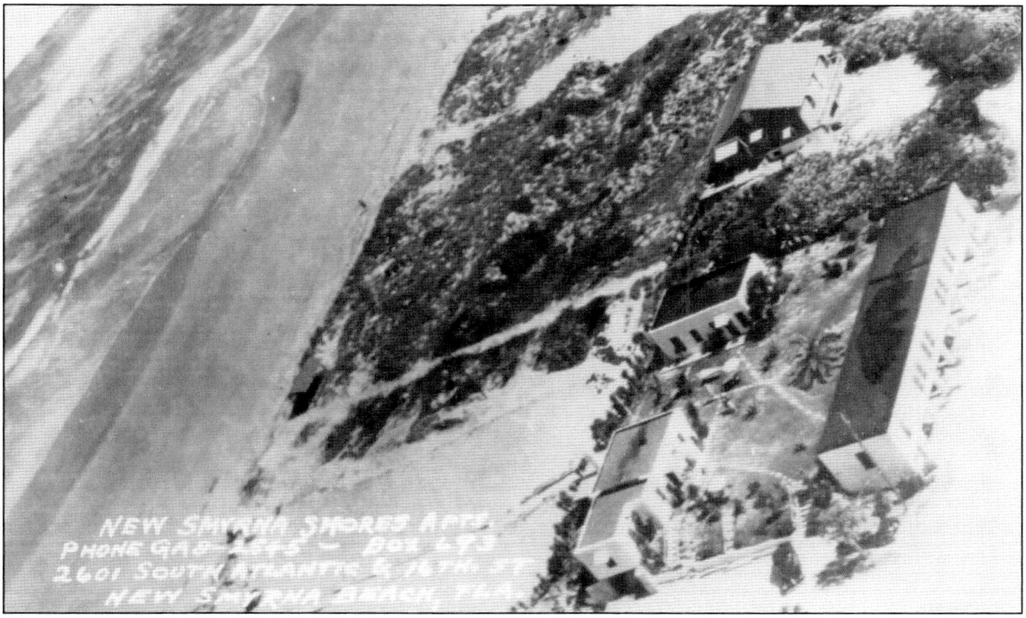

New Smyrna Shores Apartments. Located at 2601 South Atlantic Avenue at the corner of Sixteenth Street, the New Smyrna Shores Apartments provided excellent ocean views. The skewed north-south view of this card shows the beach and ocean on the left, or east. The owners were Vista and Fred Seth. The address provided on the card is currently a vacant lot.

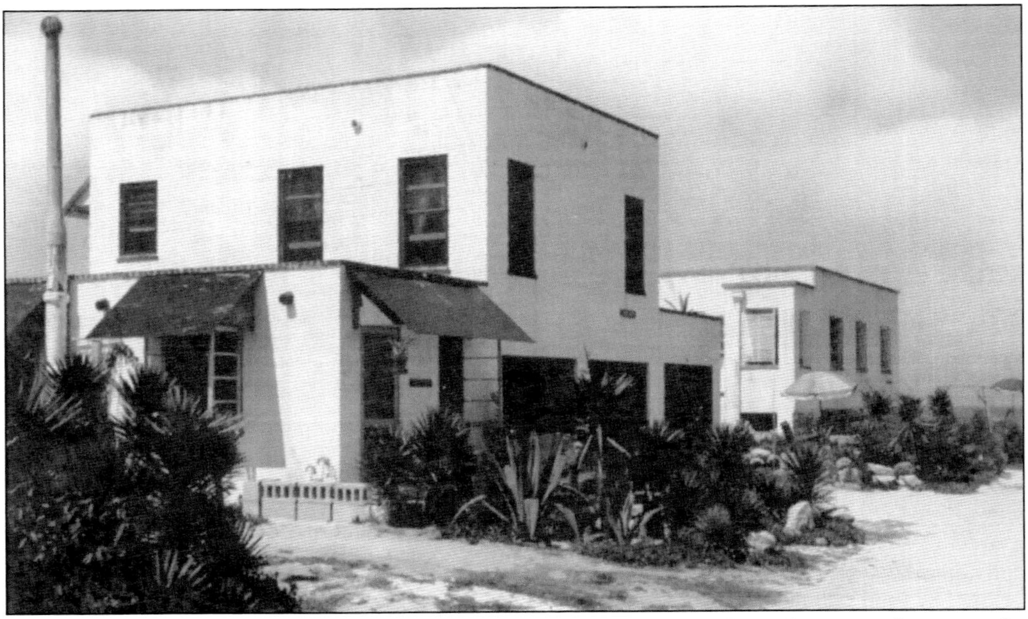

Horizons on the Ocean. Whether travelers wanted to stay for a day, a week, a month, or a season, Horizons apartments and cottages were able to accommodate the needs of guests. Horizons on the Ocean was owned by James Reginald Wilson and his wife, Winifred. Reginald was born in Canada and served in the Royal Air Force during World War I with the rank of lieutenant. Reginald and Winifred are both buried in Edgewater–New Smyrna Cemetery. The Wilsons' son Reginald Stuart Wilson served in the Army during World War II, earning a Silver Star, Bronze Star, and Army Commendation Medal. He retired with the rank of major.

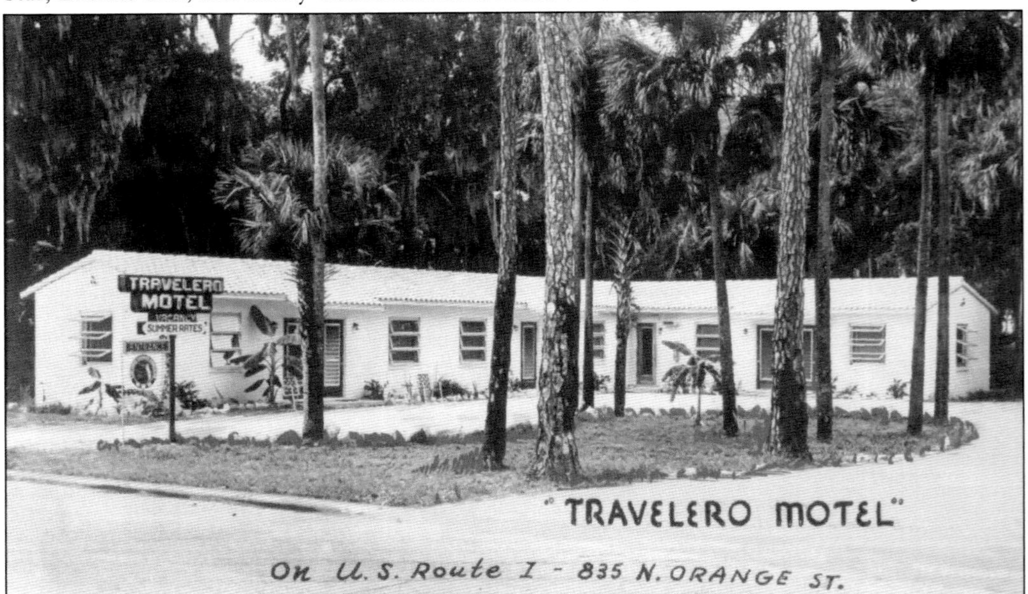

Travelero Motel. "Where friends meet friends in the sunshine" was the motto of the Travelero. The Travelero Motel was located at 835 North Orange Avenue, as US 1 used to be called, and boasted eight modern rooms, private tile showers, air-conditioning, and Hollywood beds. The card advertises summer rates. The motel has been enlarged and renamed the Tuscan Inn.

Five

Not All Fun and Games

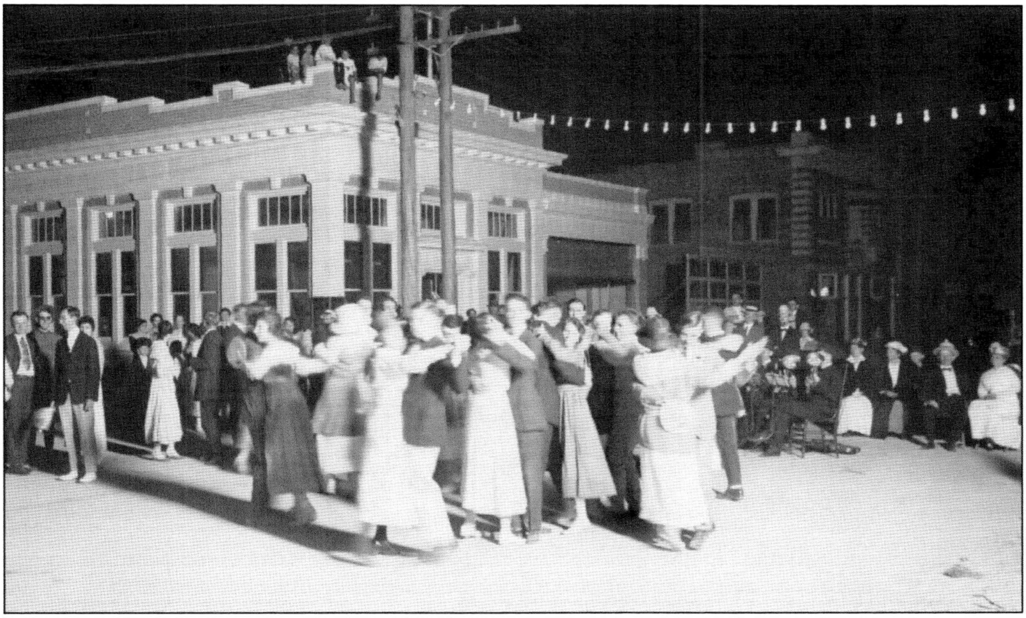

State Bank of New Smyrna. The building that is highlighted here served as the State Bank of New Smyrna, then opened as the Bank of New Smyrna in 1936, and today, it is home to the Utilities Commission. Constructed in 1926, the building is considered to fall within the Beaux-Arts Classical style, which consisted of elaborate decorative details. In addition to the bank building and the dancers in the street, note the live band at right and the partiers hanging over the rooftop. How they got there after business hours is lost to time.

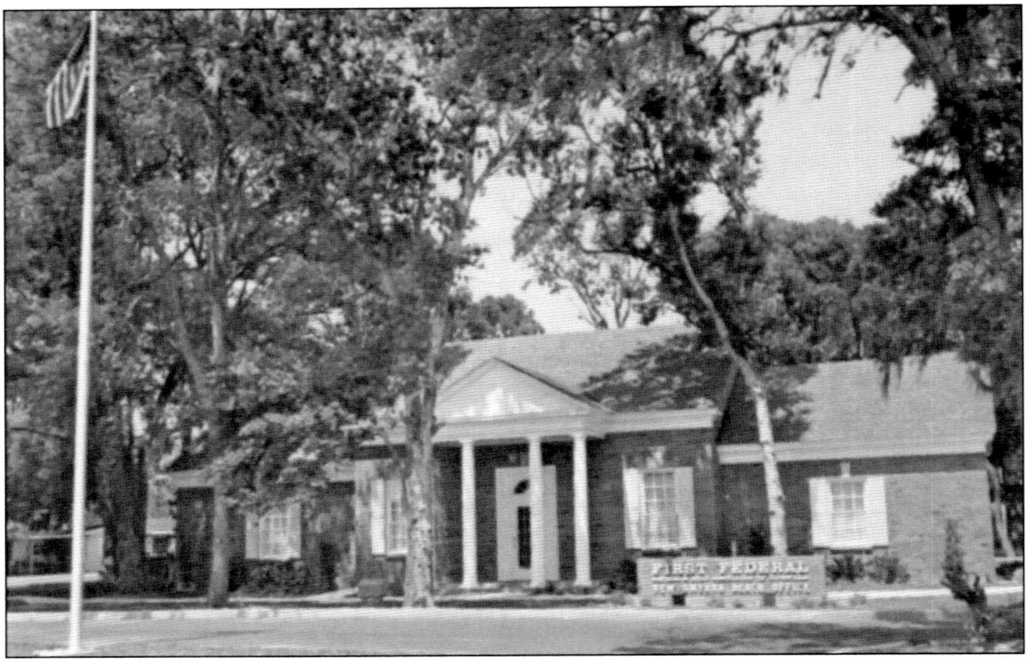

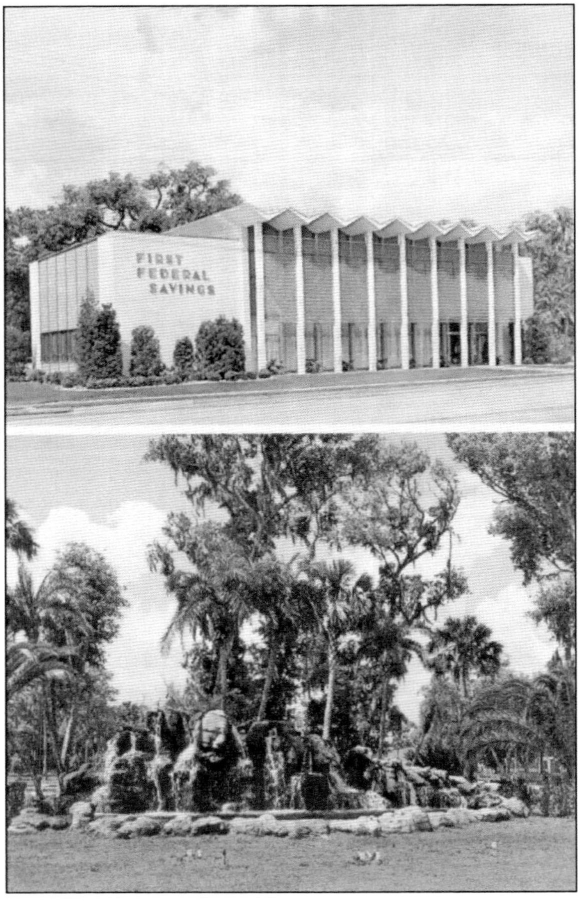

First Federal Savings & Loan. First Federal Savings & Loan was established in July 1935. In 1991, the name was changed to First Federal Savings Bank of New Smyrna, and in September 1997, it was merged into Regions Bank. The card above shows its former location at 1701 South Dixie Freeway, which is now a Launch Federal Credit Union. The card at left, featuring waterfalls, is the 900 North Dixie Freeway location, which still houses a Regions Bank.

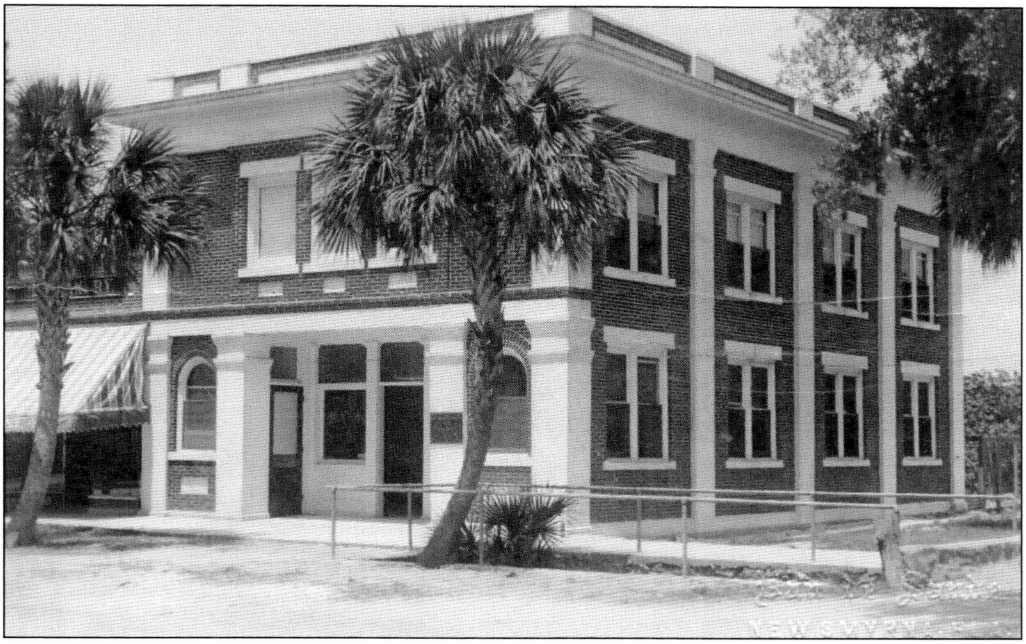

FIDELITY BANK. This beautiful brick building sits at the corner of Canal Street and Sams Avenue. Over the years, it has been home to several popular businesses. Originally, it was Fidelity Bank. Since then, it has been the Hofreiter Bakery, Davis Corner Store, and currently, Jason's Corner restaurant. (Courtesy Southeast Volusia Historical Society.)

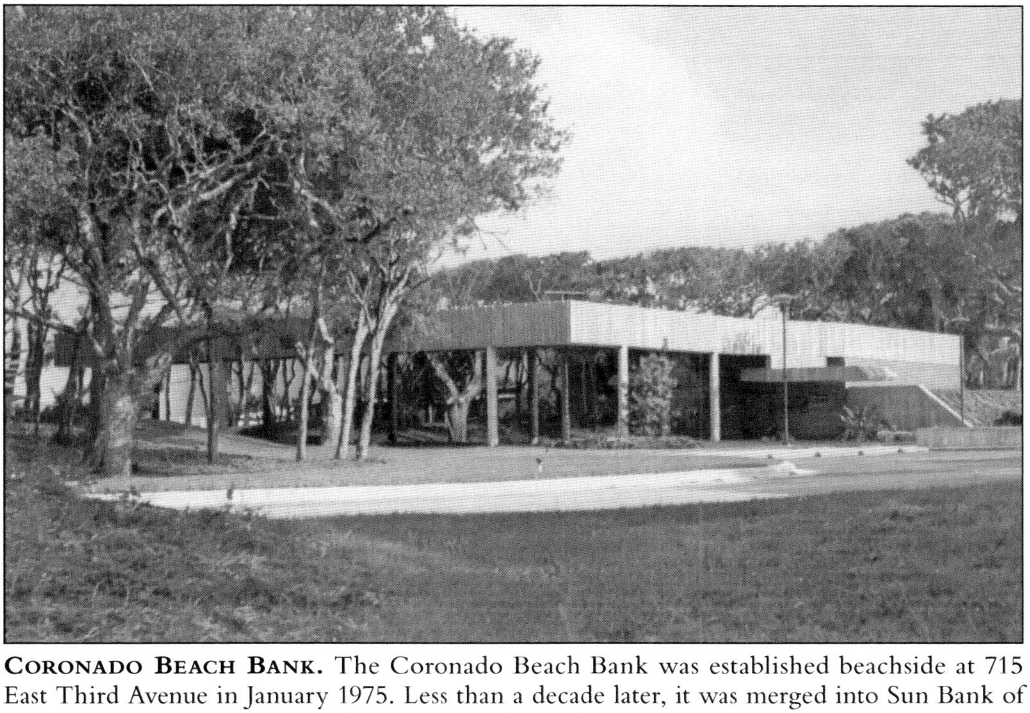

CORONADO BEACH BANK. The Coronado Beach Bank was established beachside at 715 East Third Avenue in January 1975. Less than a decade later, it was merged into Sun Bank of Volusia County, and in 1995, the name was changed to SunTrust Bank East Central Florida. In January 2000, the name was shortened to SunTrust Bank. Due to address changes, SunTrust Bank is now located at 705 East Third Avenue.

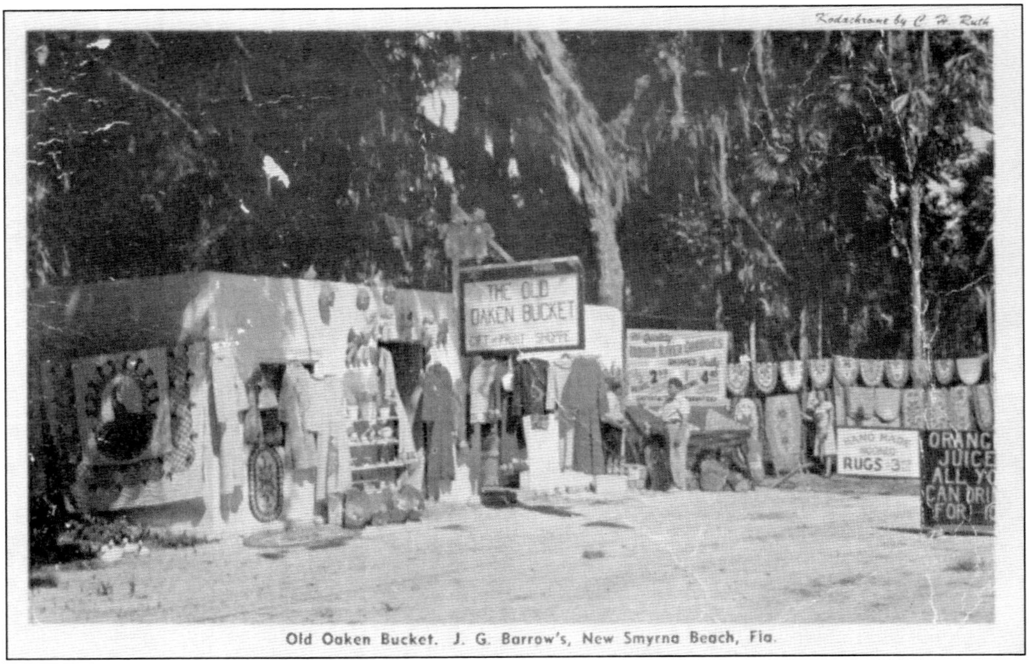

OLD OAKEN BUCKET. This gift shop and fruit stand was owned by J.G. Barrow. In addition to offering unlimited orange juice and hand-hooked rugs, the Old Oaken Bucket was well known for shipping fresh fruit. Indian River oranges cost $2.69 per half bushel and $4.48 for a full bushel. Daily shipments were made November 1 through May 1, assuring buyers the freshest-quality citrus possible. (Courtesy Dorothy Moore.)

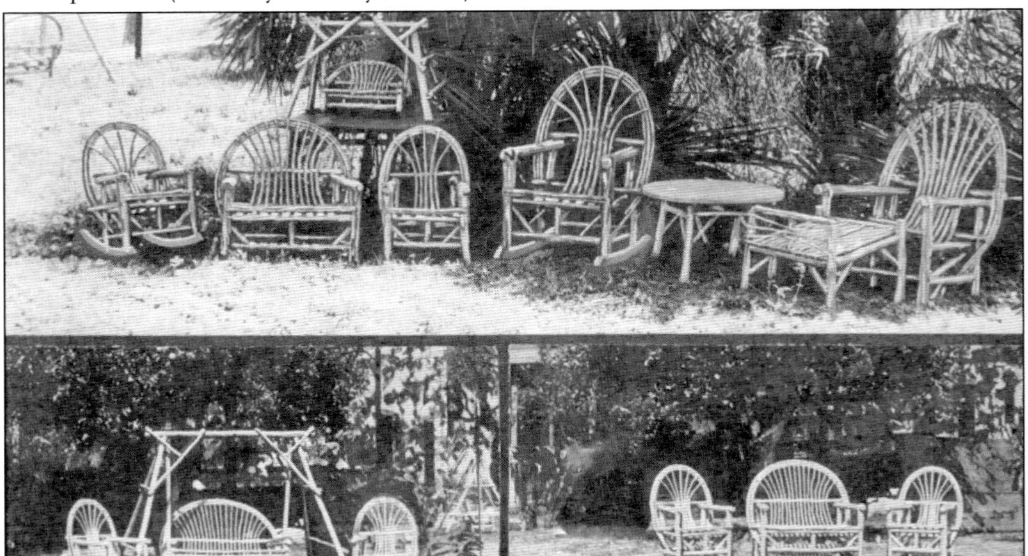

E.A. MORRIS RED CYPRESS FURNITURE. Located next to Redland Court cottages on US 1, E.A. Morris Genuine Handmade Red Cypress Furniture specialized in rockers, swings, tables, and other handmade furniture. Morris advertised a "naturally acquired" product with the use of "first grade zinc coated galvanized nails." Whether the furniture was sold by the piece or by the carload, Morris could accommodate all orders with "shipping costs very low."

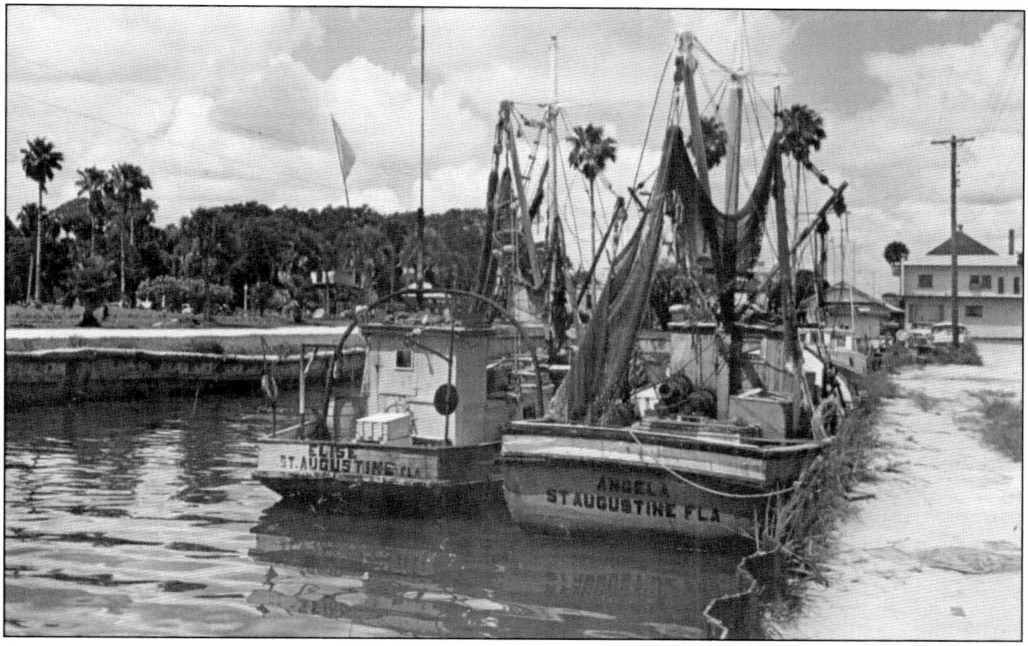

SHRIMP BOATS. Fishing and shrimping were a vital part of the New Smyrna Beach economy. Small family-owned businesses came from up and down the coast to fish and then sell their catch. These two boats, the *Elise* and the *Angela*, both from St. Augustine, are shown docked near Riverside Drive. They might have sold their catch to Feger's Fish Market, a longtime staple on the North Causeway.

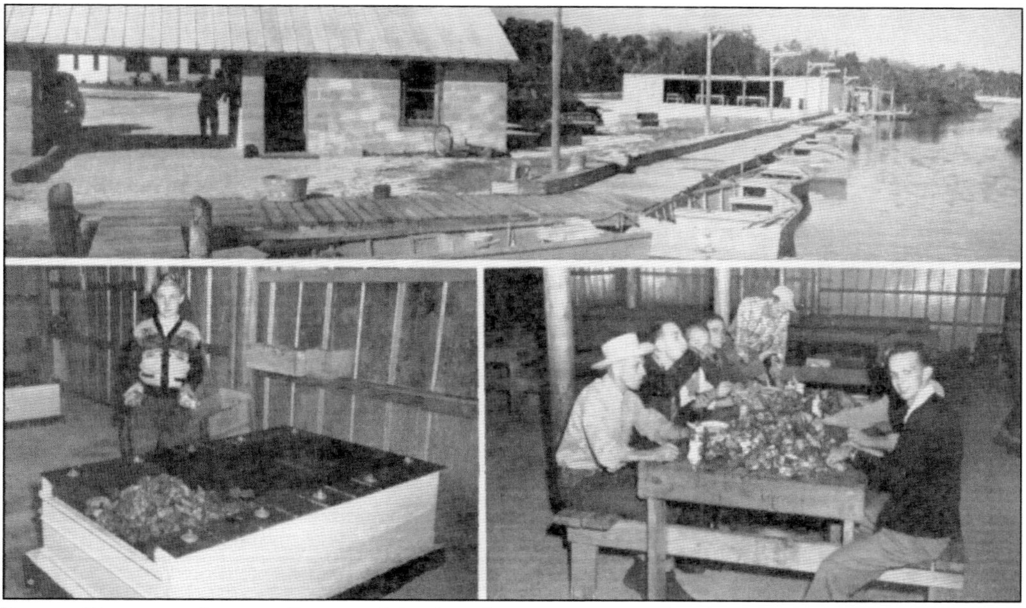

JONES FISHING CAMP. Operated by brothers Harvey and Olen Jones, the Jones Fishing Camp was located just south of New Smyrna Beach. The fish camp boasted a full-service experience, including the boat, bait, tackle, and motor, as well as an expert guide. In season, they offered delicious oysters from their own roasters. The Jones brothers are both buried in Edgewater-New Smyrna Cemetery.

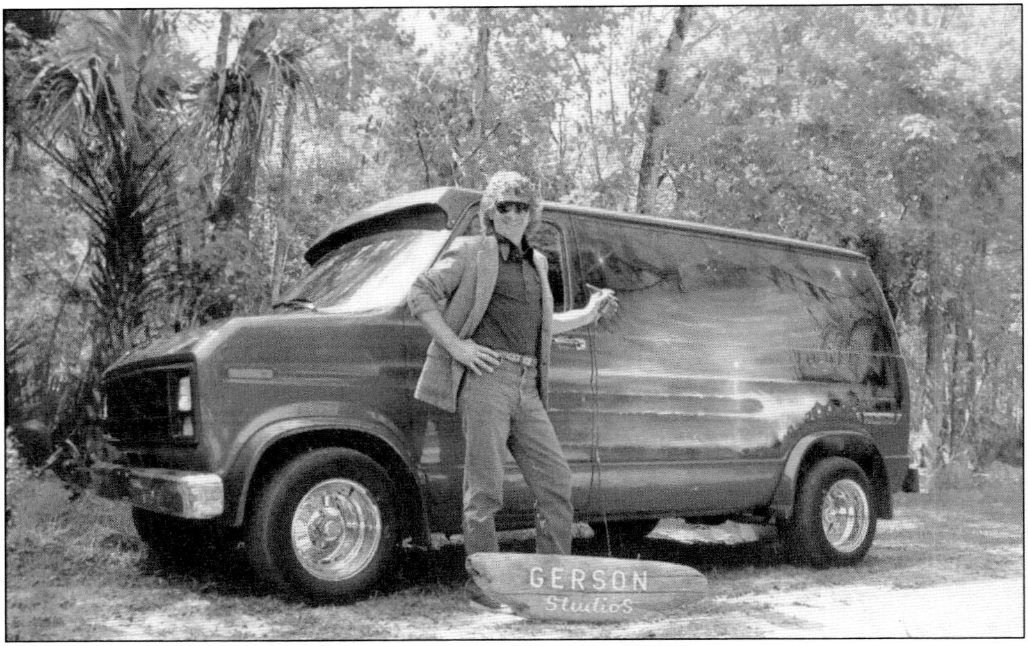

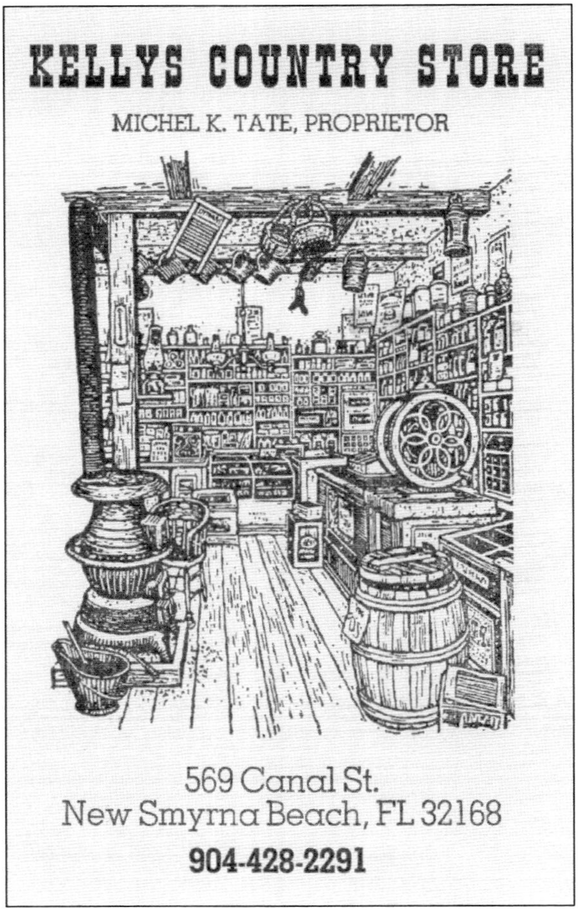

GERSON AIRBRUSH ART STUDIOS. Offering custom painting since 1965, Gerson Studios was started by Henry Gerson Jr. He specialized in all types of advertising, including vehicle art, sign painting, and wall murals. Today, Gerson Studios is operated by Henry and his wife, Mary. After having been high school sweethearts, they got back together and were married in 2011. They now offer airbrush, fine art, photography, limited-edition prints, and sculpture.

KELLY'S COUNTRY STORE. Named for owner Michel K. Tate's daughter, Kelly's was open seven days a week. Tate came to New Smyrna Beach from Naples, where he built homes and previously owned a department store. Kelly's contained a mix of country and antique items, including wicker furniture, weather vanes, and Coca-Cola memorabilia. It was located in the former Phillips Feed Store. The building is currently home to Southeastern Surfaces & Equipment, Inc.

YOUNG LADIES DRESSED IN WHITE. This real-photo postcard of two young African American ladies does not include a location. Based on their identical attire, the women appear to be in uniform. Perhaps they worked as maids or waitresses. This image was taken by well-known local photographer Theo van de Sande, who worked out of a studio on Faulkner Street.

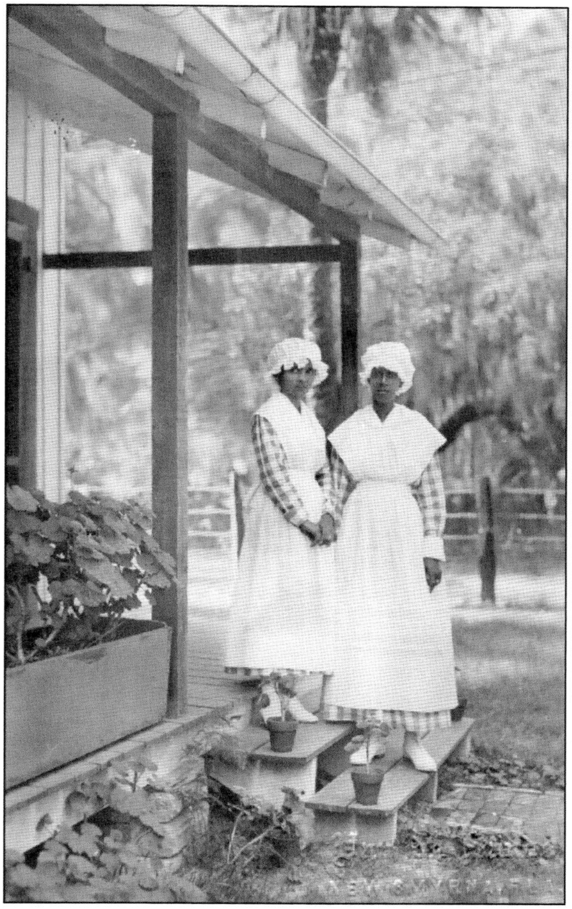

PAMPAS NURSERY. Pampas Nursery claimed to be the world's largest grower of pampas plumes, selling them for both decorative and ornamental purposes. The nursery even offered wholesale pricing upon request. Originally owned by W.S. Hughes, Pampas Nursery was located on Route 1 before moving west of New Smyrna Beach to its current location off Highway 44 on a road bearing the business name.

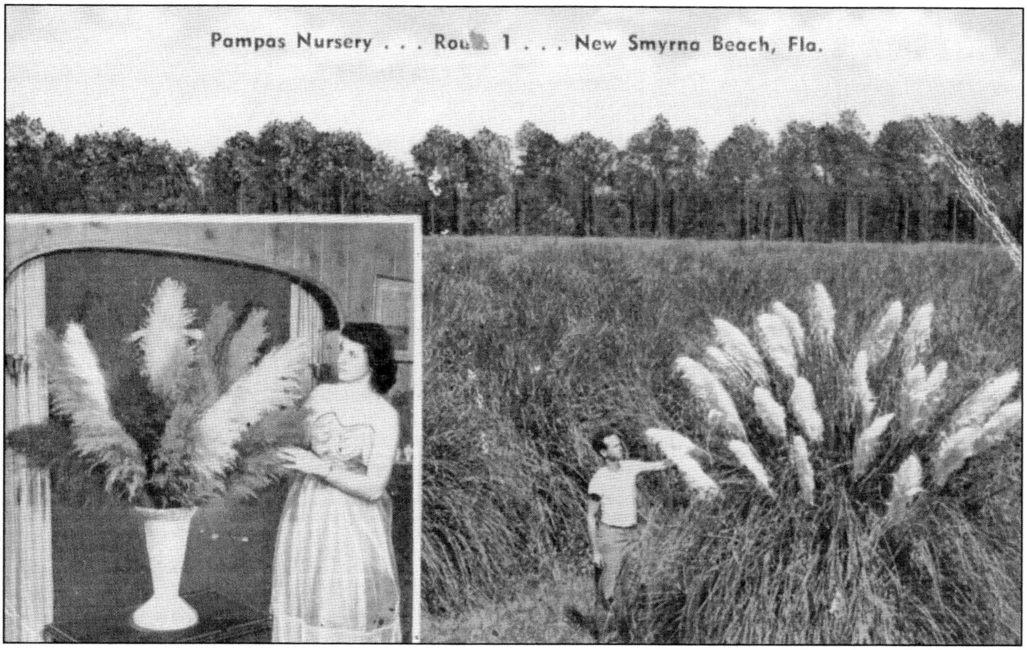

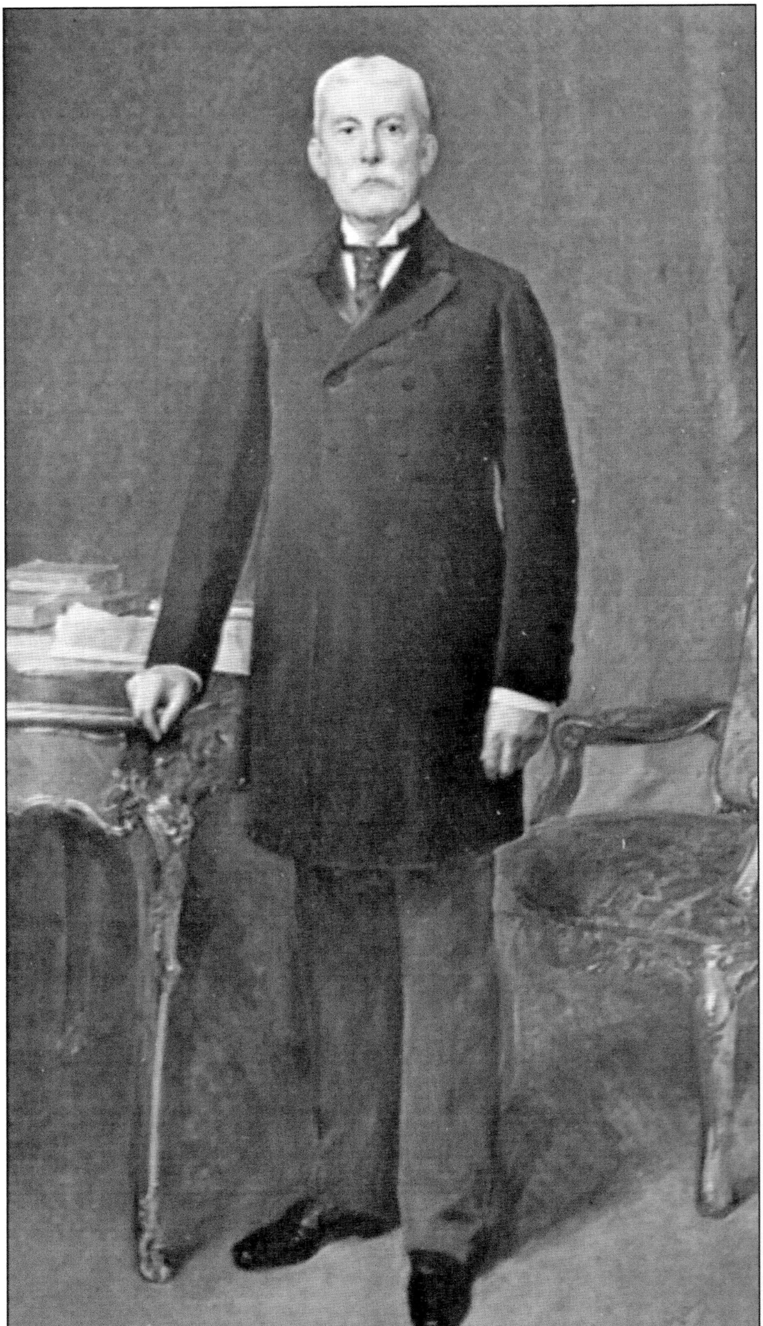

HENRY MORRISON FLAGLER. This image is from a painted portrait of Henry Flagler that hangs in the Henry Morrison Flagler Museum in Palm Beach, Florida. Flagler was a founding partner in Standard Oil, along with John Rockefeller and several other partners. Flagler left his mark in Florida in many ways. He owned several luxury hotels along the Florida coast; however, he is probably best known for founding the Florida East Coast Railway, originally both a passenger and freight line. A crippling strike in the 1960s led to the discontinuation of passenger traffic. The FEC, as it is often called, was a major employer in New Smyrna Beach for several decades.

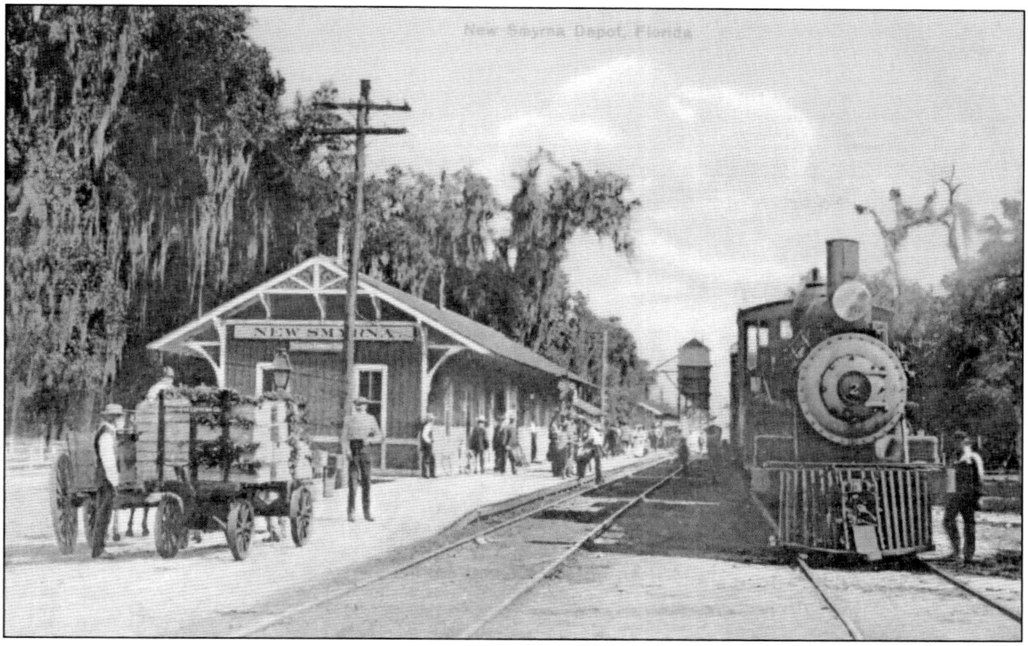

New Smyrna Train Station. These images, taken from opposite ends of the New Smyrna train station, show the importance of rail to the city. Above, take note of the cart at left. It is marked "Southern Express Co." and appears to be holding a large amount of produce that would most likely be shipped to a northern destination. Below are several lines that branch off, allowing multiple trains to come through the station. Notice the large number of passengers waiting to board. Currently, there is no depot or passenger traffic through New Smyrna Beach. The closest Amtrak station is in Deland, about 40 minutes away.

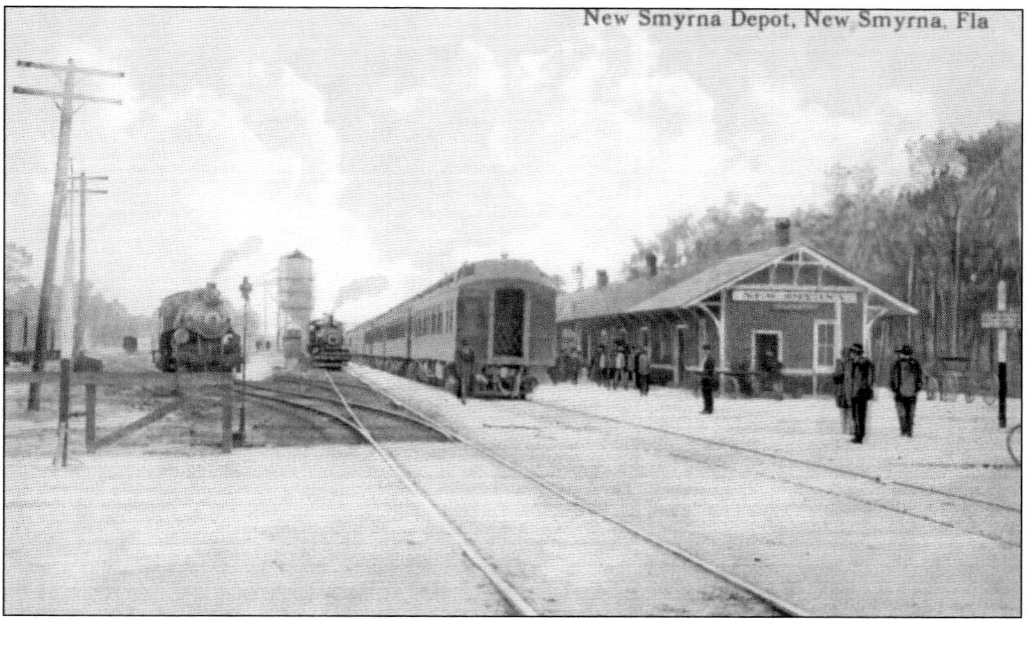

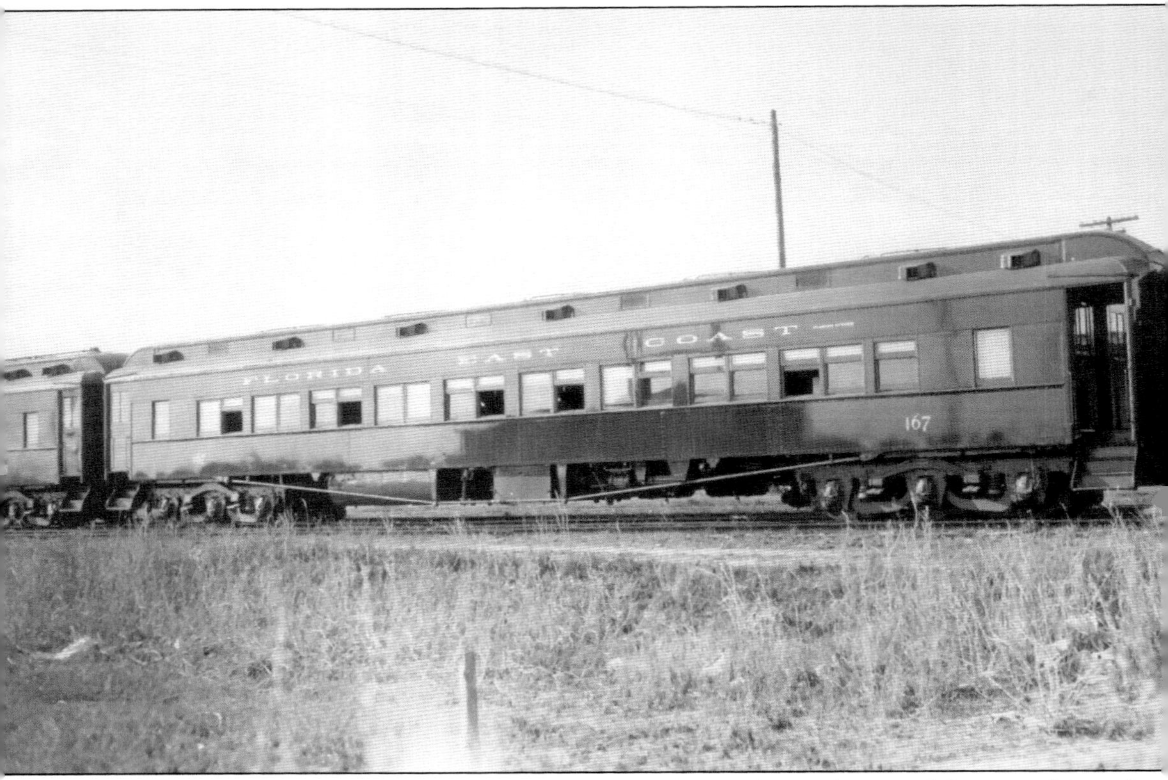

FLORIDA EAST COAST COACH CAR. In the era before widespread automobile ownership and the advent of the interstate system, rail travel was one of the most common choices for Northern visitors who would spend the cold winter months in the balmy weather of New Smyrna. Many of the exceedingly wealthy would have their own railcar in which to travel. Hotels such as the Alba Court or the New Smyrna Hotel would have a car waiting at the station to shuttle their guests quickly and safely to their winter residence.

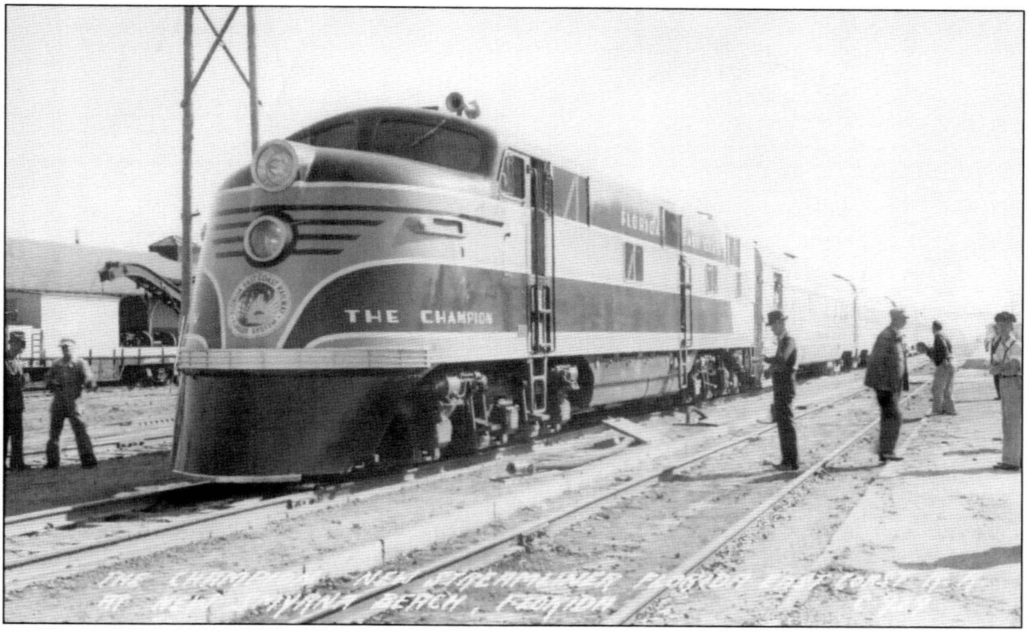

TRAIN LOCOMOTIVES. The Champion engine shown above is unusual in that it does not have an identifying number. Directly above the word "Champion" is where the number would be found. It is safe to assume this engine was painted in the red-orange and mustard-yellow color scheme often associated with the line. Below is Engine 673, which also exhibits the traditional coloring. No. 673 was one of a group of 10 Electro-Motive diesel-electric locomotives that was built in 1957. This image is from 1962, shortly before the rail strike disrupted service.

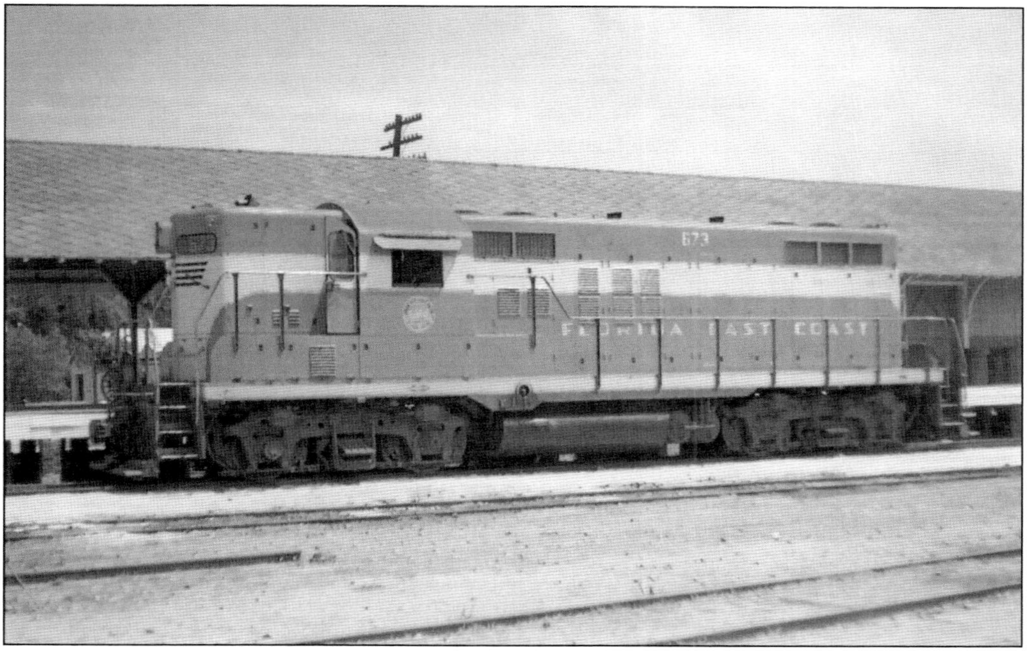

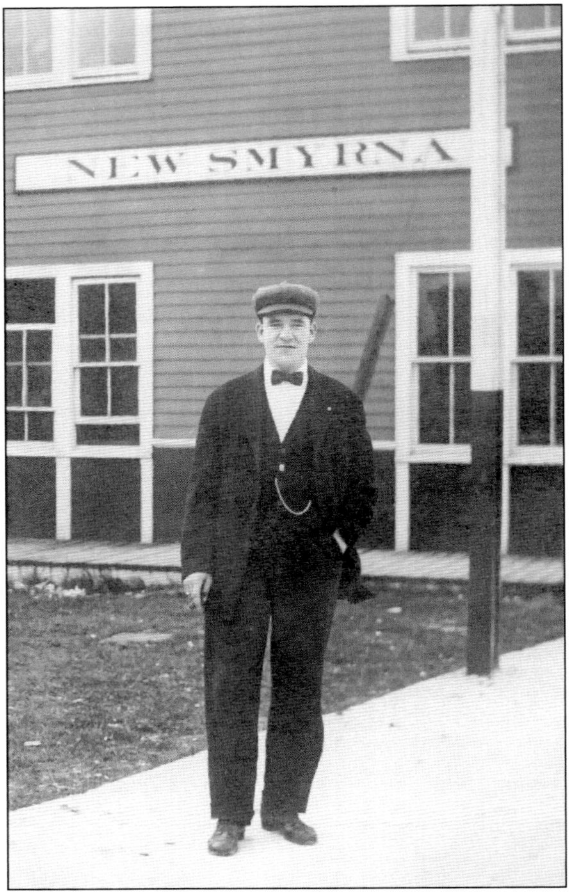

RAILROAD EMPLOYEE. The dapper-looking young man in this real-photo postcard appears to be an employee of the railway. He is standing outside the New Smyrna railroad depot that was located near the intersection of Canal Street and what is now US 1. It is easy to note where this young man was standing when looking at the card below, which shows the same windows and multicolor post. If this young man were single, he most likely would have lived in one of the boardinghouses off Canal Street in the downtown area.

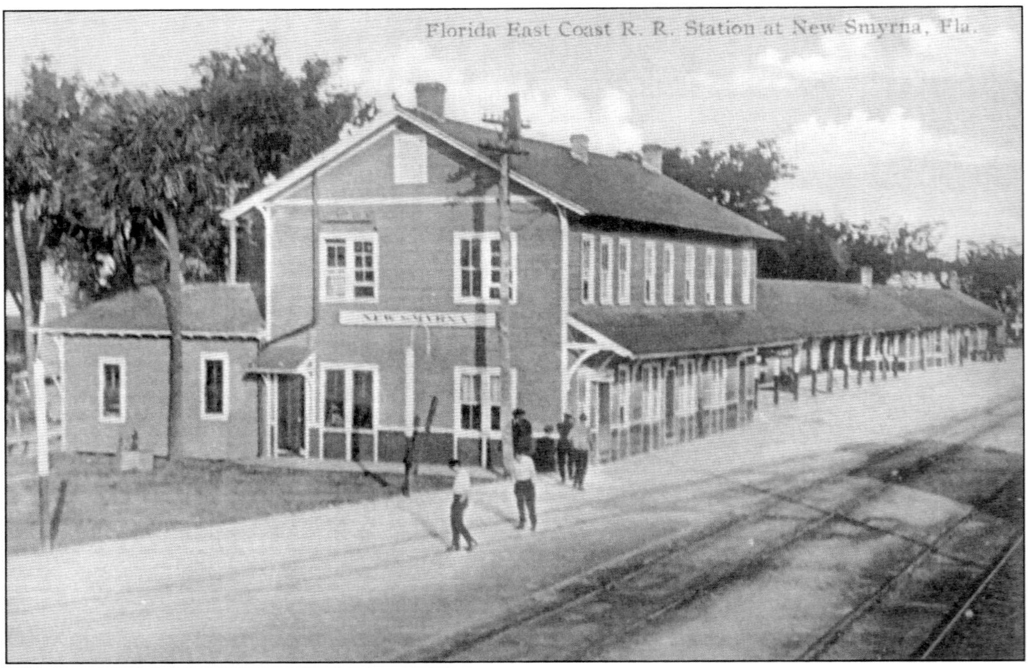

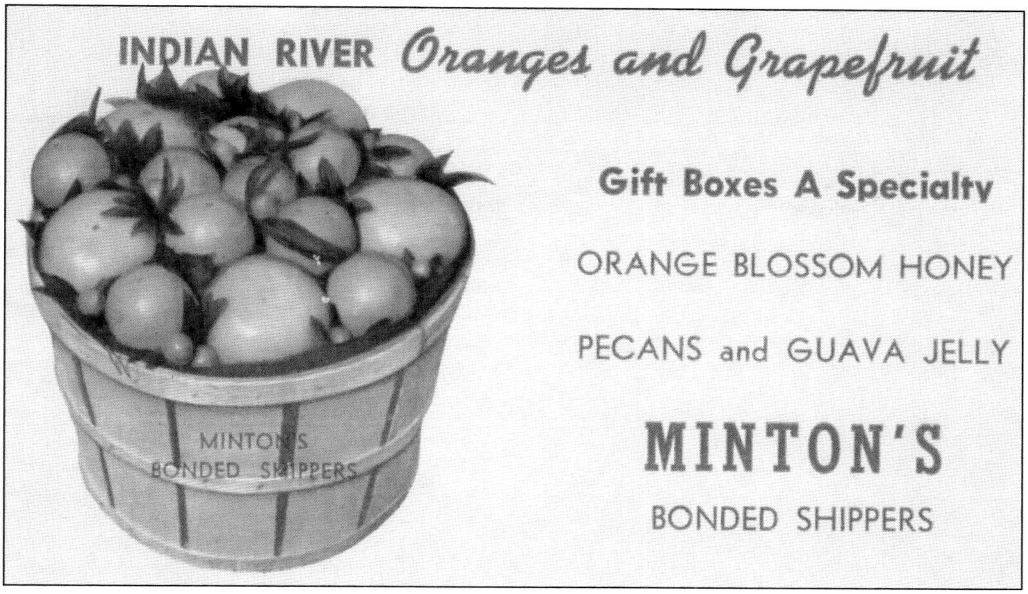

MINTON'S BONDED SHIPPERS. Businesses like Minton's can still be found up and down the roads of Florida. Located at 640 North Federal Highway, Minton's offered Indian River oranges and grapefruit, guava jelly, orange blossom honey, and pecans. One bushel of fruit cost only $6. The business was owned by Walter Ivan Minton, who is buried in the Edgewater–New Smyrna Cemetery. His headstone includes a Masonic symbol. (Courtesy Norm Shepard.)

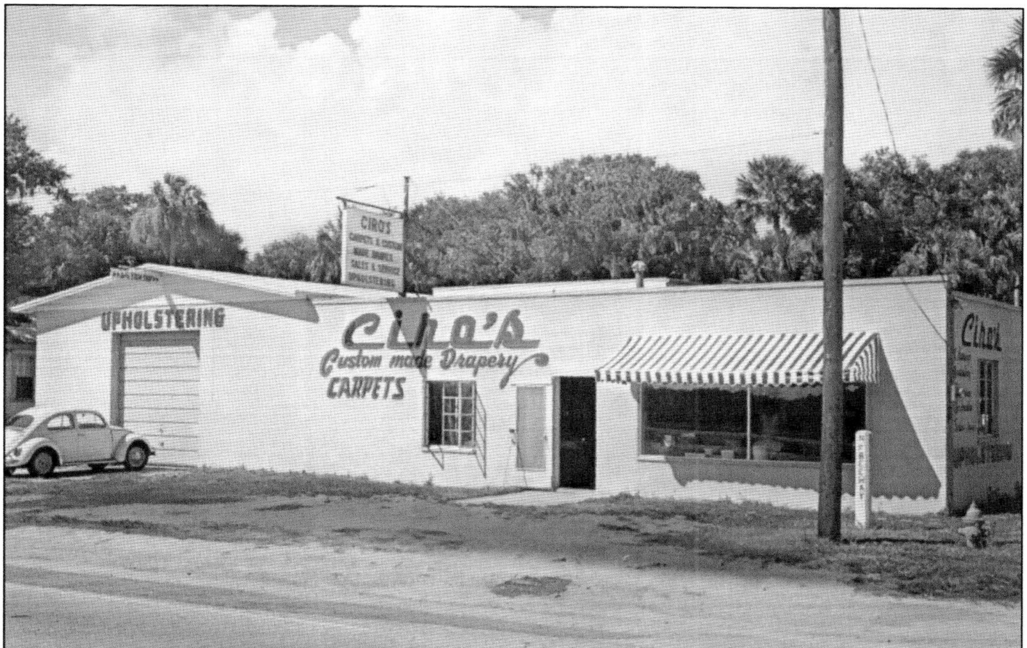

CIRO'S CARPET AND DRAPES. With the slogan "We're here to help you with all interior decorating," Ciro's specialized in carpet, custom drapes, upholstering, and wood finishing. Its former location at 2650 North Dixie Freeway is now the site of an office building that houses tenants Car People Marketing and the Council on Aging. (Courtesy Norm Shepard.)

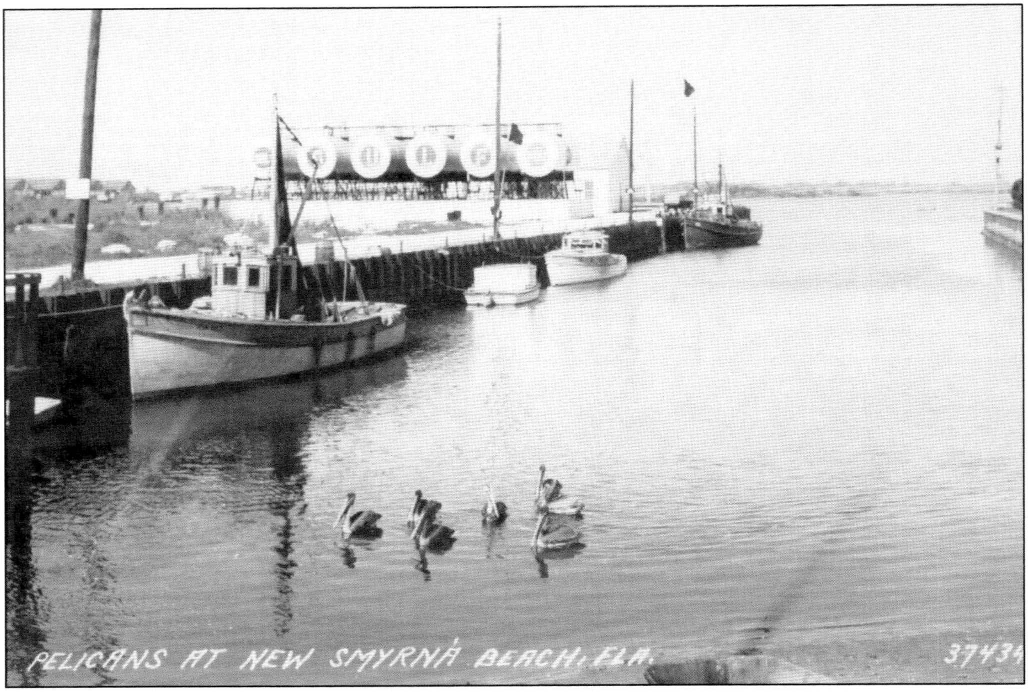

PELICANS AT NEW SMYRNA BEACH. This image is significant in two ways: first are the fishing/shrimping boats moored to the dock; second are the Gulf Oil storage tanks. The Gulf Oil plant was located at the eastern end of Canal Street and was managed by Charles H. Sams for many years. The property is now home to Captains Quarters condominiums. (Courtesy Norm Shepard.)

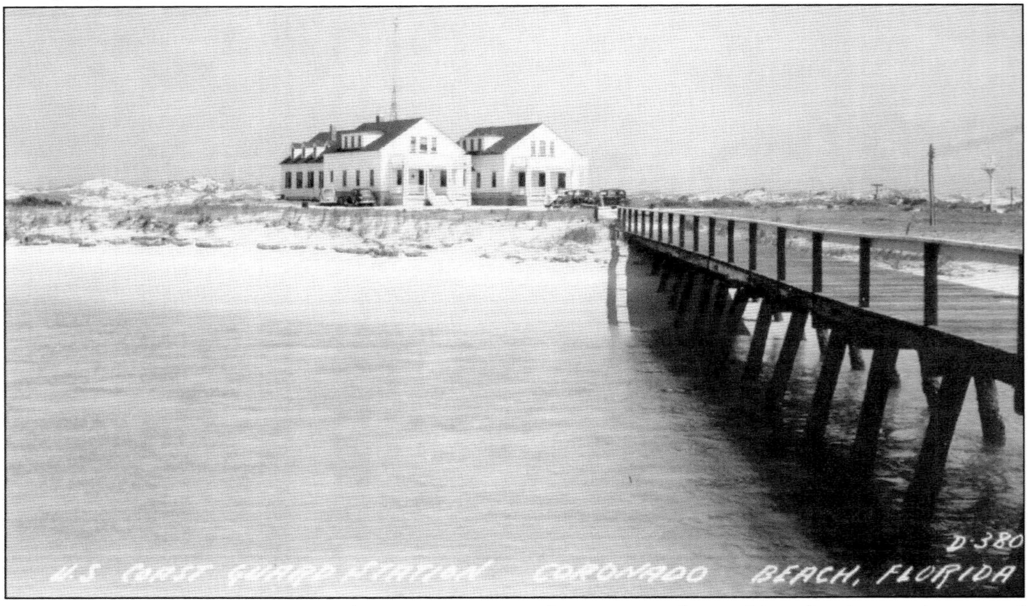

US COAST GUARD STATION. The US Coast Guard station was located in what is now Canaveral National Seashore, in a building that formerly housed the Mosquito Lagoon House of Refuge, which is no longer standing. The USCG station is now situated much closer to the inlet. The primary role of the USCG station at Ponce de Leon is to carry out search-and-rescue missions and law enforcement. This station serves under the Jacksonville sector. (Courtesy Norm Shepard.)

Six

Local Landmarks

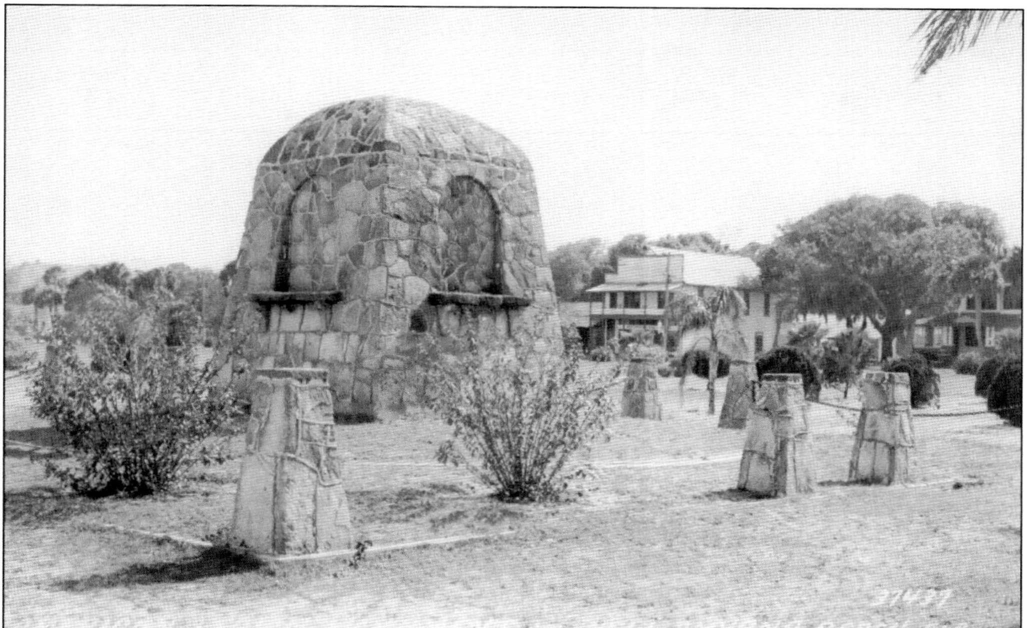

War Memorial. Located in Riverside Park, this coquina monument was originally built as a memorial to soldiers who fought in World War I. November 11, or Armistice Day, as it was called then, was a busy one with a parade, speeches, sporting events, and more taking place on the day the monument was dedicated in 1927. This image was taken prior to 1959. In that year, a six-foot-tall bronze eagle, a cross, and a helmet were added to the monument. In addition to World War I, the monument now makes mention of World War II and Korea. Off to the side is a separate monument for locals who were killed in action during the Vietnam War.

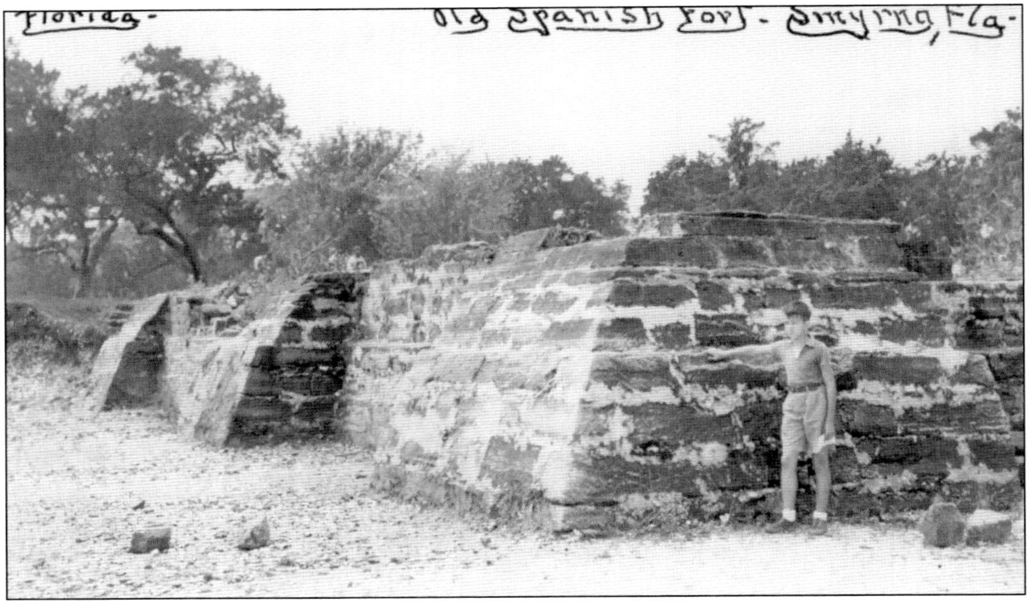

OLD SPANISH FORT. While historians and archaeologists have yet to completely solve the riddle of the coquina ruins located just off Riverside Drive, there are two facts that have been agreed upon: first, these are not Spanish ruins; second, these are not the ruins of an old fort, as notated above. The ruins are most likely the foundation of a home that Andrew Turnbull was building for his partner, Sir William Duncan. The image above appears to have been taken from the northeast corner. In addition to the boy in the foreground, notice the man in overalls and a white shirt looking down toward the camera from just above the upper level of the ruins to the left of center. The card below was postmarked in 1925, well before an uninformed Works Progress Administration (WPA) did work on the ruins to make them appear more fort-like. (Both, courtesy Dorothy Moore.)

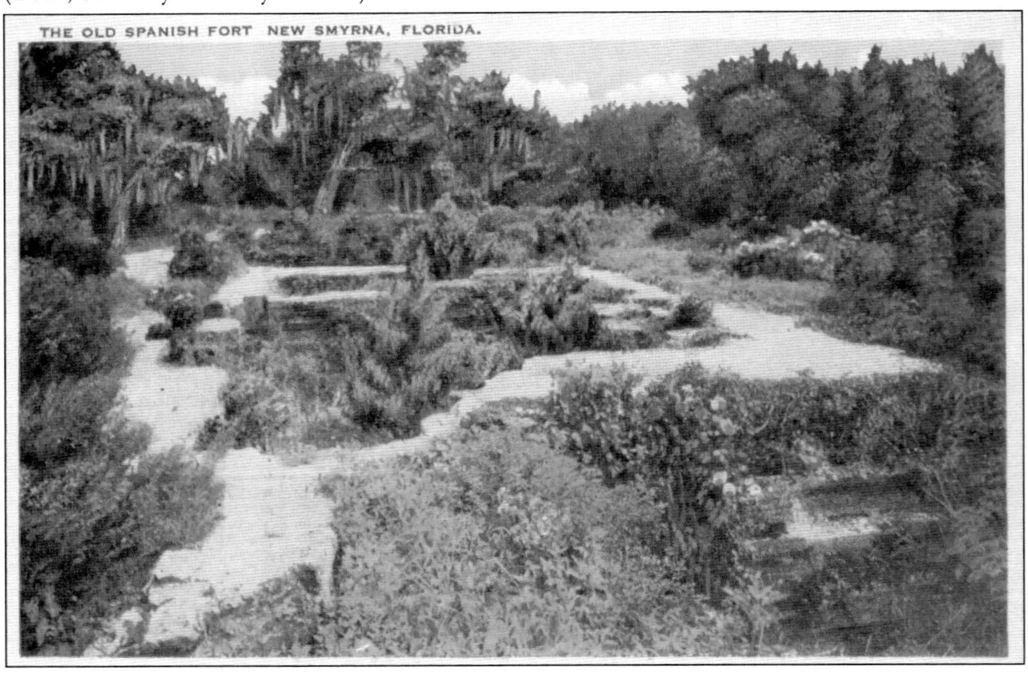

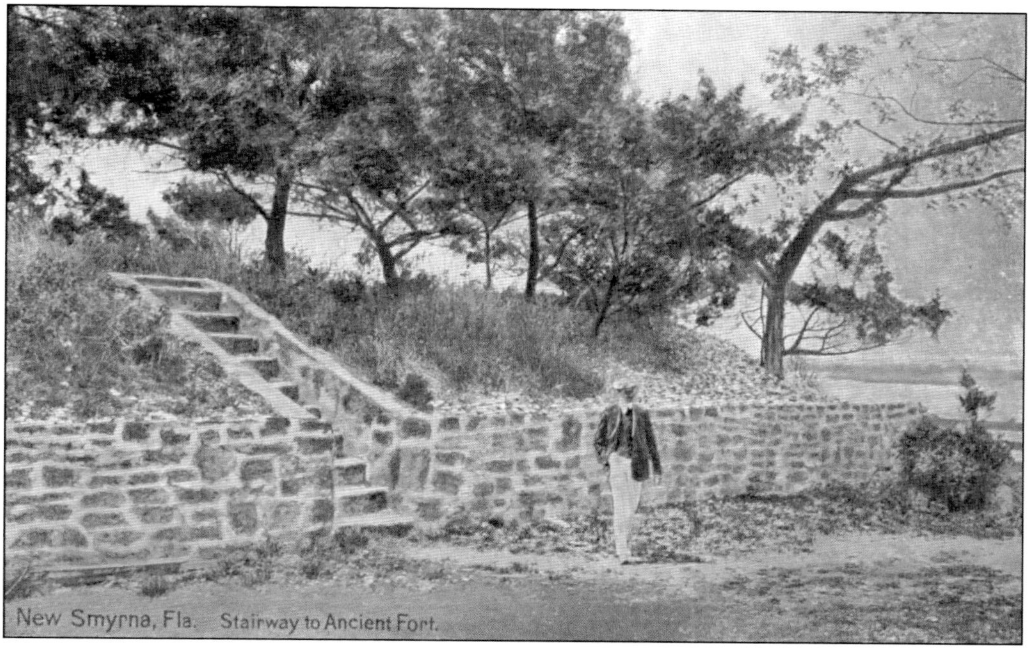

ANCIENT FORT. Taking a look at the overgrown state of Old Fort Park in these images, it is hard to imagine the pristine state in which the city keeps the park today. The statement on the card above shows just how far flung local history can become and how stories take root. According to the caption, many of the ruins were attributed to Turnbull and his colony, but growing opinion suggested that the remains were those of a fort and chapel built by Christopher Columbus on his second voyage to America.

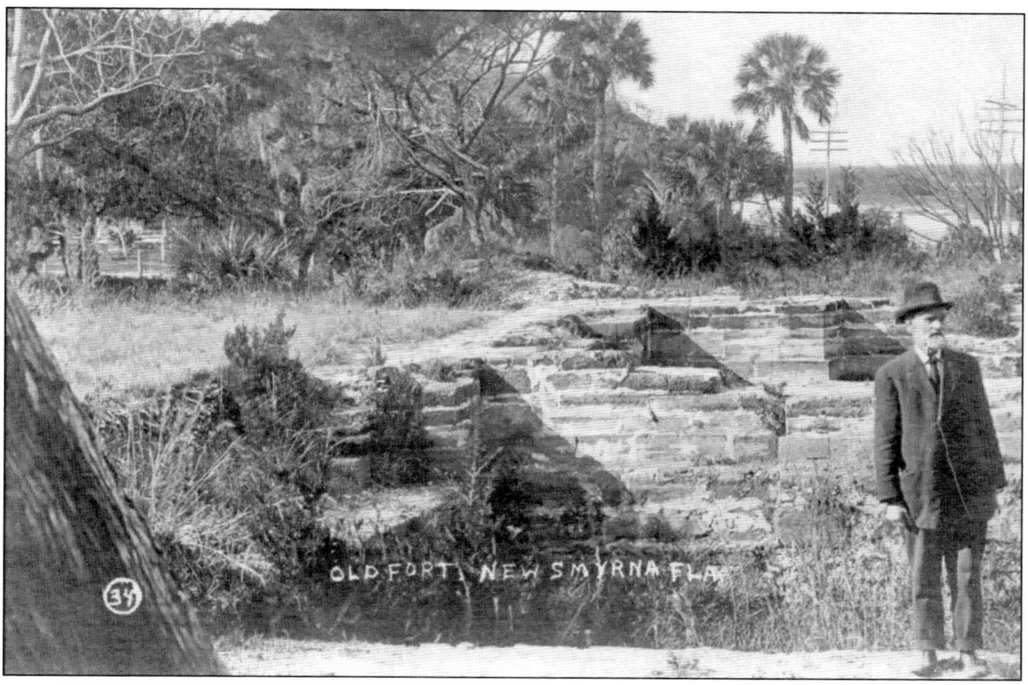

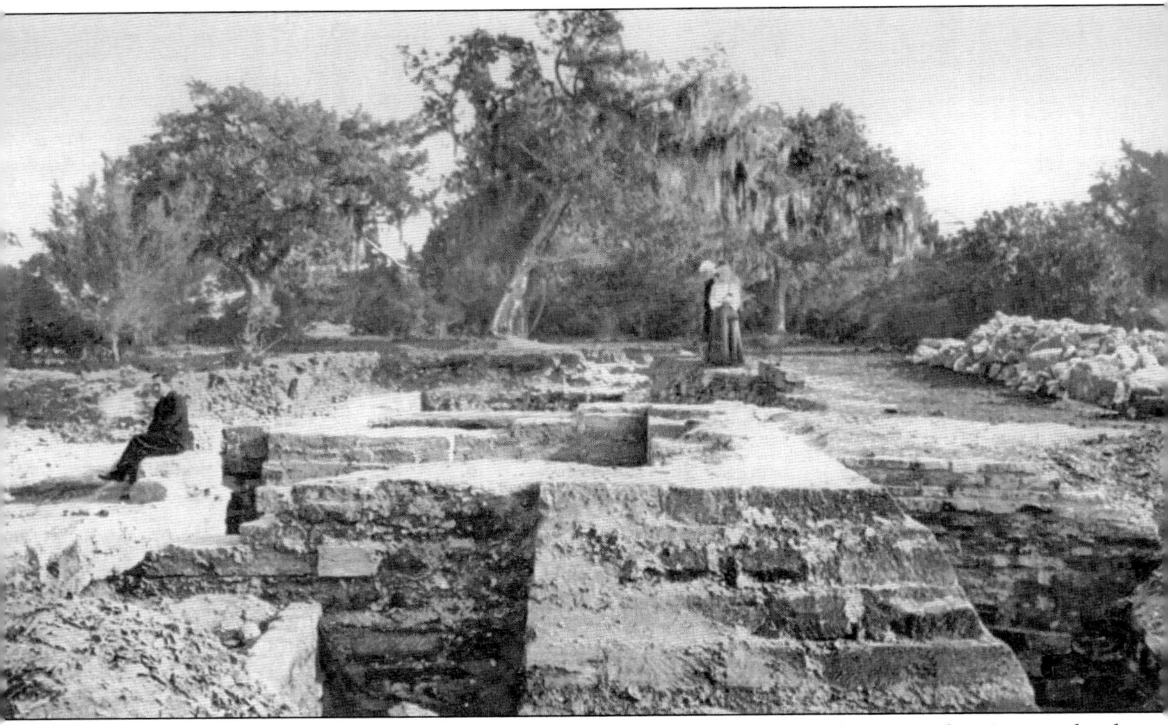

Ruins in Old Fort Park. This image can be dated to the early 1900s, but it was clearly taken after the 1903 demolition of the second Sheldon family hotel at this site. The first hotel was shelled by the Union navy during the Civil War. After the war, the family rebuilt, on a smaller scale, using whatever materials could be found. The property has changed hands several times, and it is now owned by the City of New Smyrna Beach.

Turnbull-Era Canals. The city of New Smyrna Beach is dotted with the remains of Turnbull-era canals. These canals were used for irrigation and to transport ripened crops to the wharf area for shipment. Perhaps the easiest place to locate canal remains is the city line between New Smyrna Beach and Edgewater on Riverside Drive. Another easy vantage point is on the north side of West Canal Street. This is the canal system that can be seen emptying into the river. Note the two young girls playing in the canal at right. Historian Larry Sweett has stated that these girls are Julia Dilzer and Margaret Knapp. (Both, courtesy Dorothy Moore.)

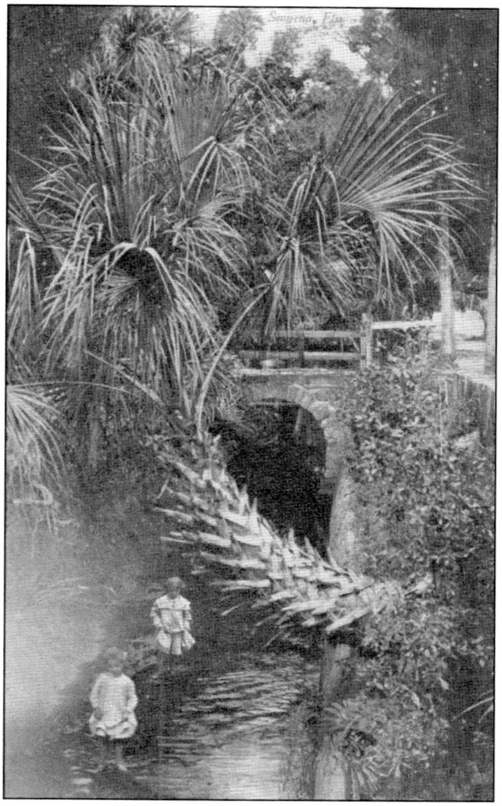

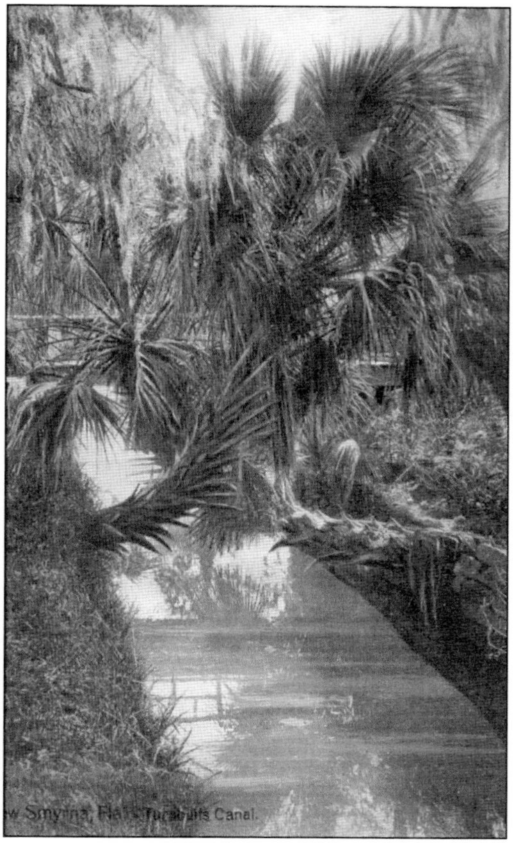

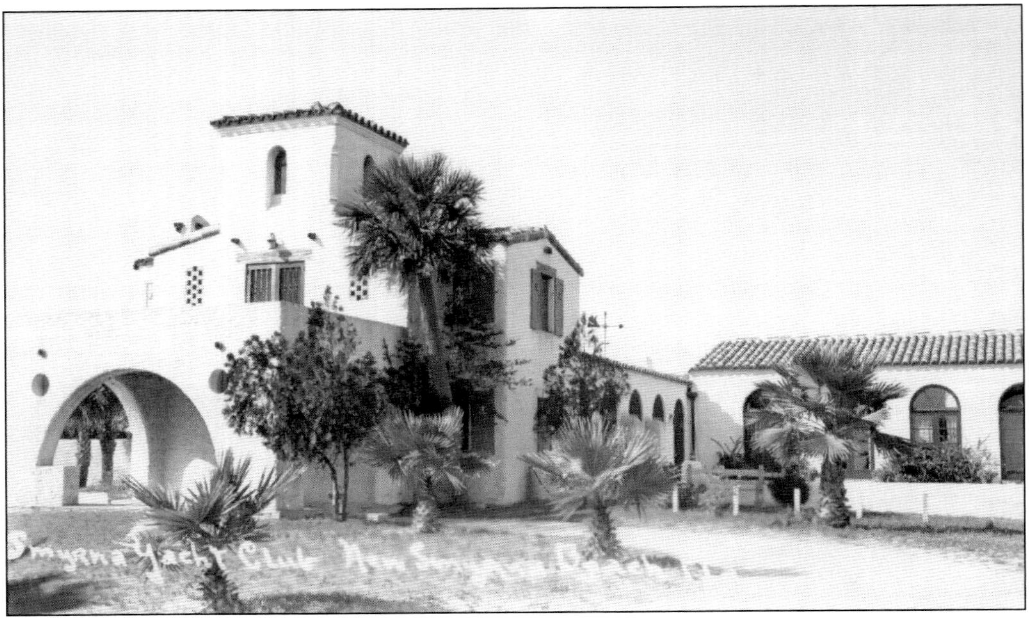

SMYRNA YACHT CLUB. The Smyrna Yacht Club, which was designed by architect Harry M. Griffin, is situated just off Riverside Drive, with beautiful views of the Indian River. The club was organized in 1928 and began holding powerboat races shortly thereafter. Winners have their names added to the prestigious Gov. Dave Sholtz trophy. In addition, the club hosts the annual Lipton Cup sailing regatta. The card below provides a good view of the club's property. The small driveway bridge is still the access point to the island where the club is located. Seen in the background is the now demolished New Smyrna Hotel.

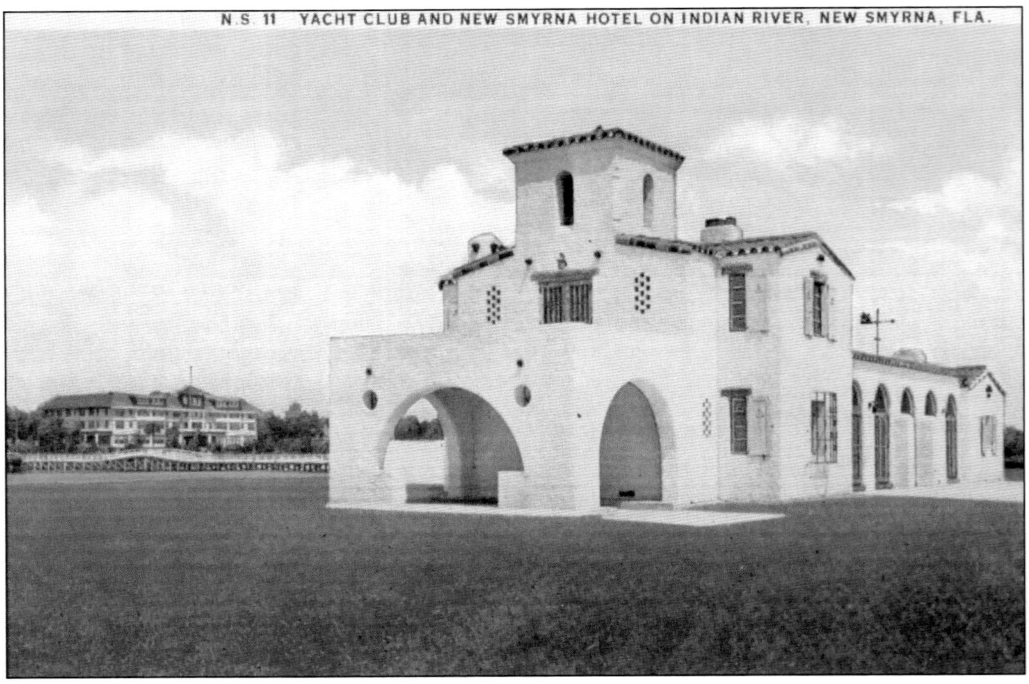

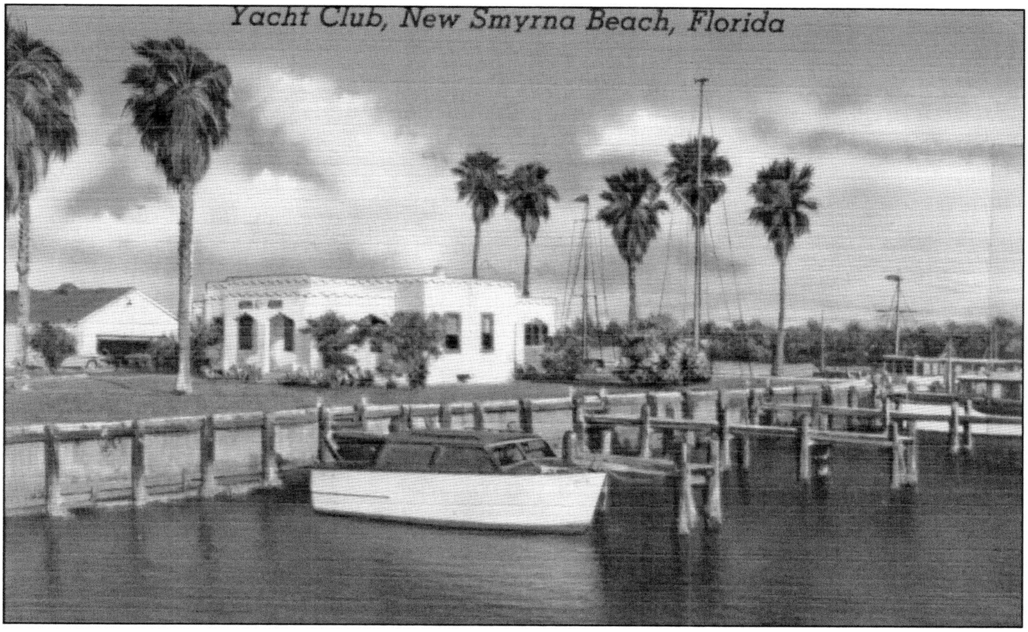

ANGLERS CLUB. This city-owned property off the ever economically expanding North Causeway has been home to the Anglers Club since signing a 99-year lease with the city in 1946. Adjacent to the city marina, the club offers beautiful views of the Indian River. Note the card above misidentifies the building as the Yacht Club, which is located off Riverside Drive, south of the Anglers Club.

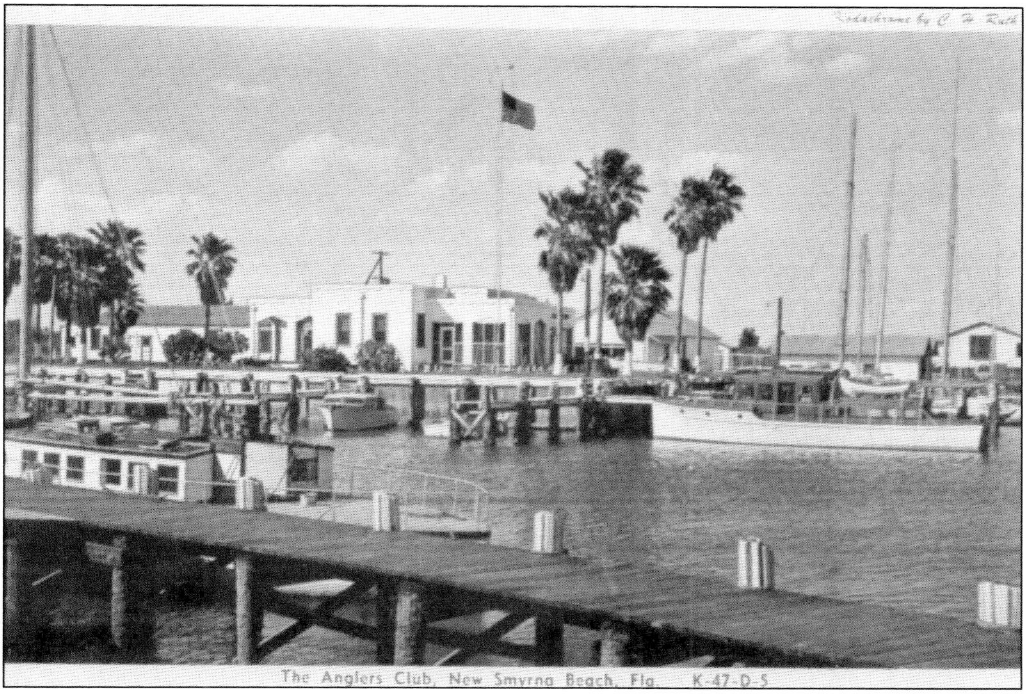

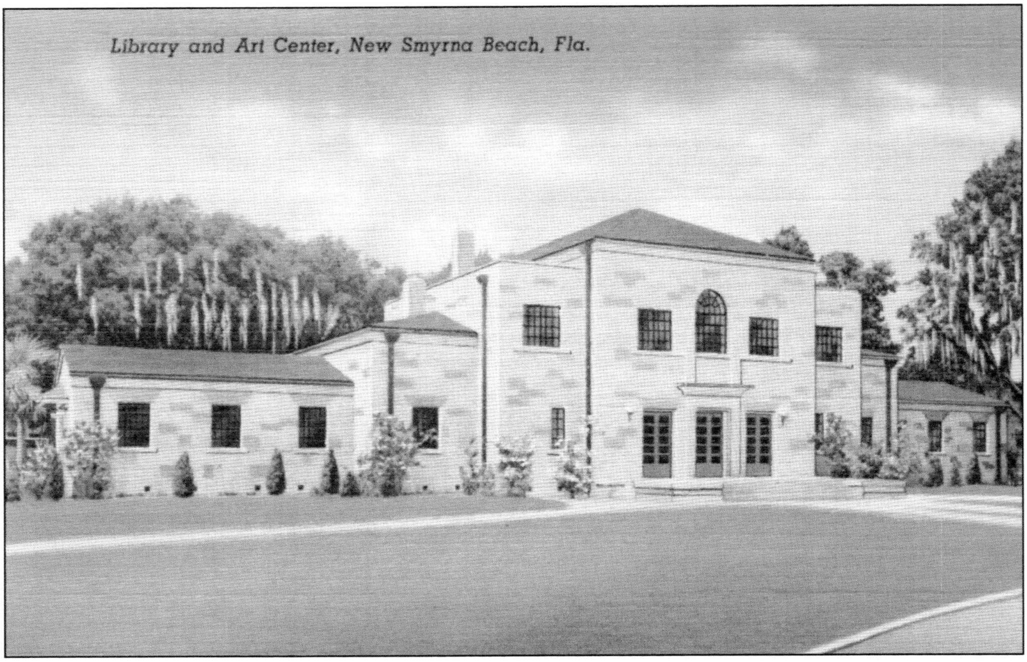

CITY HALL. The building that now houses city hall was constructed during the Great Depression using WPA funding at a cost of approximately $125,000. It was dedicated in March 1941 as a cultural center meant to house a library, museum, and art gallery. In November 1945, the city government voted to take over the majority of the space for city offices. In 1966, the library was moved to new headquarters in Riverside Park, and city hall took over use of the entire building. It is interesting to compare the size of the bushes in the two images. The circular drive in front of the building is a feature that still exists.

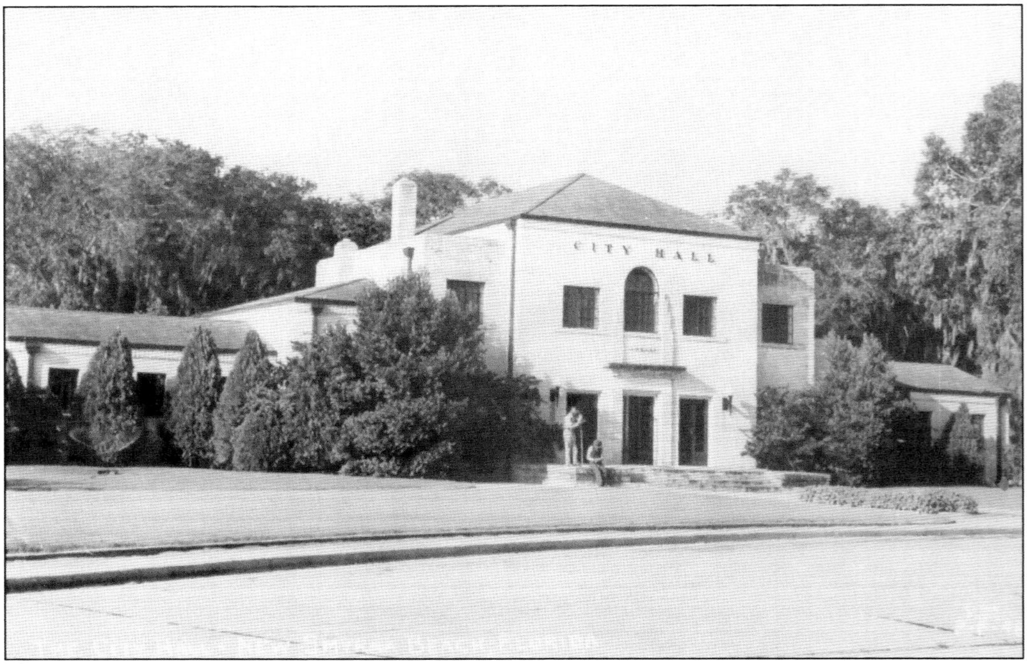

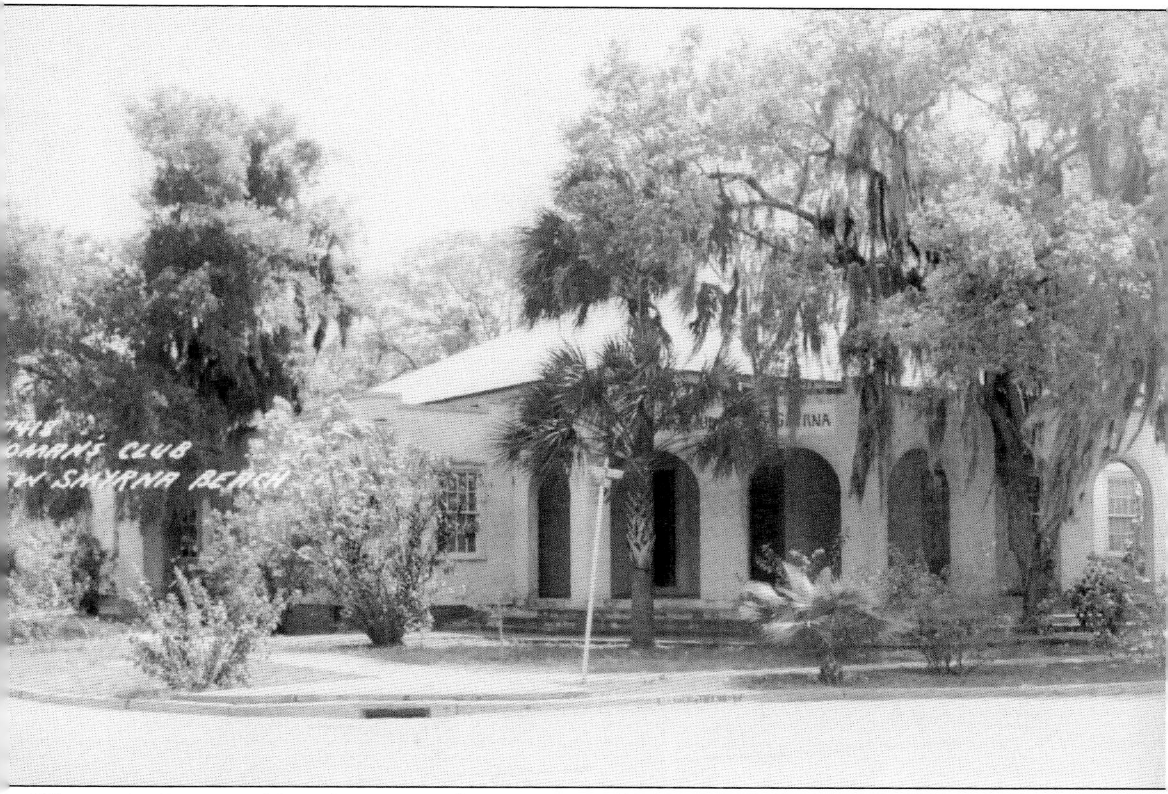

Woman's Club of New Smyrna. This property, which is listed in the National Register of Historic Places, is owned by the City of New Smyrna Beach. Classified in the Mediterranean Revival style, the building was constructed in 1924, with the interior being completed in 1934 after a fire gutted what was already there. It is also recognized due to the contributions of Harry M. Griffin, a noted Florida architect who designed the interior of the building. The Woman's Club of New Smyrna was organized in 1911 and originally met in the homes of members.

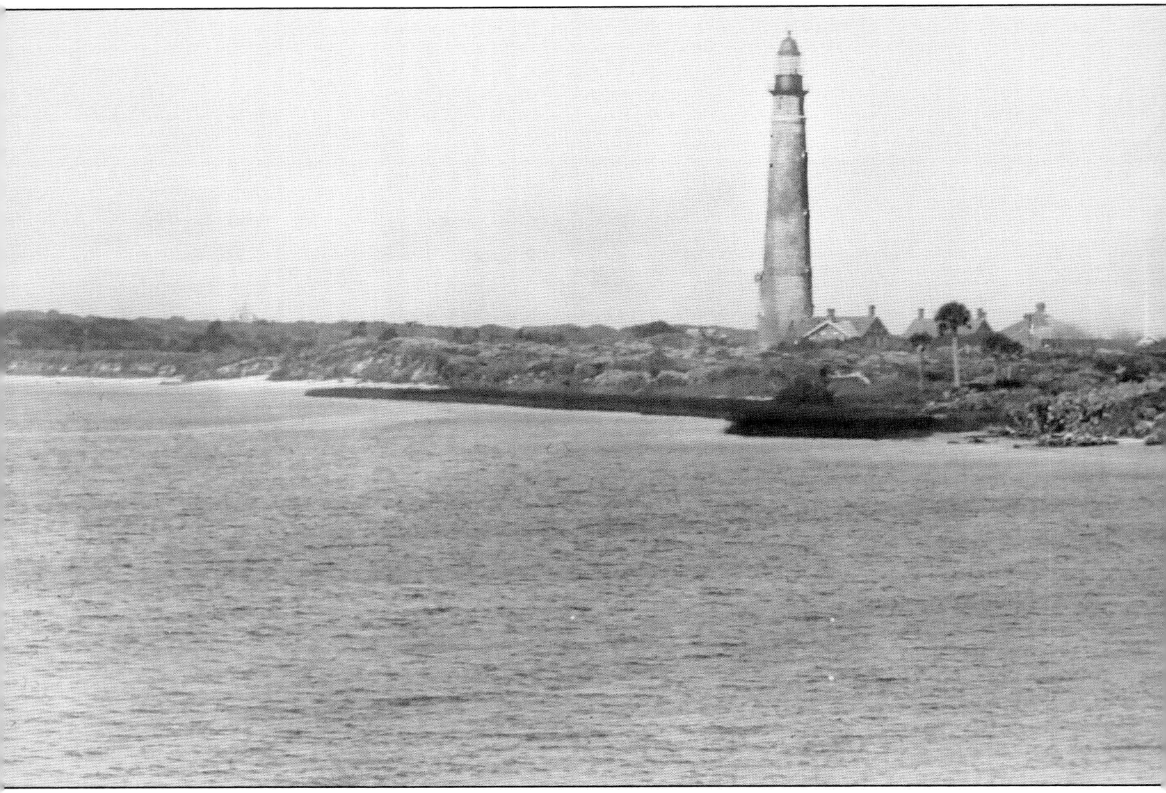

PONCE INLET LIGHTHOUSE. This real-photo postcard shows the isolation that must have been felt by lighthouse keepers in Ponce Inlet. The various buildings that can be seen around the base of the tower were all associated with the lighthouse, including homes for the keepers and storage for supplies. Further proving the need for a light at the dangerous inlet was the death of

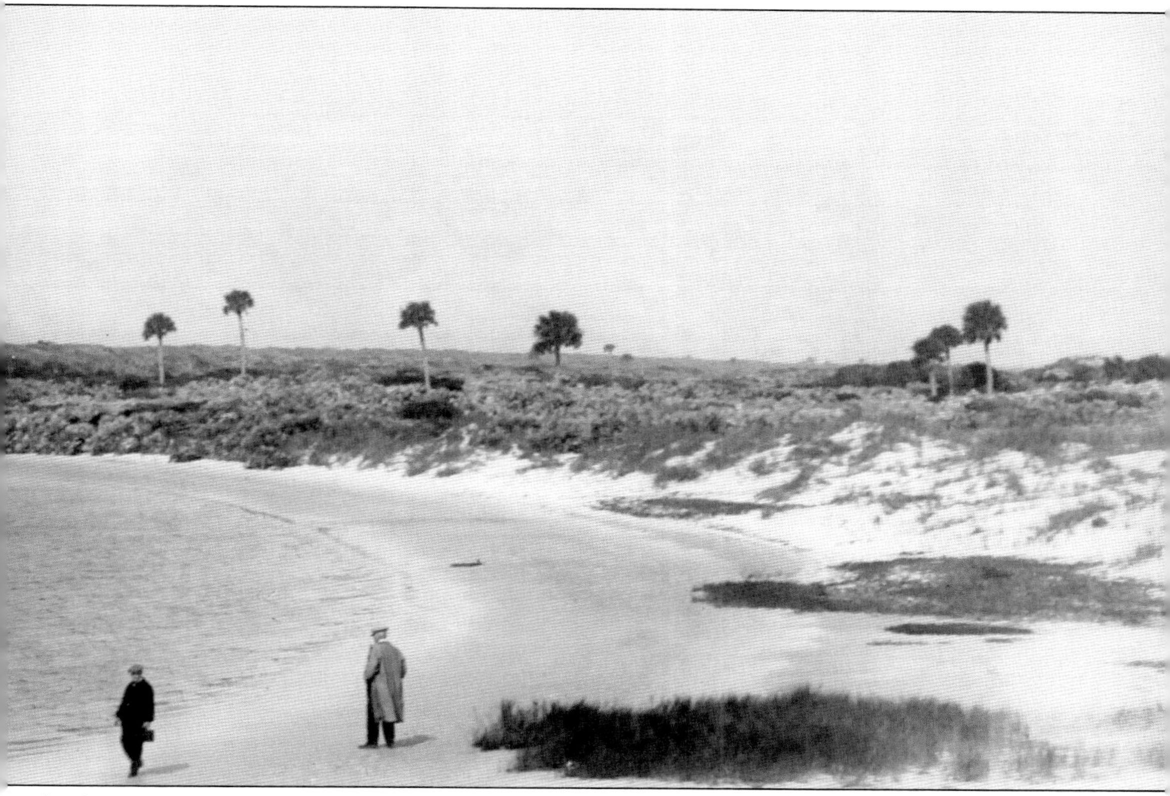

chief engineer Orville Babcock in the rough waters near where the tower was being constructed. Babcock was a close confidant of general, and later president, Ulysses S. Grant. Babcock is buried in Arlington National Cemetery. (Courtesy Norm Shepard.)

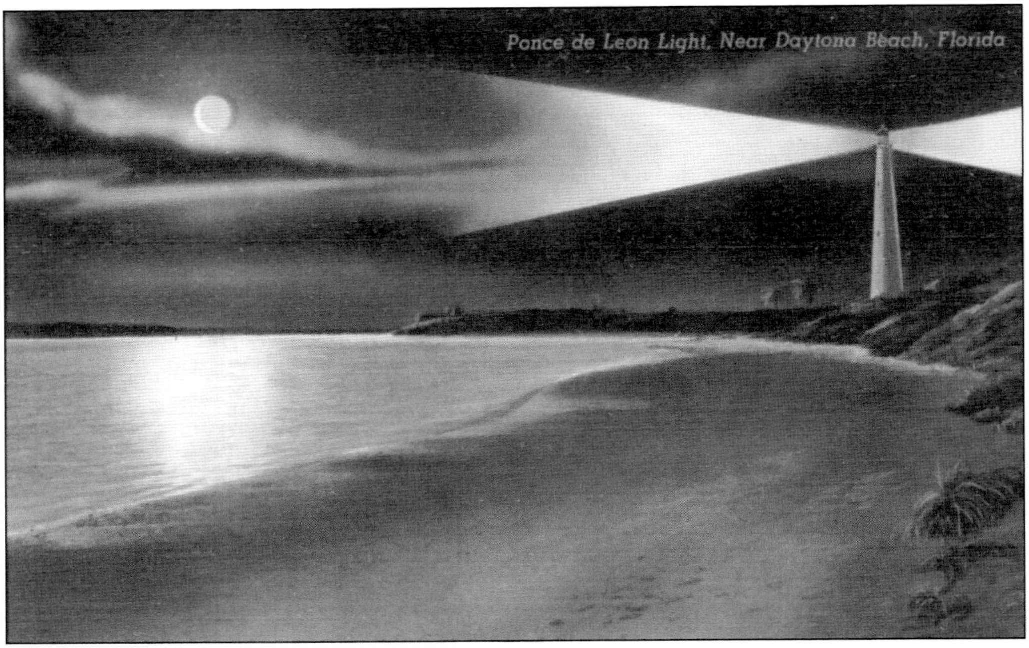

SECOND PONCE INLET LIGHTHOUSE. The Ponce Inlet Lighthouse on the north side of the inlet is actually the second to stand in the area. The first lighthouse was constructed between 1834 and 1835 but was never lit. During a Christmas 1835 raid by Seminole Indians, the house was ransacked, and in 1836, what was left toppled into the inlet. The current lighthouse was first lit by principal keeper William Rowlinski and his assistant on November 1, 1887. The tower was decommissioned in 1970 and is now owned by the City of Ponce Inlet. Visitors can climb the 203 steps to the top, as shown in the dizzying photograph below.

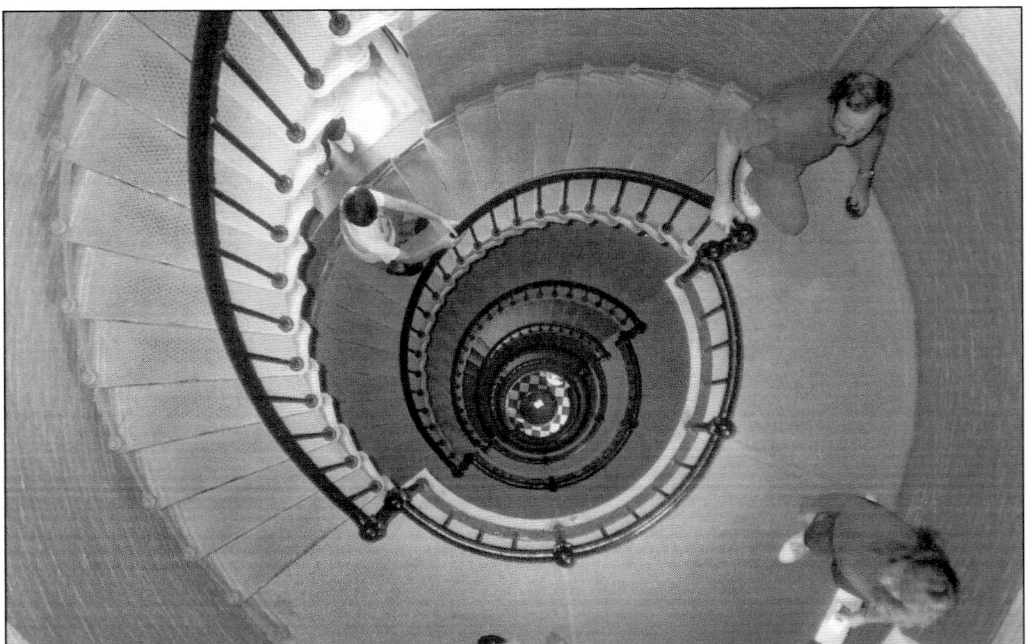

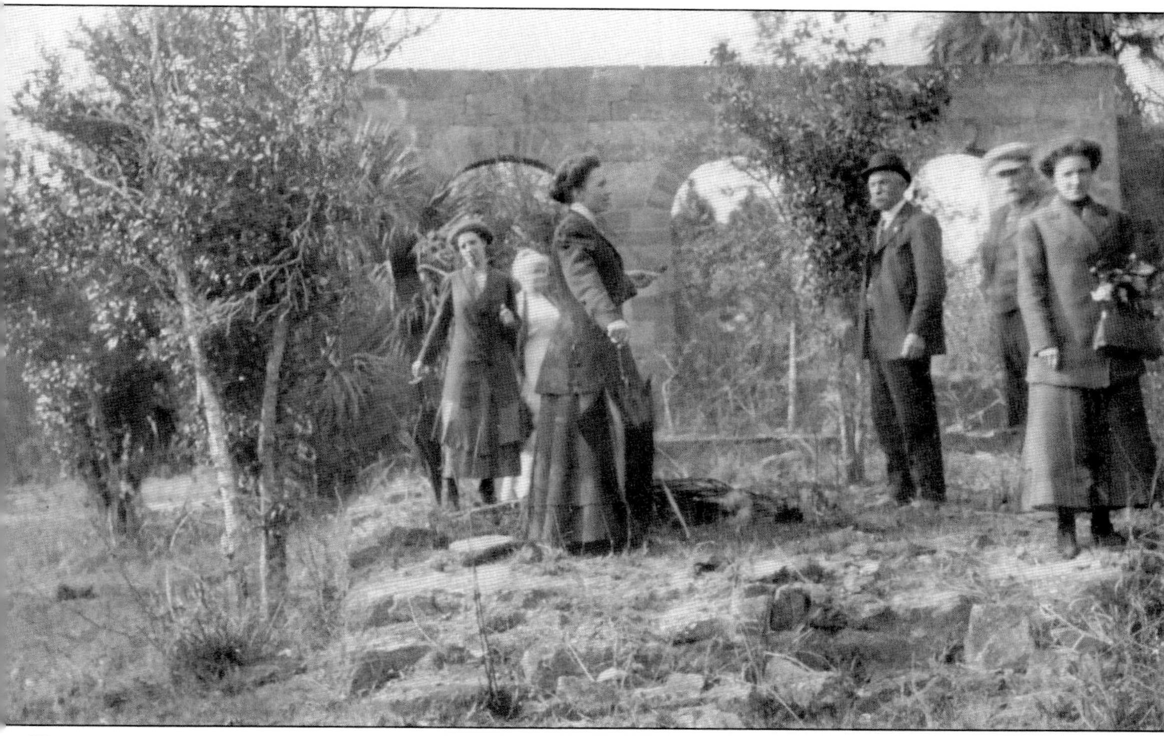

VISITORS TO THE SUGAR MILL. This real-photo postcard was sent in March 1911, showing that these ruins have always fascinated visitors. The card was addressed to family in Michigan. Demonstrating just how easy it is to spread a fanciful story, the sender notes, "This is supposed to be a mission founded by the followers of Columbus." (Courtesy Dorothy Moore.)

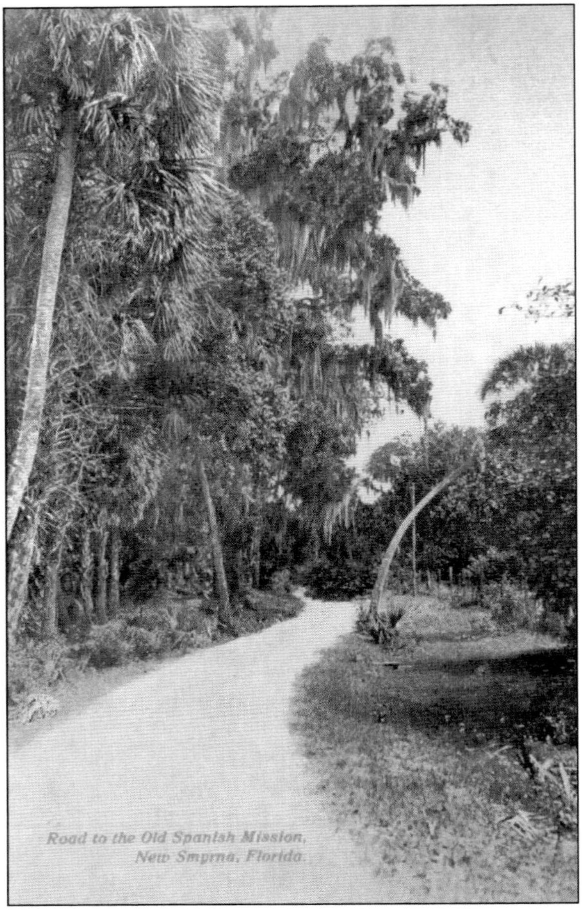

ROAD TO THE SPANISH MISSION. While history has marched on and it has become known that the sugar mill ruins were never those of a Spanish mission, some things, like the narrow dirt road leading the mill, remain the same. Old Mission Road was named for the legend that is still told by some even to this day. (Courtesy Dorothy Moore.)

SUGAR MILL. This real-photo postcard of the Sugar Mill was taken by local photographer Theo van de Sande. Here are several of the rooms used during the process of grinding sugar cane. Also note the large live oak tree that had grown among the ruins. The small white sign near the center of the image offers a $25 reward for information about something. It appears that vandalism is not just a current problem. (Courtesy Dorothy Moore.)

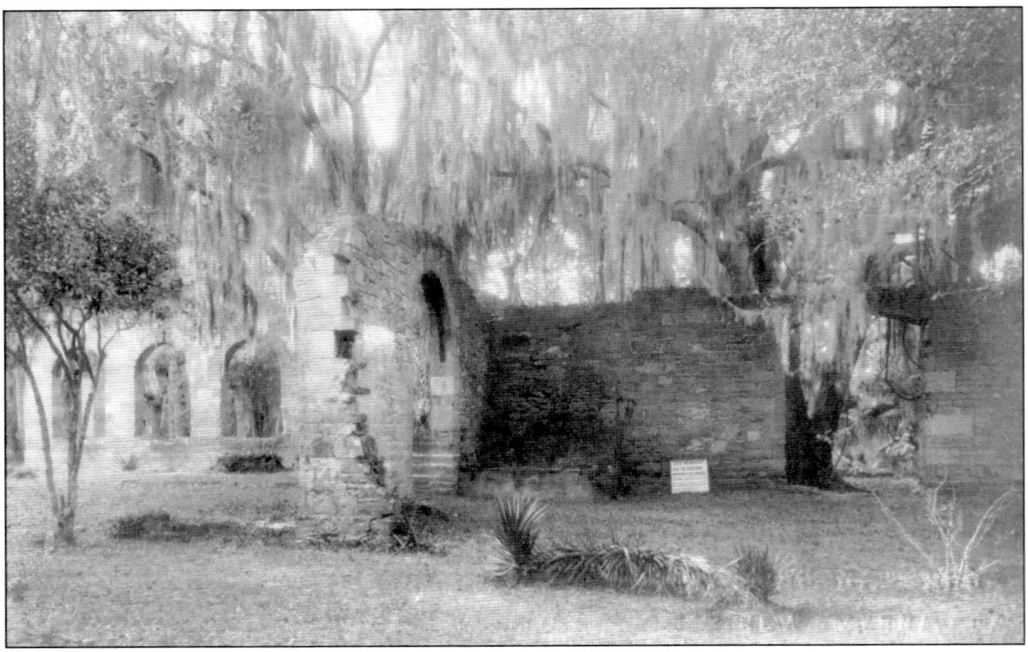

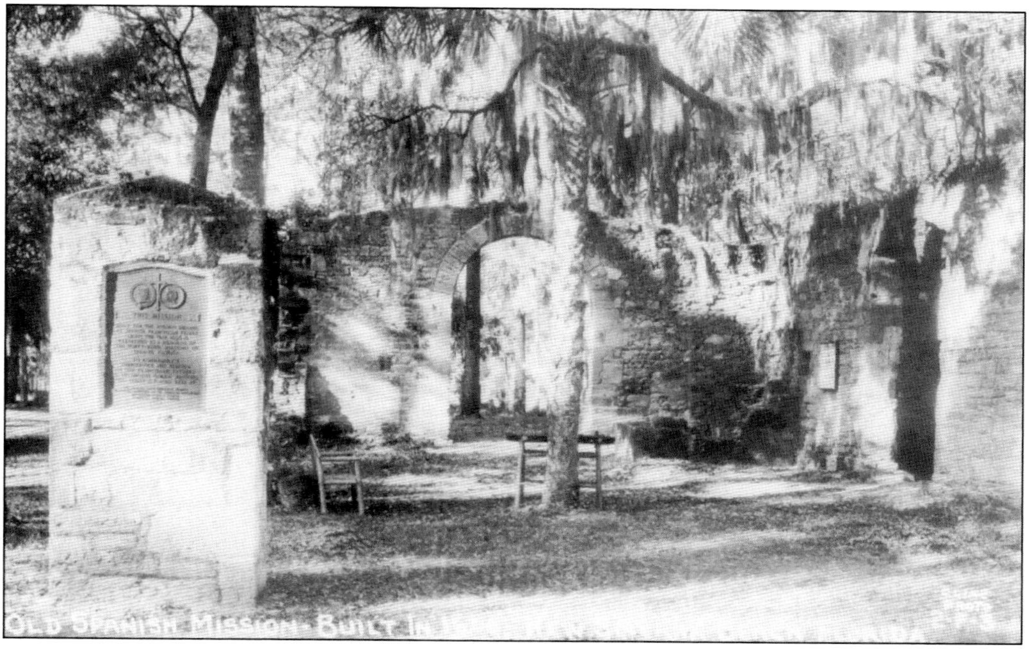

THE MISSION. Shown in these real-photo postcards is a plaque that was displayed at the ruins. This plaque outlines the theory put forth by Jeanette Thurber Connor, the second wife of the wealthy Washington E. Connor, which states that the ruins were one of 44 missions built by Franciscan friars around 1696 for the Jororo Indians. While Jeanette was known for her research in Spanish archives, she was wrong in this case. The Florida State Historical Society referenced on the plaque is not the current Florida Historical Society, but rather a defunct organization. The plaque shown in the close-up at right may now be viewed at the New Smyrna Museum of History.

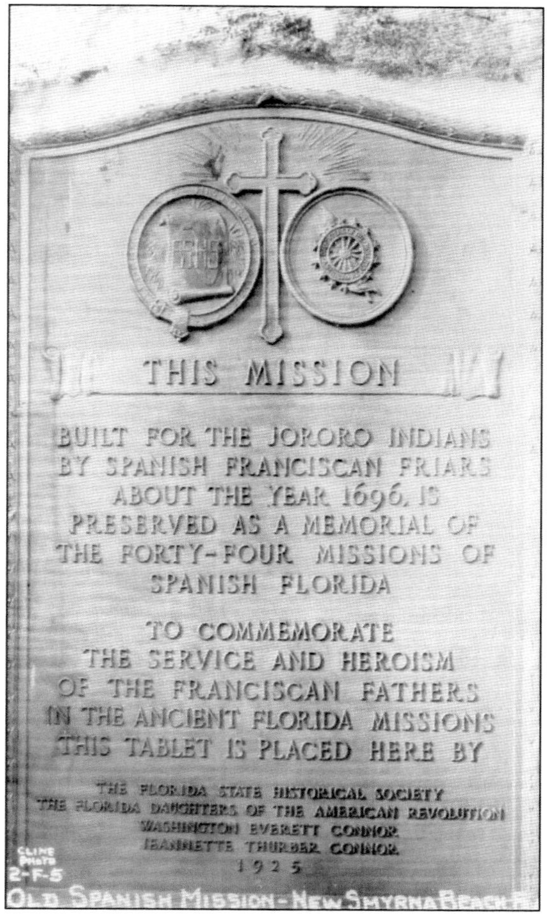

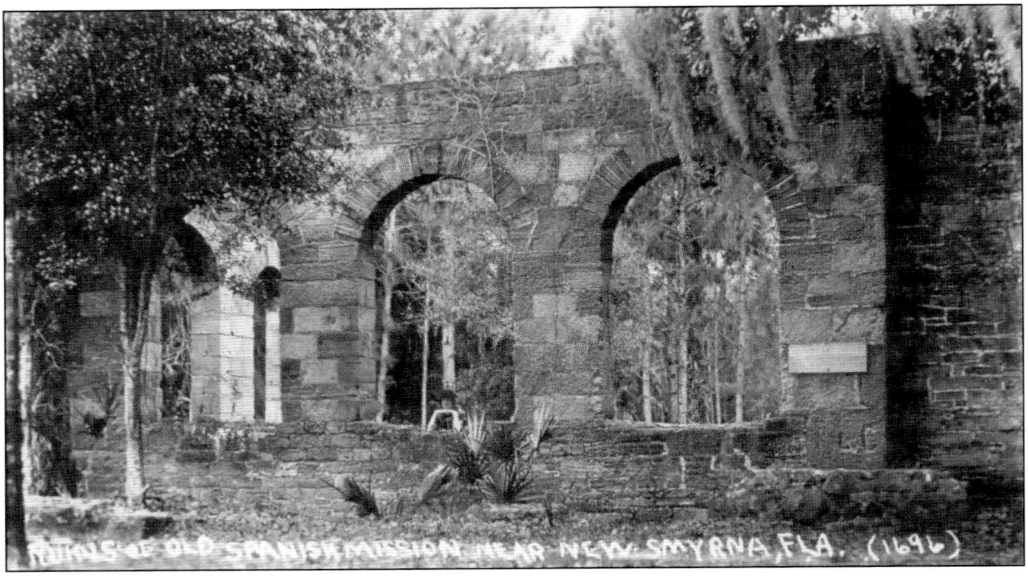

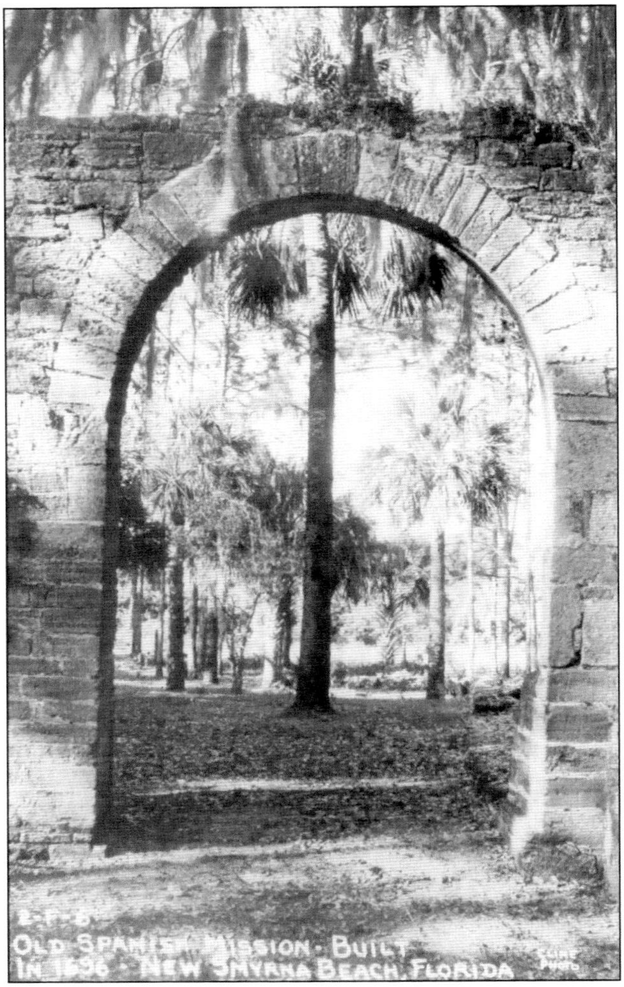

ARCHES AT THE RUINS. The architectural details of the sugar mill are quite amazing, and these images show the arch work the builder included. Above, note there is an individual, who appears to be wearing a hat, peering through the bottom of the center arch. Also notice that the caption for the images references them dating to 1696. In his 1941 booklet titled *Debunking the So-Called Spanish Mission Near New Smyrna Beach*, Charles Coe did as much as anyone to set the record straight that the ruins are those of a sugar mill and not a Spanish mission.

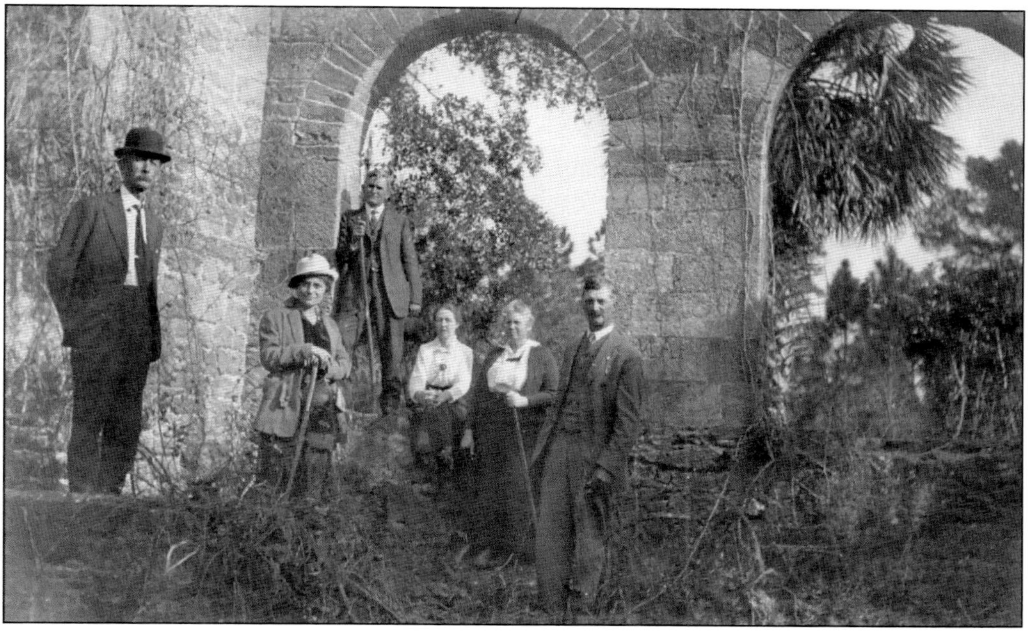

VISITORS TO THE OLD MISSION. Despite the rugged condition and overgrown landscape, those pictured in these real-photo postcards saw fit to dress up in order to visit what they no doubt considered a Spanish mission. These cards have a handwritten notation on the top indicating they are from 1916. The gentleman at left in the image above is the same individual as seen in the image below. Perhaps the heat had gotten to him and he decided to shed his sport coat. The tie remained knotted at the neck, however. (Both, courtesy Zelia V. Sweett.)

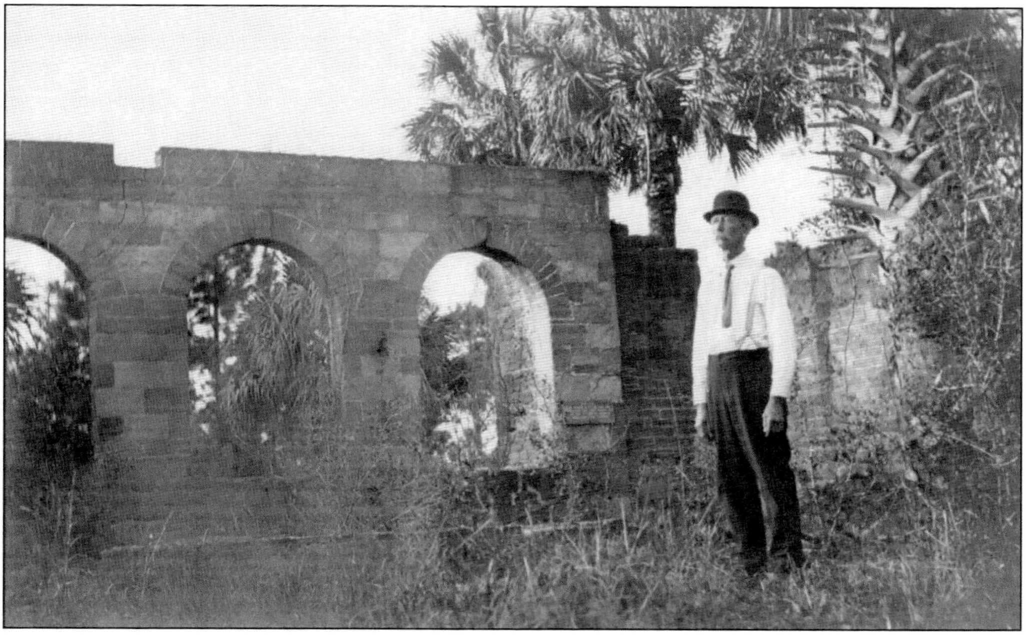

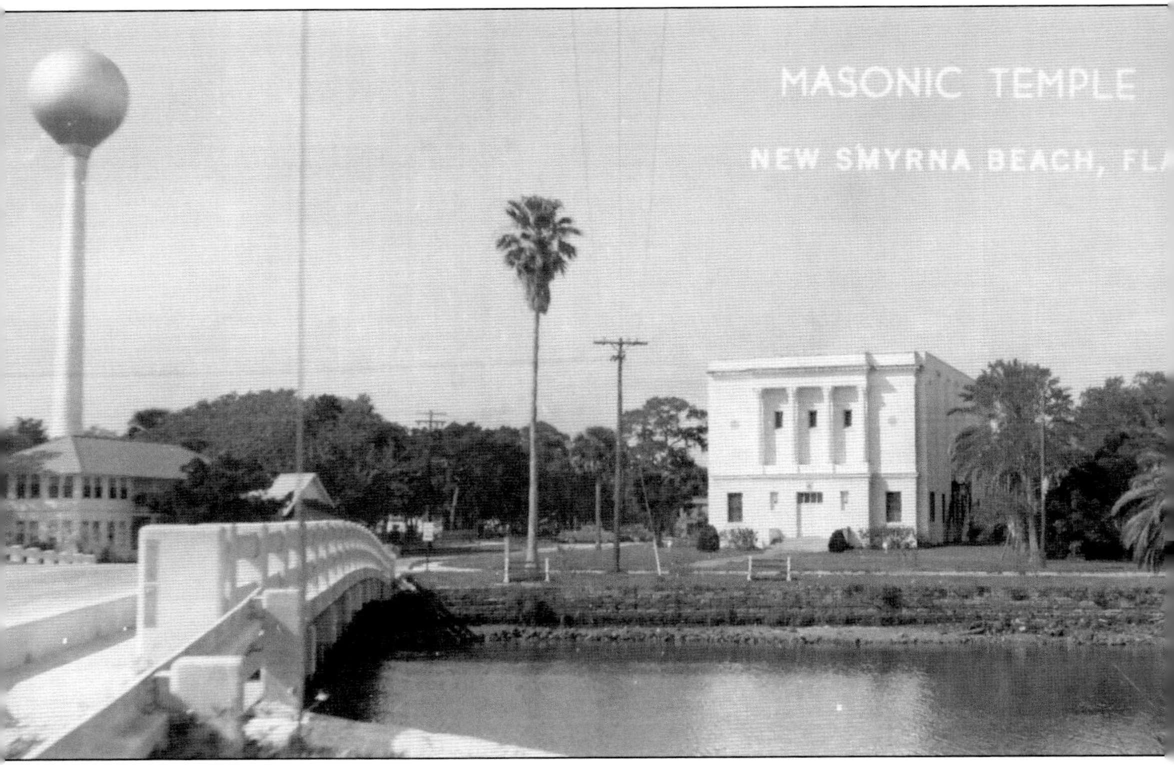

MASONIC TEMPLE. The Free and Accepted Masons Lodge 149 has been a fixture in New Smyrna Beach since receiving its charter in 1896. Situated at the western end of the North Causeway, the beautiful Masonic temple at the corner of Washington Street and Riverside Drive has been home to the Masons since December 1927. The building and water tower seen at left are no longer standing.

Seven

Friends Long Gone

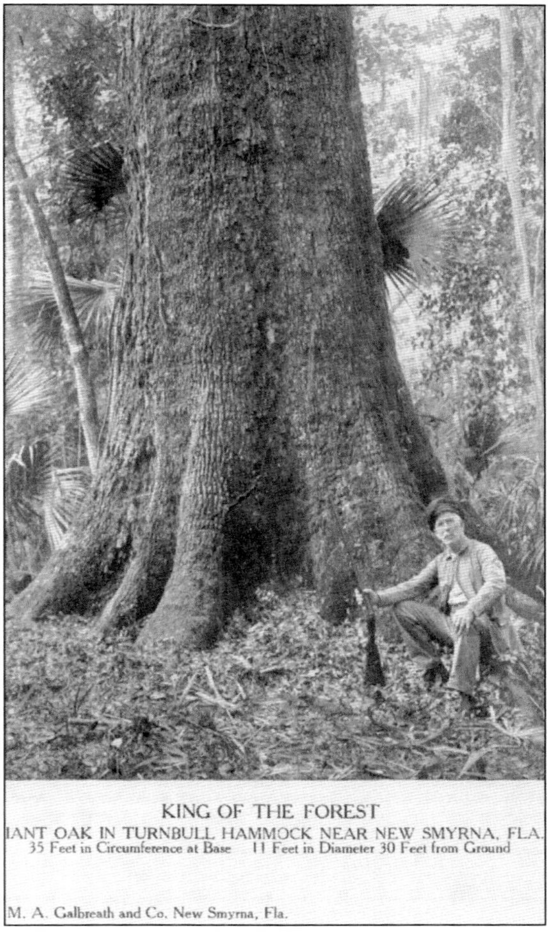

King of the Forest. This massive live oak tree once stood in the Turnbull Hammock area of New Smyrna Beach. Unfortunately, the tree was struck by lightning and later died. The gentleman pictured here is Samuel Galbreath, who appears to have been on a hunting outing. It is said the tree measured 11 feet in diameter and 35 feet in circumference. (Courtesy Susan Bergert.)

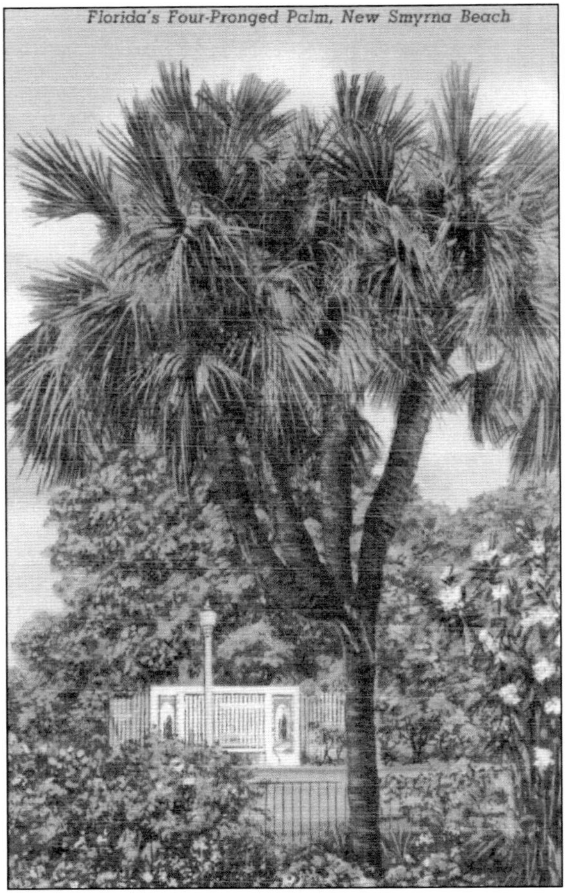

FLORIDA'S FOUR-PRONGED PALM. This unusual site was located on North Orange Street in the yard of Belle Murray. The tree was toppled during Hurricane Donna in 1960. Murray passed away in 1971 and is buried in the Edgewater–New Smyrna Cemetery.

OLD SPANISH SHELL MOUND. This card incorrectly attributes the shell mound to the Spanish, when it is in fact Native American. Shell mounds like this, or middens, as they are more properly called, dotted the coastline of Florida. Middens can provide archaeologists and historians with much information. Based on what is discovered, dietary information can be gleaned from the remains. Many middens were destroyed, and the contents were used for roadbeds or helped in laying railroad tracks. Today, Turtle Mound stands as an excellent example of a little disturbed Indian midden.

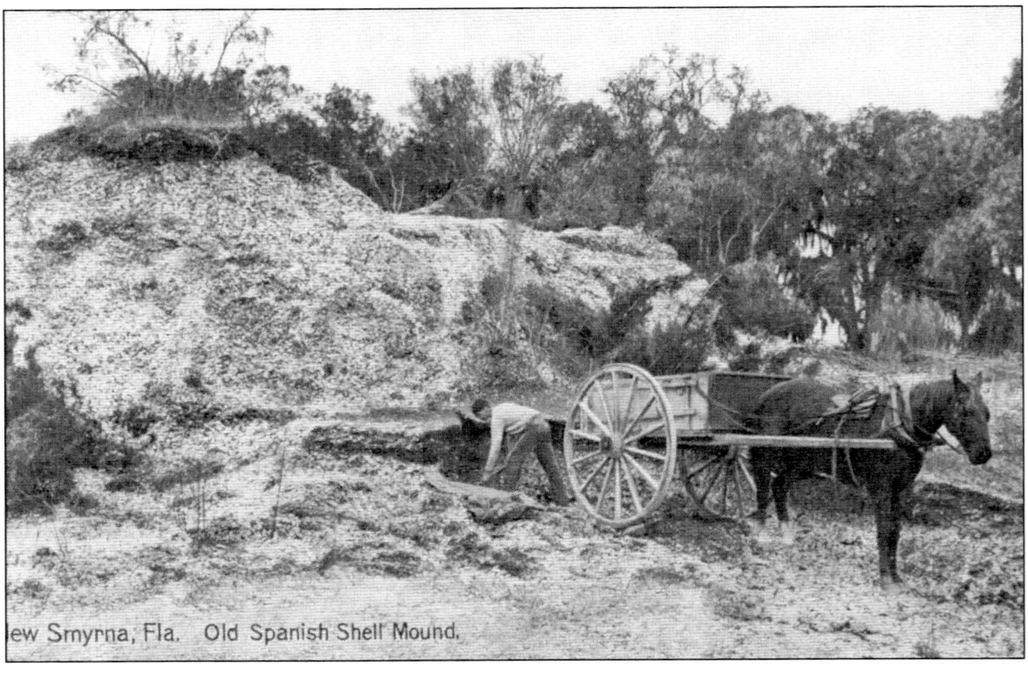

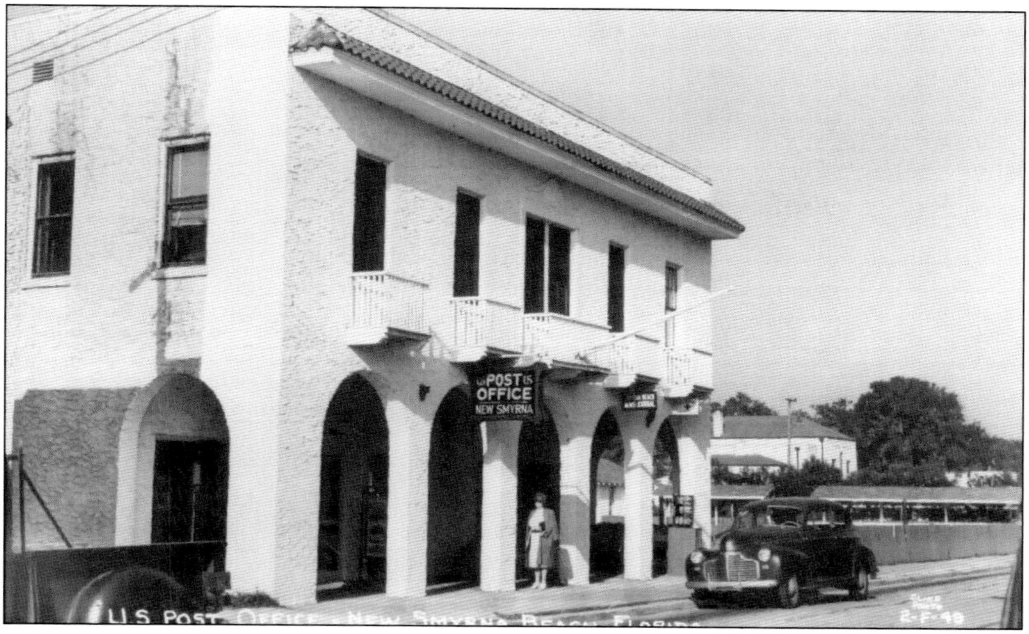

US Post Office. Shown here are two prior locations of the US Post Office in the downtown area. A new modern post office, with a large parking lot, is now located on Old Mission Road, west of downtown. Both of these buildings have been saved and converted into other ventures. Above is the Sams Avenue building, which was constructed by Edward Wilson in 1925 and served as the post office until 1967. It now houses the New Smyrna Museum of History. Below is the Canal Street building, which served as the post office until it moved to its current location in 1989. It is now home to the Corkscrew Bar and Grille.

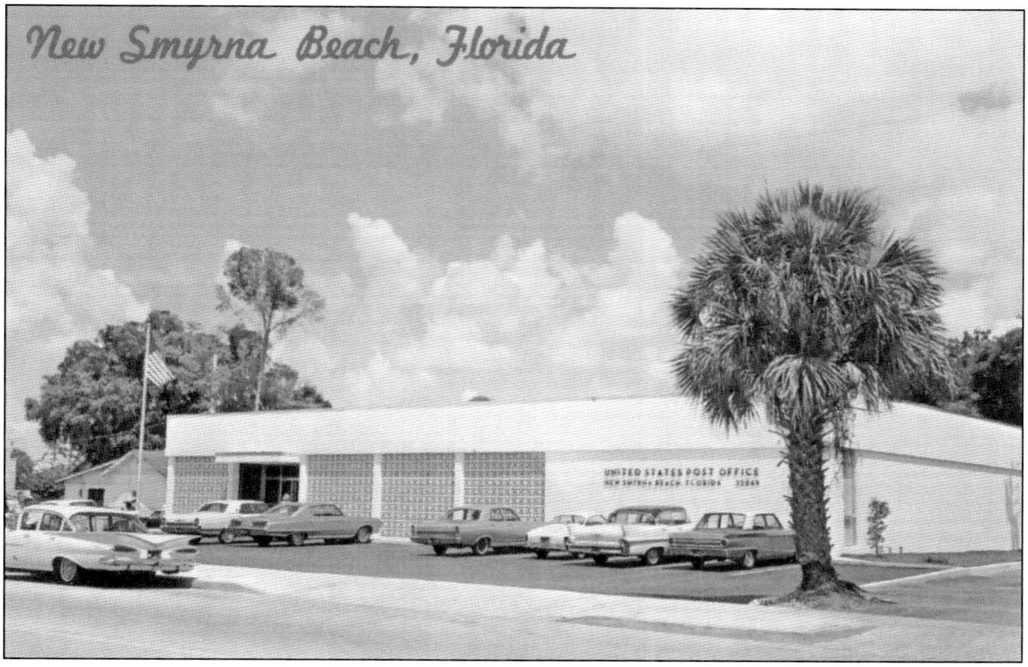

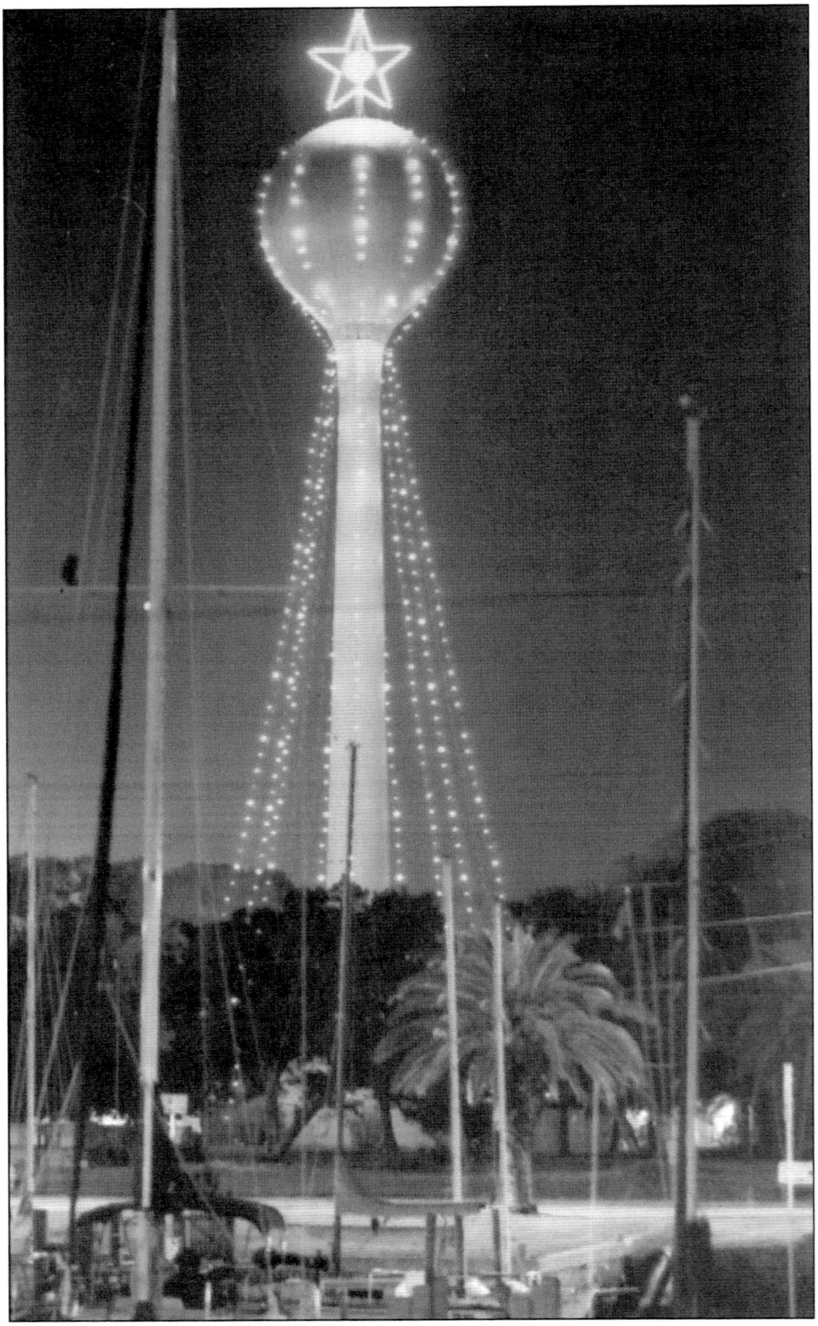

Water Tower in Old Fort Park. From 1953 until the tower was removed because of damage and lack of need in 1994, residents would always know it was the holiday season when the strands of lights decorated the tower and the large illuminated star sat atop it. The tradition was originated by Utilities Commission worker Wayne Lowe and turned into an annual event drawing thousands of visitors to the downtown area. Despite more than 20 years since the tower was demolished, the light display is still talked about to this day. The tradition of lighting the star is now carried on at the Utilities Commission building on Canal Street. The event is called Spark the Spirit and is attended by thousands each year.

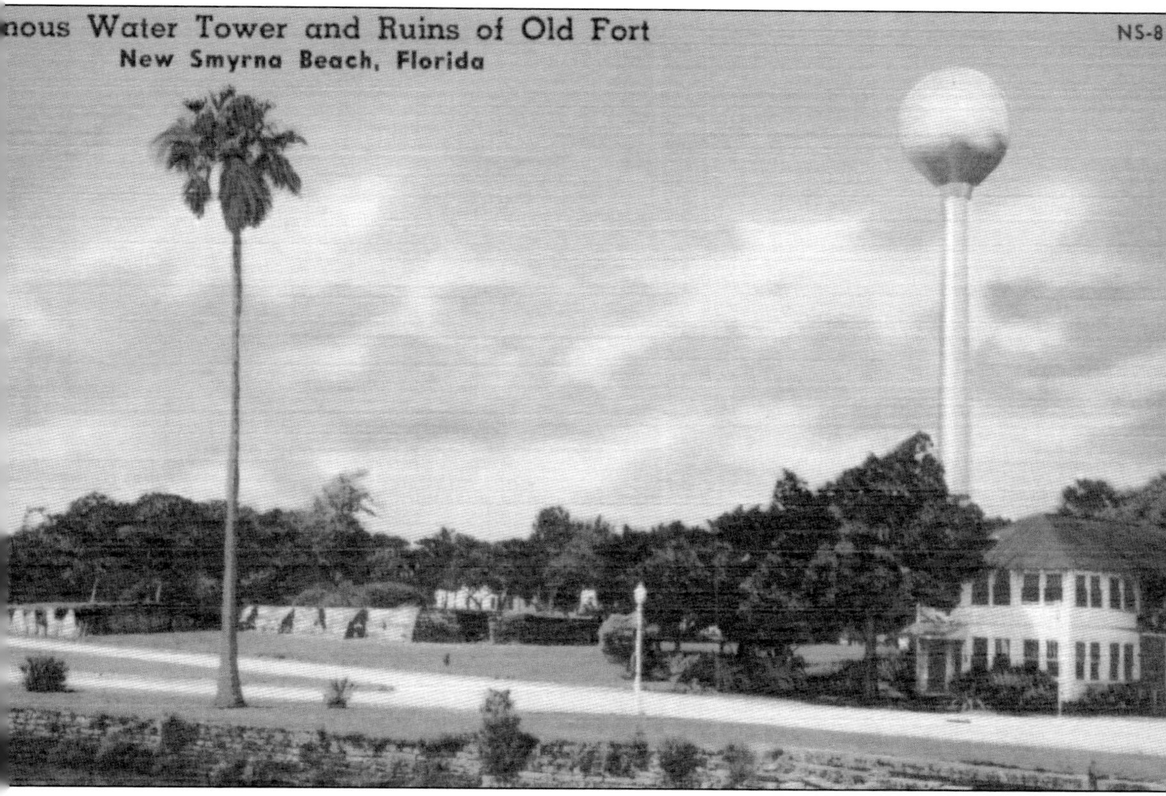

Famous Water Tower and Ruins of Old Fort. This card, with a view from the east, shows two structures no longer in existence: the water tower and the two-story building seen in the lower right corner. The caption also makes the error of stating that the coquina ruins are those of an old fort. The water tower is most remembered for the beautiful holiday light display that was attached to it each year. It has been said that on a clear day, workers on top of the tower could see all the way to Cape Canaveral. The unnamed building at right was constructed in the early 1900s and served as a home and a retail space. Some of the businesses included a soda shop, a repair shop, and a gift store.

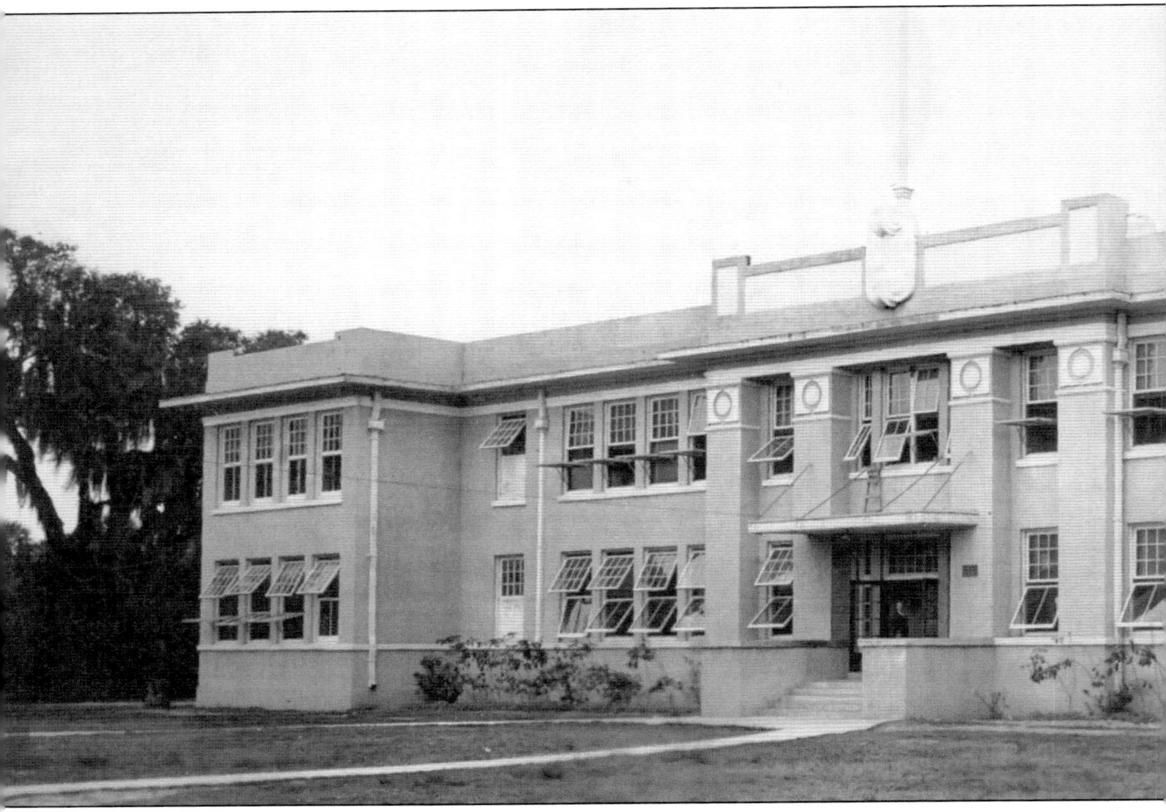

FAULKNER STREET SCHOOL. The school on Faulkner Street was built in 1916 and originally housed elementary, middle, and high school students. When the Live Oak school was built in 1925, the high schoolers moved there. Anne Patillo served as principal from 1921 until 1946,

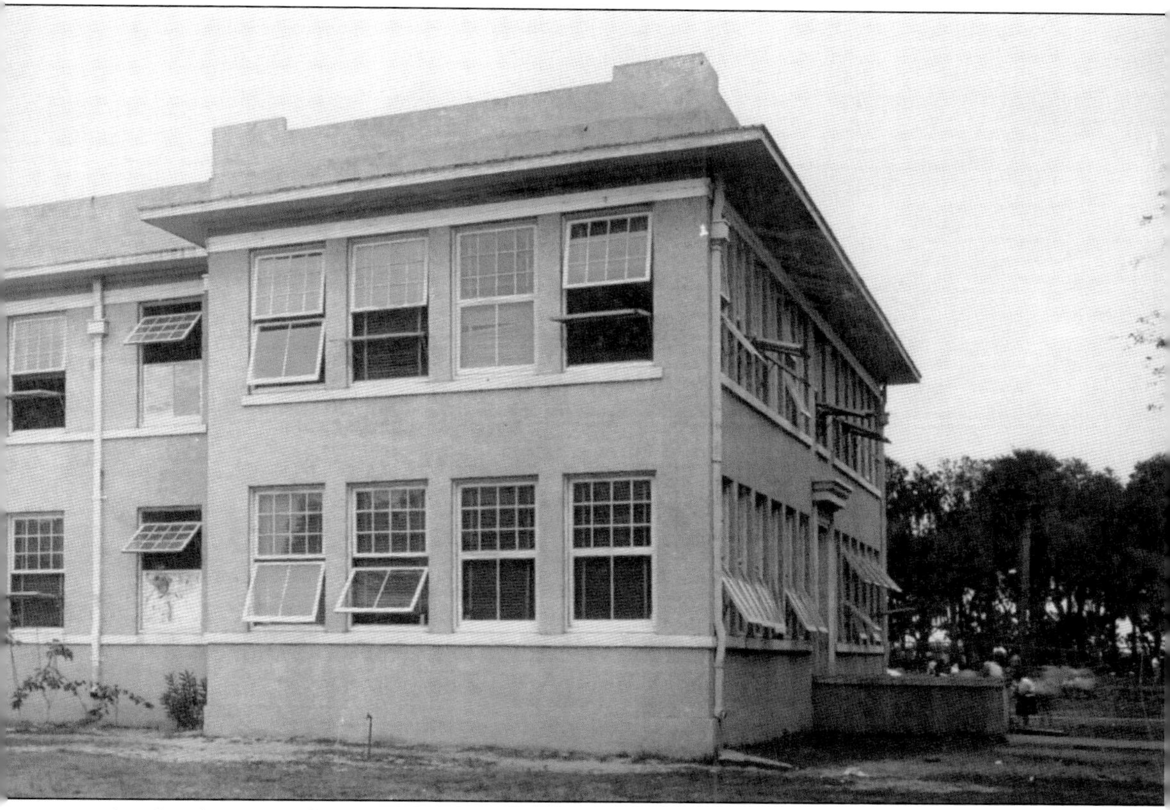

cementing her legacy in local education. The school was closed in 1986, and students were transferred to the then new Chisholm Elementary. Faulkner Street School has since been demolished. Note the open windows in an attempt to cool the classrooms.

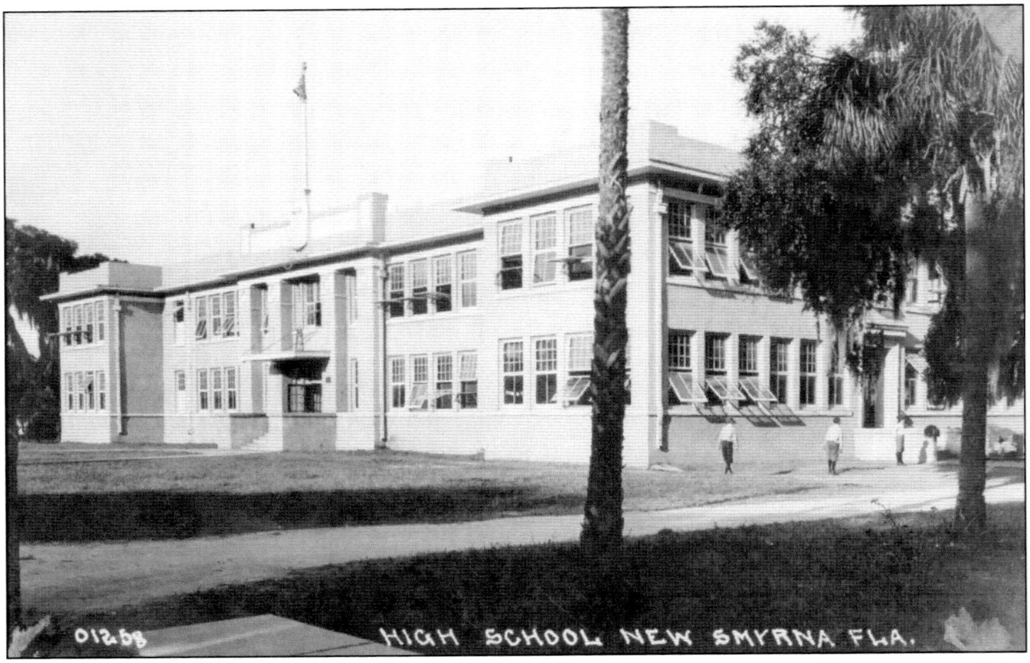

FAULKNER STREET HIGH SCHOOL. The view above shows a slightly different angle of the Faulkner Street School, where children appear to be playing a game of some sort. While the school was home to many great memories, there were difficulties as well. During the Great Depression, funds were so tight that class photographs were canceled, and the free school lunch program could not be funded by the Parent-Teacher Association (PTA). Taken by photographer Theo van de Sande, the image below shows what appear to be high school students standing outside the school. Thus, it can be dated to the years between 1916 and 1925, when high school–aged students attended the Faulkner School. (Below, courtesy of Dorothy Moore.)

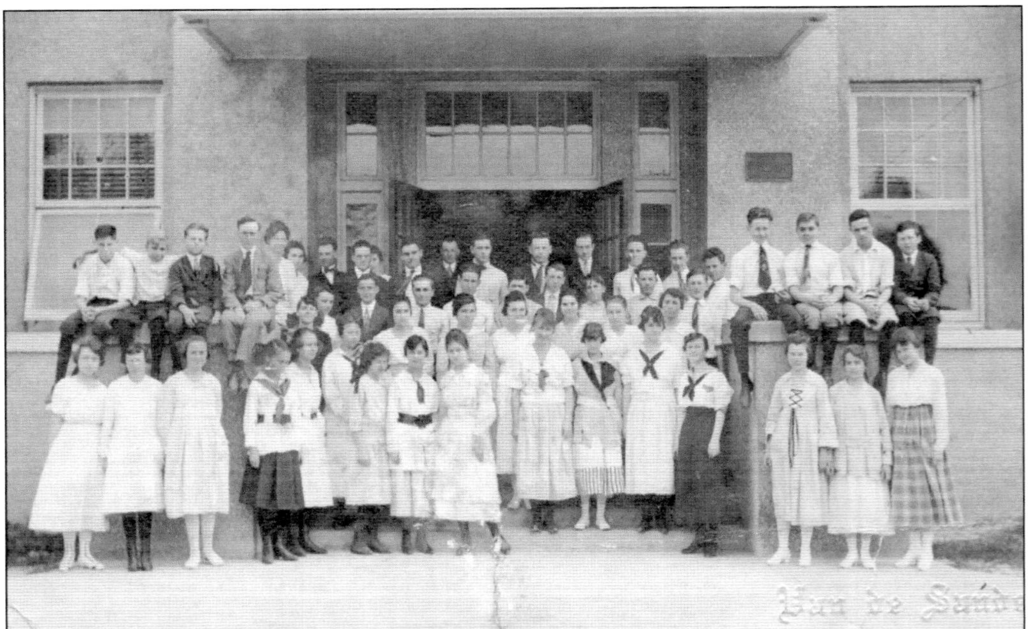

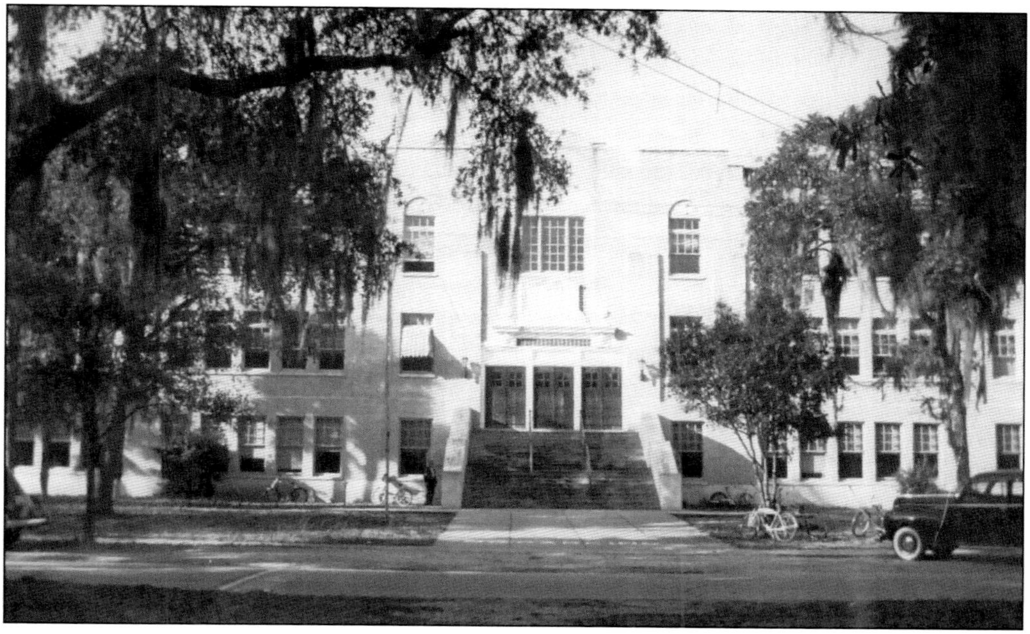

LIVE OAK GRAMMAR SCHOOL AND HIGH SCHOOL. The Live Oak School opened for the 1925–1926 school year. Students from the south side of New Smyrna and Edgewater attended elementary school and junior high here, as did all white high school students during the years of segregation. In 1957, elementary school students were moved to the new Read-Patillo School. The year 1963 saw the opening of a new high school on the North Causeway, and Live Oak became a devoted junior high school until the opening of New Smyrna Beach Middle School on Myrtle Avenue in 1983. The school has since been torn down, but the gymnasium is still used by the New Smyrna Beach Recreation and Special Events office.

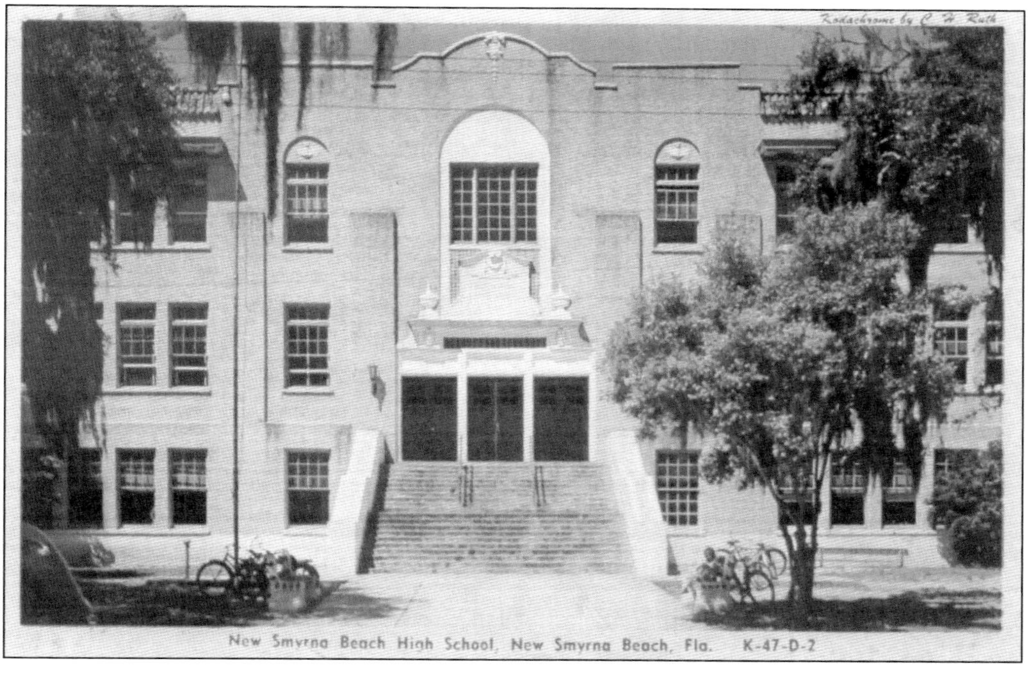

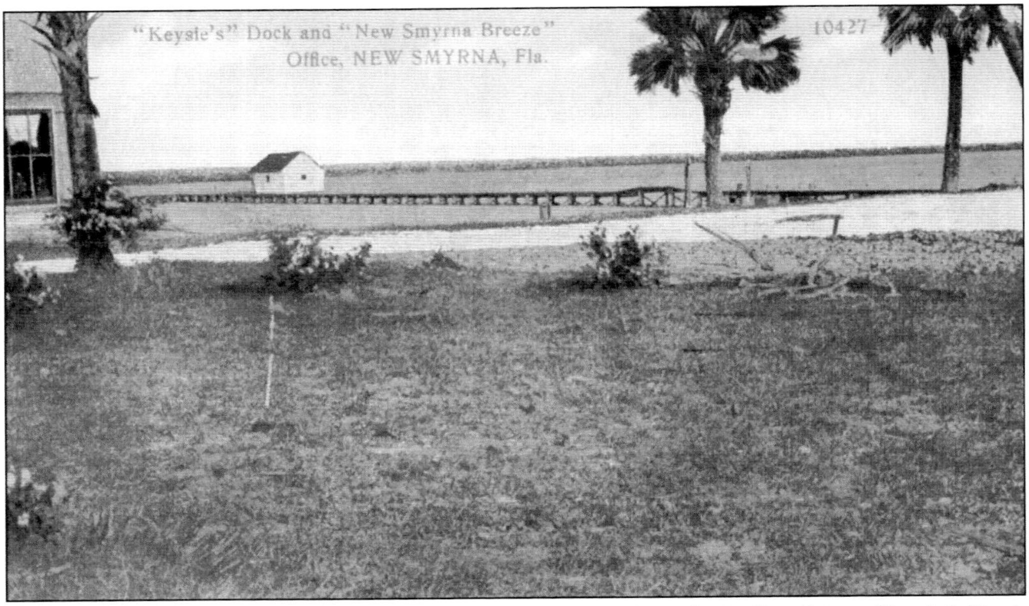

KEYSIE'S DOCK AND *NEW SMYRNA BREEZE*. Jutting out into the Indian River, Keysie's Dock provided a landing point for boaters needing to stop for supplies, for fishermen wanting to sell their catch, or others passing by. The *New Smyrna Breeze* building is seen as the left-hand side of the image. The *New Smyrna Breeze* was a local newspaper first published in 1887, with John Detwiler serving as editor. As happened across the country, the Great Depression took the *Breeze* as a victim, and it ceased publication in the 1930s. This card was postmarked in 1916.

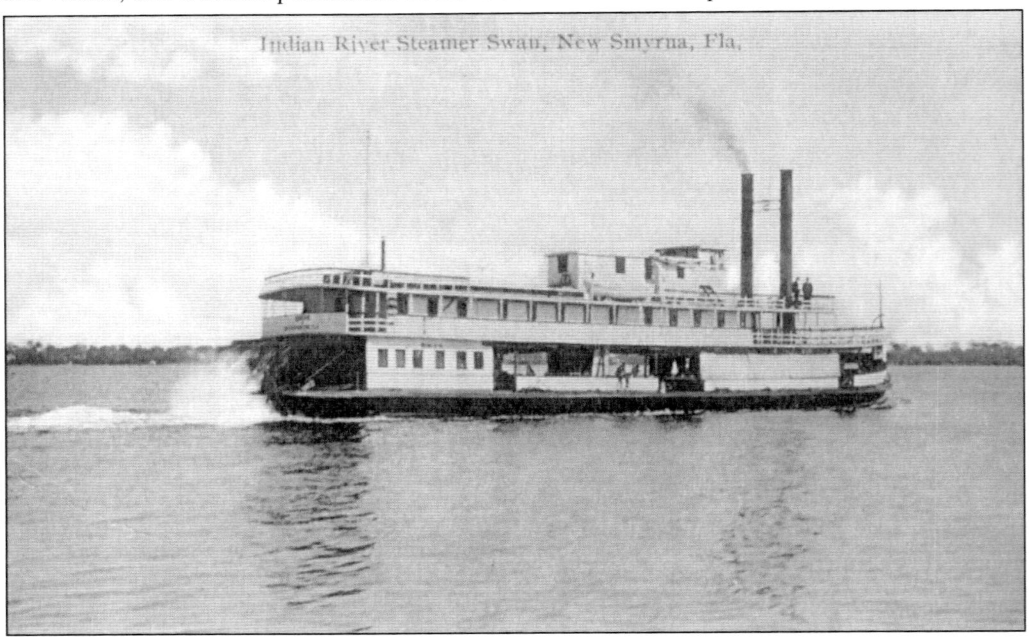

INDIAN RIVER STEAMER. In the days before trains and automobiles, ships were the most efficient way to travel and to move goods from one location to another. Steamships traveled up and down the Indian River, often helping move citrus to ports from where it could be transported farther north. The *Swan* began operations between Jacksonville and West Palm Beach in 1904. The 156-foot ship would make the trip in less than three days. J. Hatton Howards served as captain.

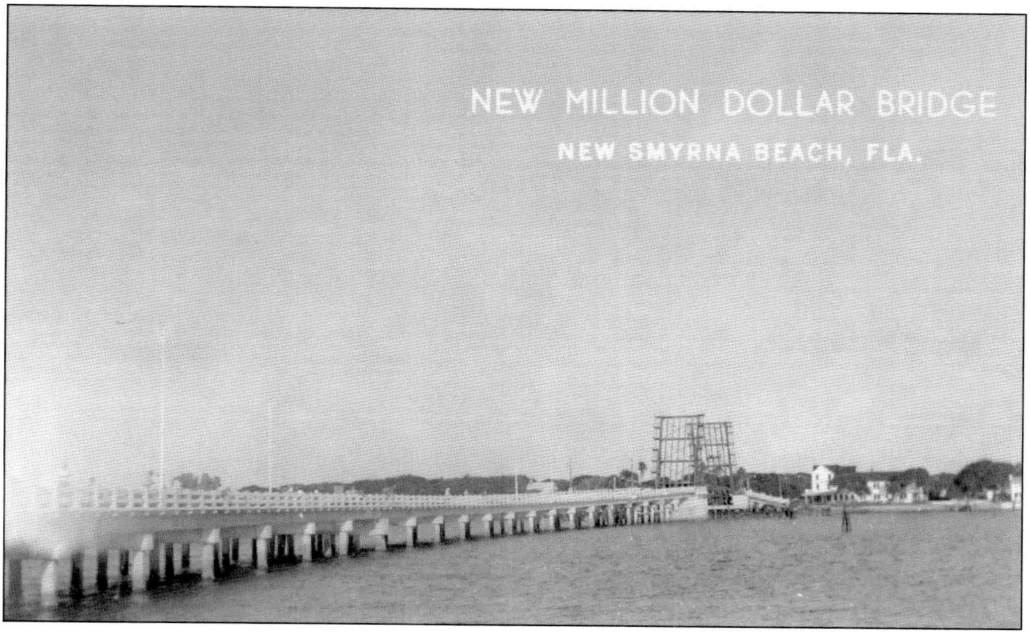

NEW MILLION DOLLAR BRIDGE. Originally built in the 1950s, the north bridge only had a 14-foot span and a width of less than 35 feet. With increased traffic, both on the river and on the road, these dimensions were not suitable for modern life, and in 1996, the new George Musson Memorial Bridge opened, featuring a 21-foot span and 65-foot width. The Musson Bridge opens three times per hour to allow for tall boat traffic to pass through. Above, the building at the end of the bridge is the Riverview Hotel.

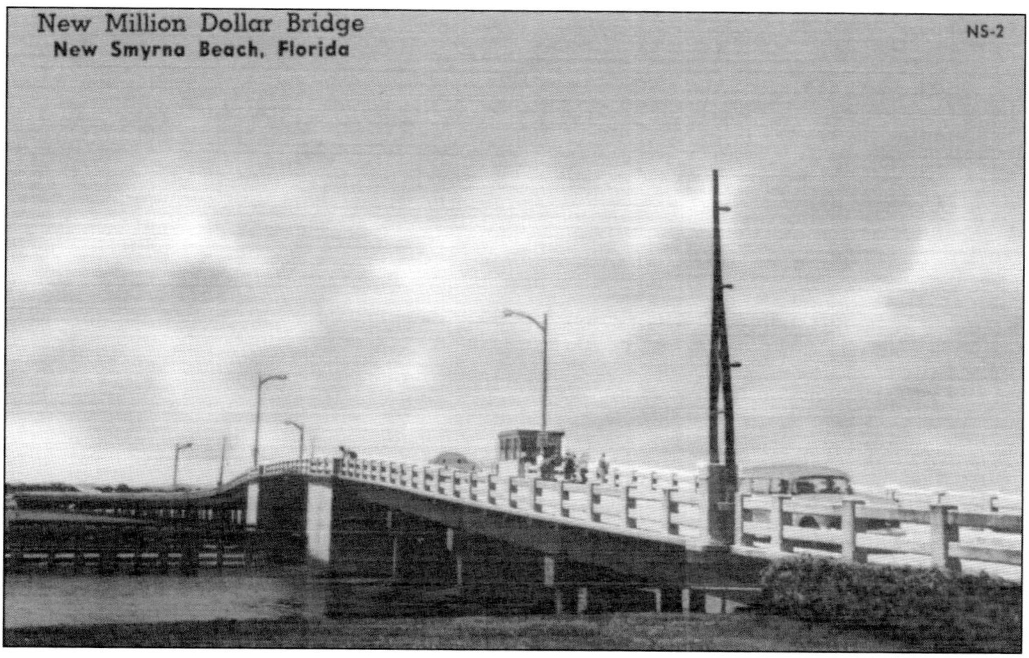

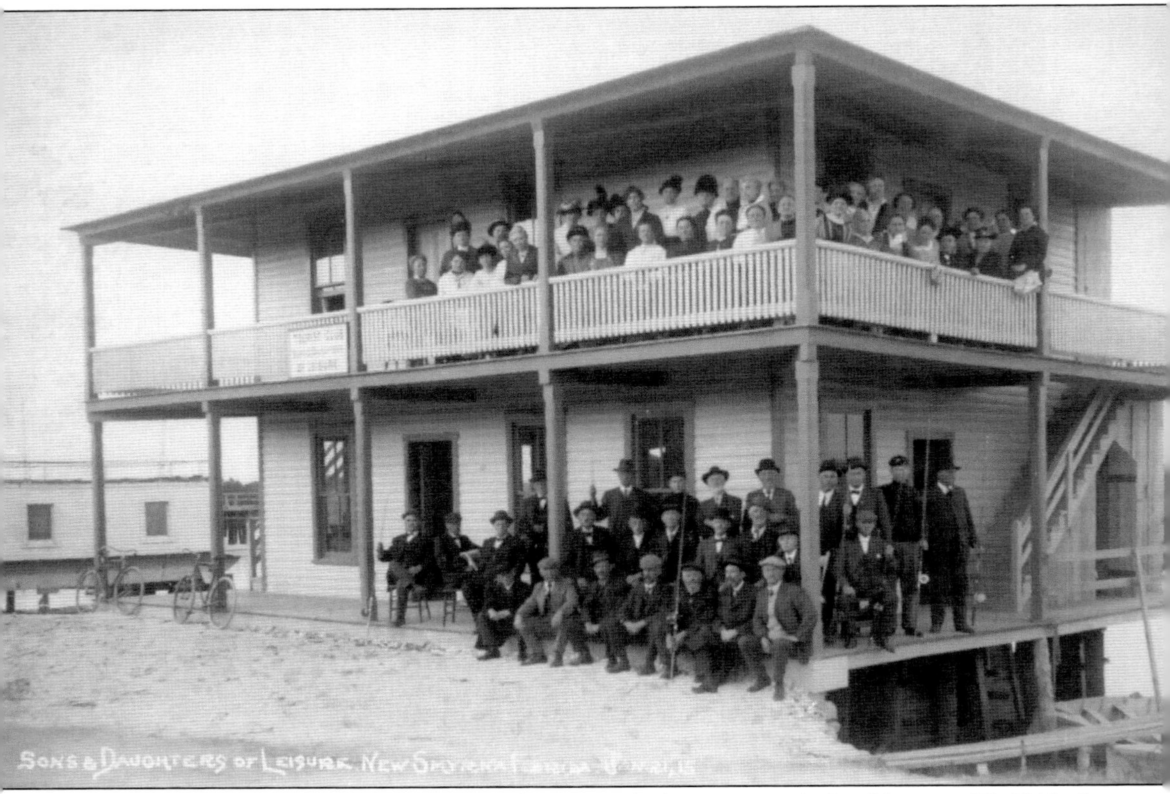

Sons & Daughters of Leisure. This rare real-photo postcard, dated January 21, 1915, shows the two-story clubhouse for the Sons & Daughters of Leisure that was located on Riverside Drive, north of the ruins in Old Fort Park but south of the bridge. This group later became known as the Anglers Club, a designation that is still active to this day. Several things are noteworthy in this image. The men are gathered on the ground floor, while the women are above on the second floor. Many of the men are holding fishing poles, indicative of the later name change. A small part of the bridge that would have led to Coronado Beach is visible between the two buildings at left. When examined closely, the sign on the second-floor railing states, "Tourist Club Sons & Daughters of Leisure." It is also interesting to note the bicycles leaning against the building, serving as a reminder of the mode of transport for many of the members.

Bibliography

1906–2006, 100 Years: First Baptist Church Serving God for 100 Years in Downtown New Smyrna Beach. New Smyrna Beach, FL: N.P., 2006.

Coe, Charles H. *Debunking the So-Called Spanish Mission Near New Smyrna Beach*. Washington, DC, 1941.

Luther, Gary. *History of New Smyrna: East Florida with Illustrations*. 3rd ed. rev. New Smyrna Beach, FL: Luther's Publishing, 2009.

New Smyrna Beach City Directory. Various years.

New Smyrna Beach Historic District National Register of Historic Places Registration Form. US Department of the Interior, National Park Service, 1990.

New Smyrna Beach News. Various dates and years.

Newell, Richard T. *A Genealogical Study of the Newells and Meares of New Smyrna*. New Smyrna Beach, FL: Luther's Publishing, 2000.

Redd, Robert. *Historic Sites & Landmarks of New Smyrna Beach*. Charleston, SC: The History Press, 2015.

Sweett, Lawrence. *New Smyrna Beach*. Charleston, SC: Arcadia Publishing, 2007.

US Bank Locations. www.usbanklocations.com.

Volusia County Schools. *The Odyssey of an American School System: Volusia County Schools 1854–2000*. Deland: Volusia County Schools, 2000.